Journalism Is War

GEORGE ARCHIBALD

Journalism Is War

Stories of Power Politics, Sexual Dalliance and Corruption in the Nation's Capital.

ANOMALOS PUBLISHING HOUSE

CRANE, MISSOURI

Anomalos Publishing House, Crane, Missouri 65633
© 2009 by George Archibald
All rights reserved. Published 2009
Printed in the United States of America.
09 1
ISBN-10: 0978845374
EAN-13: 9780978845377

Cover illustration and design by Steve Warner

Cover photographs by Natasha Curry Kurfees

Editors Michelle Warner and Royann Jordan Parker

A CIP catalog record for this book is available from the Library of
Congress

For Rusty

Mummie, great friend and mentor all her life

Would to God ye could bear with me a little in my folly: and indeed bear with me.

—2 Corinthians 11:1 KJV

———————

A friend loveth at all times, and a brother is born for adversity.

—Proverbs 17:17 KJV

CONTENTS

PREFACE

———

Wʜᴇɴ ᴏɴᴇ ᴡʀɪᴛᴇs about the stuff that fuels Washington, D.C., our Nation's Capital, there is, unfortunately, no way to avoid the confluence of politics, bureaucratic self-climbing, indolence, and sex—not necessarily in that order.

Many have watched three popular hit TV series, NBC's "West Wing" and HBO's "The Sopranos" and "Big Love." Someday, a creative producer will meld the story line of these three shows and come up with a great TV series about how Washington really works—the White House and executive branch, Congress, the federal judiciary, and media. We must not forget the dominant media elites.

Unfortunately, as a newspaperman who covered Washington for almost a quarter century, and worked for Congress and President Reagan's administration after four years in the military, I concluded that it is impossible to tell the story of "Journalism Is War" without including accounts of thievery and other self-gain by politicians, bureaucrats, state and corporate lobbyists, political interest groups (including even church groups), and their hired guns who constantly game the system for their own ideological and political policy purposes at public expense.

So my apologies to readers that much of this book is about miscreants and sexual deviants in high places of government and media, high-powered thievery, and other dishonesty. It's the continuing story of Washington in our lifetime.

I did not want to write a book that highlighted Senator Ted Kennedy of Massachusetts being caught having sex with a blonde textile lobbyist under the table of a private dining room in a Capitol Hill restaurant, but it happened when the senator and others complained that President George H.W. Bush's nominee for Defense Secretary, Senator John Tower of Texas, was an alcoholic and a womanizer. Sorry to say to budding history, political science and journalism students in high school and college that hypocrisy and deceit, unfortunately, are a huge staple of Washington culture.

The place has been full of alcoholics and womanizers going back through history, and Ted Kennedy was among the best of them as he also became one of Washington's most skilled legislative deal-makers.

When she was first lady of Arkansas, Hillary Clinton had her fling with former law partner and deputy White House counsel Vincent Foster before he killed himself. The tabloids say Bill Clinton as ex-president is still "playing around" with other women.

The late Terry Dolan, a big conservative icon who helped Republicans gain control of Congress as founder of the National Conservative Political Action Committee (NCPAC, pronounced "nickpack"), preferred gay men and leather bars and died of AIDS. Dolan was a source of mine, and I had to cover the story of his closet-homosexuality at the time he died, which brought some glares from many friends in the conservative movement when I showed up at his memorial service.

So this is a fair and balanced book that tells the story from all sides and lets the chips fall where they may.

But there is also good news in this book about wonderful people who constantly work their hearts out in Washington and state capitals, and in the heartland generally around the world, to uphold a culture of life, human liberty, good moral values, and economic opportunity for all.

Not many thought The Washington Times would survive more than 25 years as a competitive newspaper in the nation's capital. I'm frankly surprised myself, because as "an editor's paper" whose daily news focus and stories have been tightly controlled by its top tier of senior editors, The Times has had its share of eccentric characters putting out the paper and sometimes angry, abusive editors with nativist, racist, anti-immigration views that would make one's hair curl. (More about that in chapter 21.) However, these people had other good qualities that got a paper out every day. I tell that story as best I can.

This is a book about stories behind the stories and sources who made them happen. It's not a hit-job book, because I love my dedicated and talented colleagues and friends at The Washington Times and throughout the media with whom I worked side-by-side for more than 23 years. But no one has written a frank book about our counter-establishment approach at The Times and how it worked. As I was there from the beginning, before The Times actually started publication, I'm in a unique and privileged position to tell the story, warts and all.

It was mostly uphill. There were many times when we turned the tables on what Editor Arnaud de Borchgrave called "the dominant media elites." We gave it to them, gladly, and asked them to say *thank you*. They never did, so we just gave it to them again and again just for the joy of it. There's been a lot of bloodletting over the years because of personal rivalries among clever Times editors and reporters, ideological fights within the newspaper—and among newsmakers themselves.

This is one part of that story from an original staff member and national investigative reporter nominated by the paper four times for the Pulitzer Prize in journalism. Never got one, but it was a great privilege to report and write many of the paper's big stories over the years, with other wonderful reporter partners—Paul Rodriguez and Jerry Seper particularly—and with wonderful supportive editors, notably Smith Hempstone, Arnaud de Borchgrave and Fran Coombs (whose temper and racial nativism brought him down in the end).

And we had "funny ownership," as Editor Smith Hempstone used to say. The Times was founded in May 1982 by South Korean religious leader the Reverend Sun Myung Moon, who claimed to be God's chosen successor to Christ on earth and calls himself "True Father." (Lightning bolts.) Hempstone once joked he never worked for a publisher who did not think he was God. We all laughed and rolled up our sleeves; nonetheless, grateful that Moon's many successful business ventures enabled him to plow more than $3 billion into the newspaper and related publications over the years I was there.

Yet by industry standards, The Times has been a huge business disaster, in the red with low advertising and circulation—even less in 2008 than the first day the paper hit the streets a quarter-century ago. So why have its owners kept it going?

Because The Times was started as a newspaper to go up against The Washington Post, other dominant media elites, and the so-called liberal big-government establishment. Profit was not an issue. I know as the first reporter hired by Bo Hi Pak, the Reverend Moon's emissary, and Josette Sheeran Shiner, leaders of the founding group.

I had served in the Reagan administration as deputy assistant secretary for legislation at the U.S. Education Department in 1981, after seven years on Capitol Hill in various jobs and a budding newspaper career after military service before that. After falling out with Reagan's first education secretary, Terrel Bell, who refused to fulfill the president's objective to get rid of the department, I learned about plans for the new newspaper to succeed The Washington Star, which had closed down after Time magazine bought it and ran it into the ground. So I applied in February of 1982 and was the first hired by The Times' founding group.

By almost anyone's measure, the Times quickly became a pacesetter, one of President Ronald Reagan's personal first reads every day, and commanded huge worldwide respect. The owners and original editors quickly built a staff that broke stories many other news organizations did not get—or chose not to report—and a stable of commentators who analyzed national and world events every day from all points of view, as few news organizations do today.

Only days before The Times' first issue hit the streets, I coincidentally met Ben Bradlee, then chief editor of The Washington Post, in a George Washington University hospital elevator as I accompanied my pregnant wife, Blair, arriving to have our first daughter, Leslie. Bradlee was in green scrubs with glasses hanging around his neck that I thought were a stethoscope. As we walked into the elevator, Bradlee pushed the button to the maternity floor. I thanked him and asked how he knew where we were going. He looked down at my wife and me with a smile and said, "I think I know."

I said, "Thank you, doctor. Has anyone ever told you that you look like Ben Bradlee?" He laughed and said, "I hope so, because I am. I'm not a doctor. I'm here for the same reason you are." His wife, Sally, was already upstairs in labor waiting to deliver their son, Quinn.

That night, Bradlee and I paced the hospital hall together as our wives went through labor. On the nurse's station board was written in large chalk lettering: "Sally Quinn: NO PAIN!" He asked me what I did for a living. I told him I was between jobs and had just signed on with The Washington Times. Bradlee said, "Oh, I'm sorry, that paper won't last."

Then Sally started screaming multi-syllabled epithets in final labor pain. "Gotta go," Bradlee said as the outbursts started, looking back over his shoulder as he trotted off: "Come see me in six months, and I'll see what I can do for you."

A nice offer I never had to take.

George Archibald
Middleburg, Virginia
2009

INTRODUCTION

=========

"JOURNALISM IS WAR." How come the title? When covering and reporting our nation's capital, Washington, D.C., for more than two decades, there is no way to avoid the perpetual warfare fueled by constant political self-climbers and the endless, wasteful indolence of a permanent government bureaucracy entrenched within the spiderweb of federal agency offices in the capital and throughout our country.

A national news reporter faces this group of competing political and bureaucratic forces every day, both in D.C. and state capitals, and sees firsthand the efforts of political and bureaucratic powers of all persuasions to marshal corporate, media and academic powers to back their own self-interests.

It's a constant circus of egos, strong and weak personalities. Amidst this corruption, the aim is for an honest, committed print or broadcast report that tells the story as fully, completely and honestly as one can every day.

One such story involves the perpetual increased spending madness by members of Congress of both parties who shell out trillions of taxpayer dollars each year for pet political programs and projects, fueling the growing permanent bureaucracy and its constant threat to our civil liberties and national economic growth. This is a constant story that needs to be covered fully. Journalism is war. We take no prisoners. We owe the people an unabridged and truthful report. So be it.

As politicians of all parties and ideologies like to spend and spend once in office, and have to raise hundreds of millions of campaign dollars each year to get re-elected and build power for themselves, they surround themselves at every turn with highly paid people, campaign fund-raisers, powerful people everywhere, and sycophants who rely on them for political jobs, contracts, tax breaks, self-importance, and a major piece of the economic and political power in their own local communities and nationally.

It should come as no surprise that career politicians and their perpetual crowd of glad-handers soon view themselves as demigods and become less and less accountable to people at the local and state level—the people who really make our economy work—and voters who actually elect them.

They make themselves into the elite with cell phones stuck to their ears almost 24 hours a day and big expense accounts at taxpayers' costs, as they do all they can to further their own power and control in the self-serving political bubbles they live in as perpetual office-seekers and bureaucrats.

It was Winston Churchill who once said democracy was the worst form of government except everything else that had been tried. Presidents and governors of both national parties, the political organizations at their disposal, state legislators and their political apparatus, and the intergenerational sex that is a constant ingredient of the political scene in Washington and state capitols all combine as an explosive fuel for inevitable scandals that regularly emerge from the dog-eat-dog political cauldron.

It was almost 20 years ago that Washington was in a lather over charges that President George H.W. Bush's Cabinet nominee for defense secretary, Senator John G. Tower of Texas (then chairman of the Senate Armed Services Committee), was a womanizer and alcoholic, not fit to run the Pentagon.

At the time, I was assigned to do what we call in the news trade a "clip-job" story for The Washington Times about the sexual peccadilloes of Washington's high and mighty, going back almost to the hot affair between Thomas Jefferson and his beautiful slave girl-friend Sally Hemmings.

The anchor revelation of the front-page story run by The Washington Times in summer 1989 was that Senator Edward M. "Ted" Kennedy, Massachusetts Democrat, took Elaine—a female lobbyist for the textile industry—for lunch at noontime at La Brasserie restaurant opposite The Heritage Foundation on Capitol Hill near Union Station and was caught (by the waitress) having sex with her under the table in an upstairs private dining room after a sumptuous lunch of New England crab cakes and several expensive bottles of wine.

Such indiscretions of the high-powered are protected by restaurant and hotel managers of our nation's capital and state capitals throughout the country. A regular customer would be kicked out, barred from an establishment, and perhaps arrested and prosecuted for improper public behavior—but not a member of the political elite. Events like Ted Kennedy's fornication in a Washington, D.C. restaurant go on all the time as arrogant politicians push the limits with their hedonist, self-aggrandizing behavior for power and recognition.

This public show of affection by the distinguished gentleman from Massachusetts was two decades after his drunken plunge into Dykes Pond with Mary Jo Kopechne, who died at Chappaquiddick in the back seat of his car. And was Ted Kennedy among complainers in September 2006 about Florida's disgraced Rep. Mark Foley, the male teenage page-stalker, insisting that everyone in the Republican leadership resign as Democrats grabbed any straw to win a majority in Congress?

Of course not. At least the man is not a hypocrite. With Kennedy's history, having earlier defended his nephew prosecuted for raping a woman in Florida—who got off thanks to Kennedy money plowed into defending the lad and denigrating the victimized woman—the senator from Massachusetts was not going to wage war over a hapless Republican homosexual congressman who stalked teen male pages in the U.S. House of Representatives.

There have been many heterosexual and homosexual abusers and users over the years and other scandal-damaged members of Congress who Kennedy gladly welcomed into the secular club of injured political money-grubbers. Each protect their own was the motto.

The institutional congressional sex scandals, the most appalling of which are detailed throughout this book, go back decades and have been a pox on all sides of the political aisle since our nation's beginning. A few brief examples are as follows:

——Thirty years ago, to begin the litany fairly recently, Rep. Wilbur Mills, drunken Democratic chairman of the tax-writing House Ways and Means Committee from Arkansas, jumped into the Tidal Basin with bar stripper Fanny Fox just a shadow away from Thomas Jefferson's statue.

——Maryland Rep. Robert Bauman, previously a Republican telephone page in the U.S. House of Representatives in the 1960s and a leading advocate of conservative causes for morality and limited, leaner government, regularly went to male strip clubs in downtown Washington to pick up teen prostitutes and was convicted in 1980 of oral sodomy with a minor boy.

——South Carolina congressman John Jenrette and his girlfriend, Rita Carpenter, went to the U.S. Capitol steps in 1980, stripped naked, and fornicated under a full moon.

—U.S. Sen. Donald Riegle from Michigan, a Republican-turned-Democrat, was a friend of President George H.W. Bush during their days together in the U.S. House of Representatives. Visiting Bush one day at his Houston apartment, Riegle was tape-recorded by his young mistress whom he called and performed steamy phone sex from the apartment while Bush was taking a shower. The tape was obtained by The Detroit Free Press, which ran a story.

—During the 1980s, Rep. John Young of Texas had a young female aide on his payroll for constant sex.

—Reps. Joe Waggoner Jr. of Louisiana and Allan Howe of Utah both had female prostitutes serving them, fell prey to police decoys, and were convicted of sex crimes.

—House Speaker Newt Gingrich had a continuing extramarital affair with a lovely female aide on the House Agriculture Committee staff named Callista Bisek and divorced his second wife, Maryanne, to marry Bisek after he got her pregnant.

The irony was that Gingrich—as House Republican whip, before he became house speaker—was one of our keenest and best sources in toppling Democratic House Speaker Jim Wright of Texas in 1989 and in feeding us subsequent House scandal stories that ultimately gave Republicans majorities in both houses of Congress in the 1994 elections and put Gingrich in office as speaker.

—Rep. Jon Hinson, Mississippi Republican, resigned from the House in 1981 after being arrested in a Cannon House Office Building men's room for soliciting a policeman decoy for oral sodomy.

—Rep. Barney Frank, Massachusetts Democrat, had a male prostitute lover, Steve Gobie, with whom he lived in his Capitol Hill apartment. Gobie told my reporting partner Paul Rodriguez and me that he ran a prostitution ring out of Frank's apartment while also servicing a Chevy Chase elementary school principal, another homosexual client. Rodriguez and I confirmed these details and broke that lead banner story in The Times on Aug. 25, 1989.

—Rep. Donald E. "Buz" Lukens, Ohio Republican, had a black prostitute fetish and was defeated after being extorted by a young prostitute's welfare mom and slammed with House ethics violations. I walked with Buz Lukens on one rainy day from his House office building to the Republican Capitol Hill Club to hear him deny the allegations against him, and a cab drove up. He had an apartment just blocks away in southwest Washington near Maine Avenue.

A tall, beautiful, leggy black woman got out of the cab. "That's mine," Lukens said and got into the cab with the prostitute and drove off. So much for his denials. The man was a sex addict, yet had been one of the principal movers and shakers in the early conservative movement of the 1960s to draft Senator Barry Goldwater of Arizona to run for president. He was also instrumental in building the early conservative college groups—Young Americans for Freedom, the Intercollegiate Studies Institute, and ultimately the Leadership Institute, the Heritage Foundation, and a slew of other so-called New Right groups that fueled the conservative movement behind Ronald Reagan's presidential campaign engine.

—Congressman Daniel Crane, Illinois Republican, was censured and bounced from the House in his next election for having sex with a teen female Republican page.

—Congressman Gerry Studds, Massachusetts Democrat, was censured after having sexual relations with a male teenage page around the world on government-paid congressional delegation junkets called CODELS.

No journalist has done a good complete story about all the booty, tons of discounted purchases worth millions of dollars brought back from foreign lands by members of Congress and their family members on these perpetual CODELS. This is a huge continuing scandal all on its own.

——Congressman Jim Kolbe, Arizona Republican and former powerful member of the House Appropriations Committee, left his wife for sex with boys and men and became a major advocate of homosexual rights and gay marriage. The same with former Congressman Steve Gunderson of Wisconsin, known as "Dairy Queen," and outed as gay by The Advocate, a national homosexual magazine.

The House, Senate and White House in the 1980s, '90s, and up to the current time have been equal opportunity for lewd and lascivious behavior, as politicians of both parties have had sex with adults and minors of both sexes, proving they don't need Cialis, Viagra or Levitra to be naughty for four hours without calling their doctor. They have abused people of either sex regardless of age.

The dishonor roll of politicians who have committed sexual crimes and cheated on their spouses is even more extensive than has already been listed: former Senators Brock Adams of Washington state, David Durenburger of Minnesota, and Charles S. Robb of Virginia; Senator Hillary Clinton of New York with her brief affair with Rose Law Firm partner Vincent W. Foster Jr. in Little Rock before moving to Washington as first lady and orchestrating the cover-up after Vince Foster's suicide in Fort Marcy Park up the George Washington Parkway near McLean, Virginia, on July 20, 1993; and Congressmen Gus Savage of Illinois, Fred W. Richmond of New York, and Jim Bates of California all conducted sexual affairs. The list goes on and on.

Washington, D.C. has been a scandal city for decades. However, the politicians have not blinked an eye so long as contributors continue to pony up the money that they need for their re-election campaigns and voters keep them in office.

I do not believe these scandals will stop in our lifetime. This bad behavior has gone on for so long, protected by those who run Washington, paid for by corporate people who seek favor from Congress and fund the parties and sexual dalliance that occur constantly, and covered up by most of the press who hobnob socially with the political offenders and glorify them at yearly black-tie dinners.

Members and leaders of Congress, even the president and the nation's largest news organizations, protect and perpetuate this shame on our country's honor. The problem is political power run amok. And the sadness is that voters continue to elect many morally repugnant people who ceaselessly brag about bringing home the bacon, make Smithville the center of the universe, save the military base that should be closed because it's outmoded and redundant, and kiss the president's behind no matter what in order to get a photo op anywhere Air Force One can fly.

When will people get the message? Politics in our age is all about protecting those in power, regardless of their ability and regardless of their perfidy. We're walking on broken glass, as Annie Lennox croons in one of her best songs.

The Washington Times itself had its own history of sexual dalliance, adultery and harassment cases over the years that were mostly ignored, covered up by a human relations director, Randall Casseday, who now sits in jail for soliciting minor girls for sex on the company computer system.

Casseday, who had handled and covered up many sexual harassment cases brought to him during his tenure as human relations director, including one involving the paper's female publicist and managing editor, was indicted in September 2006 for propositioning an undercover policeman he thought to be a loose 13-year-old girl he found on the Internet.

Casseday had helped cover up predatory sexual antics of several Washington Times news and photo editors as well as managers on the business side of the newspaper—men who tried to seduce and sexually exploit employees, freelancers and employee applicants.

Most of these cases, as in the Catholic Church priest scandal of the 1990s, were settled at high cost to the company. We had Assistant Managing Editor Mark Tapscott—currently editorial page editor for The Washington Examiner and repentant born-again Christian—at the time in the 1980s and '90s a married man with lovely wife and children from several marriages who gypped the company of tens of thousands of dollars as he carried on sexual affairs using the company credit card.

All of the continued indiscretions of politicians and corporate/media executives have helped make journalism a greater battle-ground over a quarter century as honest news reporters and their organizations squared off with each other across the political and cultural divide.

My national editor for many years at The Washington Times, Francis B. Coombs Jr., would celebrate a breaking story that beat the competition by coming into a news meeting or into the news-room, throwing his fist into the air, and yelling, "Journalism is war!" Coombs' phrase became our mantra.

Unfortunately, Coombs was a racial bigot, and this became a growing problem for me and many other reporters in The Washington Times newsroom. Many star reporters left because of Coombs' bigotry and foul temper.

Battle lines are drawn on cultural, moral and political princi-ples among newsmakers, news reporters and news organizations in a wildly competitive news marketplace. The war is among honest, fair, and balanced news reporters, editors, and organizations of a traditional stripe (going back generations) and wild new journal-ists who know no boundaries and are pushed by advocacy-oriented media not committed to a complete, balanced and fair report but rather are concerned with only their take on the story. It's become an ugly battle.

Traditional, honest, hard-working journalists are not wed to any particular ideology or political party but instead are committed to providing a complete report to the public each day. The wild journalists have no particular commitment to truth but rather just want to make a mark each day, and they are loved by politicians who use them for their own glory and vice versa.

Traditional news organizations, regardless of their focus, have scrambled for their place versus the fervently biased and ideological advocacy media in the public square and profitability. The Internet has changed the face of global communication to favor the wild journalists, ideological media and advocacy bloggers, and truth in journalism has been the great victim.

The usual tests for factual accuracy, fairness and, ultimately, truth have been largely thrown out the window because rigid accountability and fact-checking of news stories and opinion commentary on the Internet—before publication—have gone by the wayside.

The test now is whether the Web site supervisor likes one's viewpoint and the buzz one's piece will generate. The only accountability is the Web site's fear of getting sued, which is unlikely given the dynamics of Internet Web sites with anonymity, pseudonyms, and the usual devices used by gossip-hounds and advocates from the ideological swamps who want to evade accountability. So almost anything gets published today, regardless of its authenticity.

Thomas Jefferson had a clearly stated set of principles when it came to public policy and our polity as an independent and free people with a free press. Jefferson saw the problem clearly between the time he penned the Declaration of Independence in 1776 and became America's third president 27 years later, after serving as Secretary of State, ambassador to France, and vice president of the United States.

A strong advocate of the supremacy of disaggregated state government power as opposed to national imposition of public policy on the states by the federal government, Jefferson fervently worked for separation of powers, believing that Congress, as the nation's legislature, should set policy and appropriate money specifically to implement those policies. The president, as head of the executive branch and spokesman for national policies, was to do what Congress told him to do but had an independent role to position America in the best interests of its people with the rest of the world. This model of government has worked for almost three centuries.

Thomas Jefferson strongly supported a strong federal court system and judicial review of national government actions—U.S. district courts throughout the states, appeals courts in regions of the country, all headed by the U.S. Supreme Court, whose role was to make sure the president and federal executive branch agencies implemented the will of Congress in all matters, because members of Congress in the U.S. House and Senate were elected at the state level. This, of course, goes back to state supremacy over federal power that Jefferson knew would grow if allowed.

Fast forward to Abraham Lincoln and a Republican president's use of federal power in the mid-1800s to eliminate slavery, as originally envisioned by Jefferson and Adams, in order to subdue Southern states and state autonomy against growing federal power—a splitting point in Republican Party politics that continues to this day.

Fast forward again to Barry Goldwater's election to the U.S. Senate from Arizona in 1952, his writing of "The Conscience of a Conservative," which reiterates Jefferson's vision of limiting national government so that it supports the collective wisdom of successful state economies but does not militate against the religious, moral and economic values and work ethic of most Americans and their families throughout America.

This was a formula that had worked, but a liberal realpolitik was at war to build its own political power base to change the nation's culture and politics during the administrations of Presidents Lyndon B. Johnson and Jimmy Carter.

Fast forward again to the administrations of Presidents Ronald Reagan, George H.W. Bush, Bill Clinton, and George W. Bush, where you have three obvious men of faith who book-ended the president who sought satisfaction from female intern Monica Lewinsky in the White House Oval Office.

The cabinets of Reagan, Clinton and both Bushes were mainly strong advocates of the Judaic-Christian faith, but it was President George W. Bush, with steadfast support from British Prime Minister Tony Blair and other allies, who drew the line in the sand against Islamic fascism and the present terrorist enemies of our nation-state and Western culture.

Yet under the George W. Bush administration, counter to Goldwater-Reagan conservative principles, the federal government became more powerful, spent more taxpayer money, than all prior administrations of Franklin D. Roosevelt, Lyndon Johnson, Jimmy Carter, and Bill Clinton. Federal spending and taxation under President George W. Bush exceeded any prior administration in America's history.

And for the first time since 1776, we had become an imperialist nation on the world stage that, in the name of anti-terrorism, unilaterally declared war against two sovereign countries, with the prospect of more to come, in the mirror image of Abraham Lincoln's federal declaration of war against American states that refused to buckle to federal government dictates.

It's the continuing story of Washington in our lifetime. This is a transparent memoir; you will know where I'm coming from all the way.

CHAPTER ONE

RACING IN THE BLOOD

A Thoroughbred racehorse is one of God's most impressive engines. Tipping the scales at up to 1,450 pounds, he can sustain speeds of forty miles per hour. Equipped with reflexes much faster than those of the most quick-wired man, he swoops over as much as twenty-eight feet of earth in a single stride, and corners on a dime... To pilot a racehorse is to ride a half-ton catapult. It is without question one of the most formidable feats in sport. The extraordinary athleticism of the jockey is unparalleled... Jockeys may be, pound for pound, the best overall athletes. They have to be. To begin with, there are the demands on balance, coordination, and reflex.

—Laura Hillenbrand, "Seabiscuit"

A<small>S A</small> 10-<small>YEAR-OLD</small> growing up in a Thoroughbred horse racing family in Newmarket, England, the headquarters of British racing, I was thrown from Royal Lad—my mother's retired racehorse—and sadly told myself that I would not follow two generations of jockeys before me, on both sides of my family, to make riding "a half-ton catapult" my career. I realized I didn't have the nerve you must have to ride racing, which my father and grandfathers had, and so set my sights on a different path.

I became a newspaperman instead.

I'm sad in a way, as I believe in retrospect I would have been a great jockey as were my grandfathers and father. My mother also was a terrific rider—the first woman to ride as a paid "exercise lad" at the training track near Middleburg, Virginia.

The denouement happened in 1954 when my mother had a bad knee injury from a skiing accident—tearing ligaments in her left knee—in St, Moritz, Switzerland, and after returning to England, could not ride her retired Thoroughbred racehorse, Royal Lad, for daily exercise. My dad, a racehorse trainer and former leading steeplechase jockey, six-time Grand National finisher, woke me just after dawn one morning to tell me his exercise lad had not shown up and I was to get up to ride out.

Mummie's name was Angela, but she hated it. So when my father as her boyfriend, heard a song called "Rusty and Dusty Brown," sometime in the mid-1930s, the stable lads sang it whenever they saw them together, as he ran his fingers through her red hair. Dad christened her Rusty. The name stuck, and Rusty she was thereafter.

Dad had about 50 horses in training at his Savile House stables on the drizzly day he got me up to ride Royal Lad. I was a tiny fellow with small hands and little legs that didn't grip very well, but I knew how to ride with courage on any horse I was legged up on because that was my upbringing and what was expected by my parents owing to the family dominance in Thoroughbred racing in America and Europe going back to the mid-1800s. Yet it was hard to meet the expectations.

The ground was close on my Welsh pony, Thundercloud, but the view from the saddle after Dad legged me up onto Royal Lad was so far down and scary.

The horse knew he had a fly-weight passenger with little control. His neck was like an airport runway compared to my pony, and I knew I had no control with the big rubber-coated reins for rainy weather in my little hands. Each time he moved his head from side-to-side, he almost pulled me out of the saddle. But Dad told me to buck up, and I did (his order was always my command). But the morning did not go well.

The winding walk from the stable yard around 7 a.m., in the light drizzling rain, following a dozen horses was okay, with my father telling me what to do. We headed slowly across the square and through the watercourse toward the Newmarket racecourse, on the Cambridge side of town, where the yearly 1,000 and 2,000 Guineas races are run, which helped build my confidence.

Once we got to the bottom of the racecourse, we walked and trotted twice behind two groups of horses, maybe 15 minutes each round trip, which went okay. But things fell apart when Dad told me to canter for a third trip up the hill away from town behind four other horses. Royal Lad got feisty, and I immediately felt his resistance as we again headed away from home.

When we started off, I could feel Royal Lad tugging as we increased speed. It was as though he said to himself, "Enough of this," and suddenly he wheeled around in the other direction, me helpless, and took off at high speed back toward home. I just hung on for dear life, helpless and scared to death.

Being thrown from a big horse is no fun. It's frightening and hurts. You get bruised, sometimes broken bones, concussed, knocked out, as I was when this trip ended. At the bottom of the racecourse grounds, before some box bushes at the top of town, Royal Lad stuck his toes into the ground to stop—I was poised for him to jump the bushes and keep going—and I sailed right over his head and hit the ground as he left the scene.

A motorcyclist driving down the road from Cambridge beside the grass fairway above Newmarket saw the whole thing and stopped to help me. Somehow, he got enough information about where I lived, put me on the back of his bike, and took me home. I don't know who he was and never saw him again, but I hope I thanked him.

Royal Lad cut through Newmarket's back streets, riderless, and was at our stable yard before me. The throw scared me and showed me I was a devout coward, who didn't have the metal and nerve my father and grandfathers had as champion jockeys for generations before. So at age 10, I decided I was going to do something else with my life.

My father was at first a flat race jockey and then a National Hunt steeplechase rider in England from age 14 in 1929 until approximately age 32. He rode steeplechase races over fences, including England's toughest Grand National steeplechase at Aintree six times—30 fences including the horrendous 25-foot water jump, the Chair and Becher's Brook, twice round the 4.5-mile course—coming in third on Miss Dorothy Paget's Kilstar in 1937.

Mummie remembered that Dad was thrown hundreds of times during his 17-year riding career. "Before the war, he was riding six races a day and was thrown at least once a week," she recalled. "He broke his collarbone five times. It shortens the bone, the clavicle, which leads from the neck to the shoulder."

As a result, after he gave up riding and became a trainer at age 32, Dad's left arm used to pop out of its shoulder socket if he lifted his arm too high above his chest. "He'd have to drop to the ground, and I'd put a foot in his armpit as I pulled his shoulder back into place. It made a horrible clonking noise," Mummie said. "I had to do it hundreds of times." As a child, I would occasionally watch stable people or the horse box driver pull Dad's arm back into place, usually after he had pushed up the rear ramp of the horse box after loading some Thoroughbreds for a race meeting.

At Gatwick racecourse near London, just after World War II started, a horse Dad was riding fell at a jump and rolled over on top of him. Onlookers in the stands presumed he was killed, my mother remembered. "I was sitting there and everyone in the stands stood up and took off their hats"—a sign of respect for someone killed. Dad luckily was just knocked unconscious and went on to ride again the next day.

Once, Keith Piggott, the highly competitive father of famed

jockey Lester Piggott, who rode for Queen Elizabeth II, pushed my father up against the rail in a race as they battled for the lead. My father's light leather racing boot ripped along the rail like a finger on piano keys for close to a furlong, breaking several toes. Piggott won and my father was second, but Dad jumped off his horse in the winning enclosure and gave Keith Piggott a huge pasting for what he had done, before horrified spectators. The two jockeys duked it out until trainers and owners pulled them apart. My dad had a temper and an impatient sense of justice, so I came by those traits honestly.

Four of my parents' best jockey friends who rode on the flat— Fred and Bill Rickaby, Gordon Richards, and Tommy Weston—had many memorable falls. "Flat race jockeys are very short-legged, tiny men. It doesn't take much for a horse to step aside and drop you. You don't have enough leg to stay on," Mummie told me. "When I was still riding horses for my father in my twenties, I fell off a two-year-old of his 19 times in two weeks. It used to wheel around and drop me," she said. "Dad would just help me back up and laugh, saying, 'Can't you stay on this thing?'"

With my sister, Valerie, two years younger, as toddlers at point-to-point and steeplechase races with my parents and Uncle Harry Jelliss, also a trainer, I loved hearing the hooting and siren wail of ambulances as they tore across the racecourse grounds to collect thrown jockeys. "Here comes the am-bu-lance!" I would yell out, clapping my hands, as a five-year-old on a picnic rug at Cottenham and other race meetings, my mother told me, My infant glee did not then realize some pretty grim pain and tragedy that riders endured.

Dick Francis, a great steeplechase jockey and dear friend of my parents, had a memorable fall in 1956 down the finishing stretch of that year's Grand National aboard the late Queen Mother Elizabeth's horse, Devon Loch. Having successfully jumped the 30 harrowing Aintree fences, a shadow from a nearby structure swept across the course, and the horse thought it was another jump. Hurtling to the finish in the lead, Devon Loch suddenly took off into the air to clear the fantasy fence and crashed to the ground, hurling Francis onto the course.

He was not badly injured, but fate was not so kind to him the following year when Francis was paralyzed for awhile after a particularly brutal fall and had to give up riding after lengthy recovery and physical therapy in hospital. Dick's wife, Mary, took him paper and pencils in hospital to keep him occupied, thus starting a second remarkable career for one of the world's best-known and prolific novelists in our lifetime.

My paternal grandfather, George William Archibald (same name as my father) and Steve Donoghue, six-time winner of the English Derby through 1925, both rode in the United States and Europe during the years between the two world wars and were great friends.

Laura Hillenbrand recounts in her marvelous book, "Seabiscuit," one of Donoghue's memorable falls "on a horse that clipped heels and fell, spilling him onto the track in front of a mob of onrushing horses." She says, "He was an instant from being trampled to death when an elderly woman suddenly materialized from nowhere, grabbed hold of him, and dragged him under the rail. She left him in the safety of the infield and vanished. Donoghue never saw her again."

My grandfather was an American from Oakland, California. He rode winners at Santa Anita in the early 1900s, long before Red Pollard and Seabiscuit, and rode Meridian to victory at the Kentucky Derby in 1911. That winning race catapulted him to become a winning flat race jockey for King Alfonso of Spain and later Baron von Oppenheim of Germany, a cousin of Kaiser Wilhelm. Grandfather was among the world's best jockeys in his time.

He was almost killed at the Castellana racecourse near Madrid in 1920 riding one of King Alfonso's horses. At this track, hurdle and flat races ran on the same course. During one race, my grandfather's horse, Los Cairles, got pushed by other riders to the left of the course and, at 40 miles an hour, plunged into the wing of a permanent fence, pushing a piece of timber straight through the horse's chest and out his tail.

The horse was killed instantly and rolled over on him as it dropped, and he miraculously stayed on until it hit the ground. A marvelous sports photographer caught the whole thing on still film, and the pictures are in my grandfather's scrapbook, including one of the dead horse lying on the ground as the king and others peered at the corpse. Newspapers the next day in Spain, Germany and the United States reported the story with pictures and that King Alfonso visited my grandfather at the racecourse infirmary.

King Alfonso also gave Baron Oppenheim permission to retain Grandfather Archibald to ride for him, which led the baron to introduce the good-looking American jockey to Claire Hamel, a gorgeous champion German ice-skater. They had a whirlwind courtship and came back to the United States on the Queen Mary ocean liner in 1913 to be married in New York and honeymooned in California.

Claire got pregnant after their return to Spain, and the couple returned to America for my father to be born in Oakland at Merritt Hospital on April 2, 1915. They then returned to Spain, where my dad was raised until age five.

My grandfather was riding in Germany when World War I started, and he was detained by the Kaiser's authorities as an American civilian noncombatant, much as the Japanese were rounded up in the United States on orders of President Franklin D. Roosevelt after Pearl Harbor. With the baron's help, my grandfather sent Grandmother Claire and my father-to-be to England so they could go to America, but they never made it, having purchased tickets on the Lusitania's return voyage to New York.

The ocean liner, then on its way from New York to England's port at Southampton, was believed by Germany to be carrying U.S. weapons sent by President Woodrow Wilson to the British. A German submarine sank the Lusitania in the Irish Sea before it got to England in May 1915. So my grandmother and his infant son stayed in England.

My grandfather finally got to England in 1920 to ride racing for King George V, Lord Queenbury and other owners. A constant weight problem required him always to exercise and waste to lose pounds for his flat races. In 1927, he suddenly died of cardiac arrest after five races at Newmarket. My dad was just 12 years old and an only child. His mother put him in Hillsbrow Preparatory School in Redhill, Surrey, and moved to London.

She lived in the fast lane socially and married Cecil Rhodes, nephew of the diamond mine owner who founded Rhodesia, now called Zimbabwe, in Africa. My dad told me that my grandmother died in her London flat during the Nazi's World War II blitz. This was true. But my mother told me after my father died in 1997 that Grandmother Claire was a heavy cocaine user and committed suicide during the blitz by putting her head in a gas oven. Dad was in the British army at the time.

I understand his tremendous grief and pain and why he repressed this horrible memory and could not tell us the full truth about his mother's death. My father was a wonderful man with normal frailties and habits borne of his own family history and pain he endured through young adulthood. He was a solitary man and loner in many ways but had wonderful friends in the racing world who supported him throughout, and he was a very loving and supportive father. I loved his emphasis on civility and manners in dealings with others and his eternal commitment to care of animals.

He was a wonderful, loving man, but as I look at him in the photographs jumping the 25-foot water jump and Bechers Brook in the Grand National successive times, I realize why I am so proud to be his son. There are no pictures of his 5th Royal Inniskilling Dragoon Guard tanks taking on the Nazi machine-gun nests for two years in the hedgerows of France, Belgium and Holland.

He was a hard act to follow, having been a perfectionist jockey and horse trainer, putting horses, dogs and new cars ahead of everything else. He was a difficult father and mentor, but his drive and competitive spirit were always my model as a news reporter: the race to be first, to set the pace, to best the competition, to make a record, and to make a difference.

When all is said, riding racehorses in "the sport of kings" takes pure nerves of steel and commitment but is also pure artistry, which is why it has been one of history's best-loved spectator sports. "The racehorse, by virtue of his awesome physical gifts, freed the jockey from himself," writes Hillenbrand in "Seabiscuit." "When a horse and a jockey flew over the track together, there were moments in which the man's mind wedded itself to the animal's body to form something greater than the sum of both parts. The horse partook of the jockey's cunning; the jockey partook of the horse's supreme power. For the jockey, the saddle was a place of unparalleled exhilaration, of transcendence."

My parents admonished me as a child as I jumped my pony over small fences and hurdles on Newmarket's Warren Hill or at a pony club show: "Come on, George, you're not just a passenger. Keep your eye looking through the pony's ears, grip hard, lean forward, keep the reins gathered, pace yourself. Remember to kick and push forward on takeoff. Then think ahead about the next jump. Timing and pace are most important."

My youngest daughter, Elizabeth, now at Hollins University and on the riding team there near Roanoke, Virginia, is the inheritor of these skills and carries on the Archibald riding tradition. She rides beautifully and is my pride as she carries on a long family tradition of champion jockeys and horse trainers.

Riding was terrific training for what I would end up doing in life as an investigative newspaper reporter. There are a lot of parallels between riding and journalism.

When my grandfather died in 1927, Newmarket trainer Ted Leader took my father under his wing as a 12-year-old riding

apprentice, and he lived with Walter Earl and family, another leading Newmarket trainer for Lord Derby, who became his surrogate
father. Dad won his first races at age 14.

My mother's father was Henri Jelliss, a Belgian immigrant whose
father, Charles, was for 13 years leading jockey in Belgium. Henri
rode for Lord Astor and a number of other great owners, twice won
the famous English race, the Oaks, at Epsom—England's equivalent
of the Kentucky Derby—and the 2,000 Guineas at Newmarket, second leg of the British Triple Crown. He later was a leading racehorse
trainer.

In his teens, Dad rode for "Mr. Jell," who had 50 horses in training at Newmarket in the early 1930s. Henri Jelliss' daughter, a lovely
looking red-headed teenager, Angela, would watch young George
Archibald early mornings as he rode out in the mist with a string
of horses for daily exercise and training. My dad nicknamed her
"Rusty" because of her lovely red hair.

"I would watch him out of my bedroom window," Mummie
told me. "He looked so good on a horse. I would go to the stable
yard just to see him when they came back [from exercise]. I was a
tomboy and good on a horse myself. I caught your father's eye—I
was thought of as one of the boys. We got along well, had a great
time with all our friends, dated for many years, and got married,
even though my father never thought your dad was good enough
for me."

They were married in June 1938 in a fashionable wedding. Even
their wedding presents were listed in detail in the Newmarket Journal newspaper. It was the town's social event of the year. "We honeymooned in the south of France, and your dad brought along five
of his steeplechase jockey friends—Rip and Jack Bissill, and I can't
remember who else," Mummie told me." I do remember when we
played Baccarat at a casino in Cannes, and your dad and a Frenchman were losing, the Frenchman taught your dad how to swear in

French, and he taught the Frenchman how to swear in English. The Frenchman was Maurice Chevalier."

Mummie's maternal grandfather was George Blackwell, trainer of Rock Sand, English Triple Crown winner—who sired the mare of Man O' War, America's great champion stallion, and Sergeant Murphy, who won the Grand National (the world's most difficult steeplechase) in 1923. Blackwell is the only trainer in history whose horses won both the English Triple Crown and the Grand National steeplechase. Both horses were bought by August Belmont, founder of Belmont Park racecourse in New York, and moved to stud in the United States in the early 1920s.

While at boarding school in 1929, my mother, not quite five feet tall, would go into the gymnasium and hang by her arms from the bleachers, believing that would make her taller. Apart from always being a great rider, she also was an accomplished skier and skied from the top of the Matterhorn in her early twenties. She also was a magnificent tennis player and qualified to play at Wimbledon in 1934, but the judges disqualified her in the final cut because she had fibbed about her age—then 16—and was too young to compete.

As a toddler in England, I still remember her wheeling my pram up to the edge of the grass tennis courts as she and Daphne Gaskell, daughter of another prominent Newmarket trainer, and others played. I remember so well the pop, pop, pop sounds as the balls went back and forth. Mummie was a fierce tennis competitor and fast on her feet, so she got around the court quite well. Another trait that taught this budding journalist.

She also drove an ambulance as a volunteer throughout the war during German bombing air raids against England—we had several air bases near Newmarket that were constant targets. She and her friend, Daisy Adams, would go off in the ambulance each day when the air raid sirens started to take injured to hospital. After the attacks, she came back home, would take off her uniform, have a

bath, and returned to normal. She read me Christopher Robin stories every night before bed from A.A. Milne's "When We Were Very
Young," Enid Blyton's "Noddy" stories, and from the Bible. She read
so well, with such expression. She had taught me to read and count
by the time I was two and to ride a pony.

At age seven in England, she had to pull me off my white Welsh
pony, Thundercloud, as he reared up at a fox hunt meeting. I'll never
forget her jumping on his back, grabbing the reins, getting into the
stirrups, and kicking the pony, whip in hand. Thundercloud immediately knew who was boss and calmed down right away. She had
total control. I watched in awe.

When World War II broke out in 1939, my Dad and many of
his jockey chums joined the 5th Royal Inniskilling Dragoon Guards,
an Irish regiment that was a horse cavalry regiment in the Kaiser's
war, and went to Sandhurst, England's equivalent of West Point.
The regiment still had stables of horses, so they'd have animals for
polo.

But Winston Churchill, prime minister of England and co-
inventor of the tank, decided to mechanize the regiment, so my dad,
best friend Jack Bissill, and other jockeys soon found themselves in
training maneuvers in England's northern Yorkshire moors to test
the new tanks as they came off the assembly lines.

With my dad as tank commander, the regiment landed at Normandy just days after D-Day on June 6, 1944, six weeks before I
was born, and followed General George Patton's Third U.S. Army to
within 140 miles of Berlin by war's end, liberating villages from the
Nazis along the way in France, Holland and Belgium.

Dad, still an American citizen, was drafted into the U.S. Army
four years after the Japanese invasion of Pearl Harbor. Already in
combat in France, he sought and received a battlefield order from
General Patton's field headquarters to stay with his allied Irish regiment as tank commander.

Yet when the war ended, and he sought renewal of his American passport so he could travel abroad and start riding racing again, diplomats at the American Embassy in London refused to issue him a new passport because he had fought with a British regiment. They said he had sworn allegiance to a foreign power. Stupid bureaucrats.

Dad got annoyed, having been brewed-up in his tanks and almost lost his life many times after the Normandy invasion. "I was on our side, not Hitler's," my dad angrily told a Foreign Service officer at the American Embassy at Grosvenor Square in 1946. He told them to stuff it, and went to the British Home Office to become a naturalized British subject so he could get a passport and continue his steeplechase riding career.

This made a profound impression on me as I was growing up. I have forever remained impatient with indolent bureaucracy, government stupidity, waste and corruption—and politicians who use the system to advance themselves instead of the best interests of the people they claim to represent.

In the news business, I'm grateful for having been able to provide readers with a complete report on each story I've worked, with the help of supporting editors who shared my values regarding our birthright of freedom and creative enterprise and the need to pass that on to generations to come. But it's a heavy burden we carry as we try to live up to that kind of legacy.

When Dad made the decision to move our family to the United States in 1955, he was assistant trainer for Queen Elizabeth II— essentially "traveling head lad" who took her horses to race meetings. He had met Canadian horse breeder J. Elgin Armstrong at the Newmarket bloodstock sales. They struck up a conversation as horses were being led round a ring, and before we knew it, my dad agreed to become Armstrong's yearling trainer in Brampton, Ontario, and we moved to Canada as a stepping stone to the U.S.

Mummie handled our entire move from England by ocean liner in 1955—packing all our household goods, wrapping Dad's German Luger (confiscated from a captured German officer in World War II) and shotguns in a rolled carpet, getting us and two terriers through a two-week voyage across the Atlantic and to safety, having the dogs vaccinated in Manhattan in the dead of night after we cleared Ellis Island, and shepherding us all into Canada by train.

Financier and art patron Paul Mellon, who owned Rokeby Farm in Upperville, Virginia, brought my father to America in 1956. So we immigrated to America from Canada when I was 12 and my sister, Valerie was 10. Mummie became the first woman in Middleburg, Virginia, to break the barrier as an exercise lad riding Thoroughbred racehorses at the nearby training track.

My values were hewn by mother who taught me everything and was a pretty terrific can-do person in every area and by father who was heroic and suffered greatly at the hands of bureaucratic fools and who modeled great values.

Dad went through a string of owners, changing jobs almost yearly. First he trained for John Hay Whitney's ex-wife, then Liz Lunn,—at Llangollen Farm in Upperville—who fired him after Queen Elizabeth II and Prince Phillip recognized and greeted Dad, not her, on a visit to the Middleburg training track in 1957. Then he teamed up with leading Middleburg trainer Sydney Watters for awhile, trained for Singer sewing machine heir Stephen Clarke and James Mills (who had married a duPont), and a succession of others, including Hubert Phipps, who owned Rockburn Stud in Marshall, Virginia. It was Phipps who introduced me to the smell of newspaper ink.

I was just taking it easy in high school, working on the high school newspaper as an English requirement and participating on the school debate team. I had kept my English accent because the girls liked it, and my debate coaches encouraged it to keep the judges awake late in a day's competition with other schools. That worked.

We won state forensic honors, and I got into a lovely college that otherwise frowned on my mediocre high school grades.

Hubert Phipps and brother Ogden were part of the powerful New York Phipps publishing and investment family, but Hubert had escaped to rural Virginia, as did Paul Mellon, many duPonts, and others of hugely rich families who were sick of all the demands placed upon them and few joys except having lots of money. So they came to the rural agrarian horse country in northern Virginia, where you still can't find a McDonald's or 7-Eleven for many miles.

Phipps had bought the Fauquier Democrat newspaper in Warrenton, Virginia, now owned by publisher Arthur J. "Nick" Arundel, another horse-racing lover and loyal patron of the annual Gold Cup races at The Plains. One Saturday in 1960, when I went to the farm with Dad, he boasted to Phipps that I had a story about the week's high school activities published in the Loudoun Times-Mirror. Phipps asked me if I had ever seen a newspaper printed and would I like to go with him the next Wednesday to see his paper printed in Warrenton. Dad wrote a note to the school to get me a day off, and that experience was another turning point that helped snare me into the world of journalism. From that day, I wanted newspapers to be my life.

Dad's time with Phipps also was a turning point for Valerie, who was a much better rider than me. She acquired her great hunter show pony, Guinevere, from Lady Phoebe Phipps, who had brought some of the first great Welsh pony stallions to America from Britain. One of her Welsh stallions at Rockburn jumped into a field with a Thoroughbred mare and got her in foal. Lady Phoebe donated the lovely roan filly to Valerie, who broke her with Dad.

She named her Guinevere and went on with her to win many ribbons at area shows until she went to college and sold Guinevere to raise tuition money. The new owners changed the pony's name to Prim 'n Proper, and she was grand champion large pony for three years in a row, showing at prestige shows in Harrisburg, Pennsylvania,

Madison Square Garden in New York City, and the Washington International Horse Show in D.C. Valerie's other superb pony, Massassoit, a Connemara, was bought by a diplomat in McLean, Virginia, and later became a school pony at Madeira School for girls near McLean.

During our years at Loudoun County High School in Leesburg, my mother got a job in Washington with longtime Mutual radio news commentator Fulton Lewis Jr. The Mutual Radio studios were in the old Sheraton Park Hotel, now the Wardman Park, and I worked summers for Mr. Lewis. He took me under his wing, gave me books to read—John Chamberlain's "Enterprising Americans," Whittaker Chambers' "Witness," Arthur Koestler's "Darkness at Noon"— and took me to lunch after finishing each book to discuss them. He was like a second dad and helped teach me about America and fashion my values and future aspirations.

At Randolph-Macon College in Ashland, Virginia, where I was a freshman, friends Kenneth Y. Tomlinson and Henry Hurt got me involved in the school newspaper, the Yellow Jacket, and also the Draft Goldwater movement. Barry Goldwater, Republican senator from Arizona, was our hero. His little book, "Conscience of a Conservative," ghost-written by Brent Bozell (partner with William F. Buckley Jr. in the founding of National Review magazine), was a short, libertarian, conservative manifesto that made so much sense to us. We were young Goldwaterites and spent a lot of time to promote Goldwater's presidential nomination and candidacy.

It was the era of John F. Kennedy's presidency and assassination, leading to Richard Nixon's downfall in the Watergate bugging and cover-up scandal—the fall of two presidents who vied against each other for the White House following the 1950s era of good-feelings under "Ike," President Dwight D. Eisenhower, who led us to victory as allied commander in World War II.

The 1960s through 1990s was a period when people throughout the country worried whether those in political power really had the best interests of the people in mind or just themselves—political ascendancy and growth of centralized government, to make themselves more powerful by using the taxing power of the state to redistribute income and the product of people's work.

After college and four years as a military draftee in the U.S. Air Force during the Vietnam era as a young newspaper writer and editor at the country's largest undergraduate pilot training base at the time, William's Air Force Base in Arizona. I spent three years with The Arizona Republic newspaper in Phoenix, followed by six years on Capitol Hill as a staff assistant for two Republican congressman from Arizona—John Conlan and Eldon Rudd.

Called to serve on President-elect Ronald Reagan's Transition Team at the National Science Foundation from November 1980 until the president took office in January 1981 and then to serve a few months as budget analyst at the U.S. Department of Health and Human Services, it was my major pain then to spend six months as deputy assistant secretary for legislation at the U.S. Department of Education under Secretary Terrel Bell, who Larry Uzzell, an aide to National Institute of Education Director Edward Curran, labeled "Terrible Bell."

Those six months at the Department of Education were among the worst of my life because the hatred for Ronald Reagan permeated the civil service, and Secretary Bell and the civil servants within the Education Department undercut the president in every possible way. It was a great disappointment. That department has proved over the years since to be a tremendous waste of billions of taxpayer dollars.

I joined The Washington Times in January 1982 as the paper's first hired reporter before its May 17 launch and an unanticipated decade as one of the newspaper's lead scandal reporters during the late 1980s and early 1990s when we blew the lid off a series of congressional scandals that brought a sea change in congressional political leadership from Democrat to Republican.

CHAPTER TWO

THE COURAGE IN KING'S EYES

There is seldom, if ever, in the history of the world as a socio-political document expressed in such profound, eloquent, and unequivocal language, the dignity and the worth of human personality. This is the meaning of the American dream. And we can't afford to stop now because our nation has a date with destiny.

—Martin Luther King, August 28, 1963,
at the Lincoln Memorial in Washington, D.C.

━━━━━━

MARTIN LUTHER KING, in his "I Have a Dream" speech, is talking of the Declaration of Independence, written by Thomas Jefferson with help from John Adams and Benjamin Franklin, which states in part: "We hold these truths to be self-evident, that all men are created equal, that they are endowed by their Creator with certain unalienable Rights, that among these are Life, Liberty and the pursuit of Happiness—That to secure these rights, Governments are instituted among Men, deriving their just powers from the consent of the governed—That whenever any Form of Government becomes destructive of these ends, it is the Right of the People to alter or to abolish it, and to institute new Government, laying its foundations on such principles and organizing its powers in such form, as to them shall seem most likely to affect their Safety and Happiness."

After emigrating from England to Virginia with my family as a young lad in the mid-1950s, my first impression of Martin Luther King from new friends and their parents was that he was a socialist rabble-rouser. My father mocked King for supporting socialist welfare programs and lazy people who wouldn't work because they were on food stamps and other government assistance that deterred working to earn a living.

It was a struggle for me to sort things out. I liked King's message of equality and dignity of all people regardless of race or background, but I resented people who loitered outside our local Safeway and refused my dad's daily offers of honest paying work by helping him to feed and exercise Thoroughbred horses at the Middleburg Training Center.

"Lazy good-for-nothings," my dad would say, using the "n-word" to underscore his resentment—my introduction as a 12-year-old to the racist epithet. But my dad made a good point: Why did people prefer food stamps and state welfare payments over a good day's work and a paycheck? My parents and those of my friends worked hard to support their families and did not appreciate the rising taxation to support a growing welfare class of able men who would not work.

These memories lingered and made a larger impression as I grew older. My father was correct about the laziness and refusal of able men to work, but he was wrong to make it a racial issue. Just as many poor whites as blacks took advantage of the social welfare programs put into place by the government. We just needed to change the system that created incentives not to work and for a growing welfare class to rely on working taxpayers to carry them through life.

Another part of the culture shock after moving to Virginia was the racial segregation, which was anathema to me after going to school at St. Louis Convent in Newmarket, England, with black American children from nearby Lakenheath and Mildenhall U.S. Air

Force bases. Lucille, my first girlfriend at age six, was the daughter of a black Air Force master sergeant who gave me my first stick of Wrigley's chewing gum, something that her parents could buy at the base commissary.

I can't count the number of times that Sister Edith rapped my hand with a ruler and made me stand in the corner to say Hail Marys because she caught me chewing gum in class. Once I heard Sister Edith's rosary clacking as she marched down the aisle behind me in class and quickly buried my piece of gum in Lucille's fuzzy hair. But I was caught anyway and then given another walloping when I went home for having to say more Hail Marys. We were Church of England, even though my sister Valerie and I went to a Catholic school. The concept of double jeopardy was a big part of the discipline in our family as we were growing up.

But when I started eighth grade at Loudoun County High School, and had to travel 16 miles by school bus, there were always two buses following each other down the road, morning and afternoon—one carrying us white kids and another carrying the black children who went to a separate school.

We saw the black kids in town on weekends, but we were separated by the social and legal segregationist system that drew a line between us and kept us apart. I instinctively felt as a child that this was terribly wrong, but it took time for me to sort things out, as our country did as well, thanks in large part to Martin Luther King, who was speaking out for equality and civil rights for blacks.

So was my rector at Emmanuel Church in Middleburg, the Rev. Earnest A. de Bordenave, called Froggy, who decided to integrate a local soda fountain and restaurant when President John F. Kennedy and wife Jackie rented Glen Ora Farm in Middleburg as a weekend retreat after his election in 1960. I was an acolyte at church, and Froggy announced one Sunday as we donned our surpluses in the undercroft that he was going to lead a sit-in to take advantage of the media interest in the Kennedys' regular trips to Middleburg. I played hooky from school so I could be there.

It was uneventful, except for the fact that no local blacks would participate in the protest, apparently afraid their local employers would disapprove. So Froggy brought in several dozen blacks from nearby and called the press to get coverage. It was on the nightly TV news and gave me a firsthand lesson about the intersection of social action and the media in achieving needed change.

The sit-in also brought Martin Luther King into my life as a new hero. This was a sea change for me as a teenager because I realized that the bigotry supported in my community was wrong. As I saw King pushing for social justice on the national level, I privately cheered him on, not being able to admit in my own home or at school that I admired his courage. I was silent but grateful as events unfolded for King's unflinching, strong leadership and persistence, which made a real difference and marked me forever.

After King's speech at the March on Washington for Jobs and Freedom on August 28, 1963, Coretta Scott King revealed in an interview that he told her the experience was life changing for him. "Martin said to me, 'At that moment, I experienced the presence of the Divine as I have never experienced him before. It seems as though I could hear the quiet assurance of an inner voice saying stand up for righteousness, stand up for truth, and God will be at your side forever.'"

Michael Bolton paid tribute to King in a song that grabbed me, "The Courage in Your Eyes," which beautifully expressed the source of my gratitude for King's courage and sacrifice:

> The courage in your eyes
> The wisdom in your smile
> The strength within your heart
> To walk the endless mile
> The years have only shined upon your face

And showered you with dignity and grace
The way you lived your life
And the light you've always shown
More than the world, more than this world
More than the world
Has ever known.

CHAPTER THREE

COOLIDGE, GOLDWATER
AND REAGAN

Liberty is not a means to a higher political end. It is itself the highest political end...liberty is the only object which benefits all alike, and provokes no sincere opposition....The danger is not that a particular class is unfit to govern. Every class is unfit to govern....Power tends to corrupt, and absolute power corrupts absolutely.

—Lord Acton, John Emerich Edward Dalberg,
Letter to Bishop Mandell Creighton, 1887

═══════════

IT WAS IN 11th-grade government class at Loudoun County High School in Leesburg, Virginia, in 1961 that I first heard Lord Acton's memorable statement that "power corrupts" and that human liberty "is the highest political end...which benefits all alike."

Teacher Stanley Kelley was an inspiring cynic who made students consider the various forms of government through the ages ranging from authoritarian regimes of the Caesars in Rome; monarchy and parliaments in Great Britain and Europe; and tribal regimes in Africa, Asia, and in the Americas before our own republican democracy was formed as a federation of separate states called the United States of America.

G. William Whitehurst, my history professor at Old Dominion College in Norfolk, Virginia, told stories about the founding fathers and heroes of the ages in riveting lectures about their lives and values that shaped and inspired them.

In one lecture, my class notes show that he quoted President Calvin Coolidge, our 30th president, who the press called "Cool Cal," a stoic, little-remembered president who nonetheless said many memorable things that made sense to an eager burgeoning American who emigrated across the same Atlantic route taken by the Mayflower pilgrims three centuries earlier.

Coolidge said: "We do not need more material development, we need more spiritual development. We do not need more intellectual power, we need more moral power. We do not need more knowledge, we need more character. We do not need more government, we need more culture. We do not need more law, we need more religion. We do not need more of the things that are seen, we need more of the things that are unseen."

Coolidge was a great supporter of public schooling but a greater advocate of the development of personal character. "Education will not take the place of persistence," he said. "The world is full of educated derelicts. Persistence and determination alone are omnipotent. The slogan 'press on' has solved and always will solve the problems of the human race."

As the Vietnam War ground up hundreds of thousands of young American lives over almost a decade, young soldiers who slogged it out with the guerrilla Viet Cong in the rice paddies and river tributaries of Southeast Asia and in the skies over Hanoi, this budding reporter and editor of Old Dominion's Mace & Crown student newspaper was seriously influenced by Coolidge's emphasis on the power of observation and listening. I realized from his wisdom that the person who soaks up information, perspective, and context can responsibly pass that on to others for the good of the order. "It takes a great man to be a good listener," Coolidge concluded. "No man ever listened himself out of a job."

Coolidge also championed moral and spiritual development that reinforced my own "cool Christian" values from early upbringing in the Church of England and later the Episcopal Church in the United States. As a college student, I was not a fan of hot Baptist, evangelical, born-again, Pentecostal types. But moral and spiritual direction became important to me during those years as I rejected both narcissistic libertarian selfishness and judgmental pointy-nosed religious types who told us what God wanted us to do with our lives, quoting selected passages of the Bible.

The fact is, American conservatism is a melding of religious belief in a Creator of life and liberty, libertarian thought articulated by American Founders Thomas Jefferson and John Adams, and crystallized in our lifetime by intellectuals such as Russell Kirk, author of "The Conservative Mind," politicians such as Arizona Sen. Barry M. Goldwater who with writer Brent Bozell Sr. authored "The Conscience of a Conservative," and William F. Buckley Jr., prolific author over the past half-century who founded National Review magazine.

Goldwater libertarianism and Kirk traditionalism "jostle against one another," notes Wilfred McClay, professor of history at the University of Tennessee Chattanooga. "There are bridges between them—both have a strong anti-totalitarian, anti-statist thrust, for example—but certain issues tend to drive them apart. Libertarians tend to be anti-authoritarian and individualist in all things, while traditionalist conservatives are deeply concerned about the loss of authority and community in modern American culture."

Social conservatives with strong religious beliefs tend to favor "a static, ordered, devout, unplugged, homogenous and autarkic agrarian world that they probably would not want to inhabit for more than a few days," McClay concludes. When it all boils down, McClay concludes, American conservatives—Christian or secular—

are prepared to live in an imperfect world and confine themselves to issues and government incursions when it really matters, while liberals push for collective, government, tax-funded solutions at almost every turn without allowing people to work things out for themselves in a climate of individual freedom and the most limited government possible.

I realized the world has a lot of ideological wackos who take religious nostrums to an extreme. These would include secular so-called reverends, such as media hound Barry Lynn of Americans for Separation of Church and State, who take narcissistic anti-religious beliefs to an extreme in order to prevent public display of the Ten Commandments, the Christmas Nativity scene at Bethlehem, or prayer in schools, believing they are somehow empowered to go against people of faith throughout America for ideological and political gain in the secular political and judicial arenas.

Extremist true believers of all types have caused most of the troubles and wars in the world.

The fads of socialism, collectivism, and modern-day liberalism since World War II caused me to rebel at an early age against statism, but I didn't know why until I worked as a high school senior for Mutual Network radio broadcaster Fulton Lewis Jr., who took me under his wing and gave me books to read about the heroes of American free enterprise, the darkness of communism, and the so-called McCarthy era of the 1950s.

I got interested in politics during the Kennedy-Nixon presidential race in 1960 and campaigned for John F. Kennedy with young friends in Virginia and Maryland. My parents were for Vice President Richard Nixon, the Republican candidate, but I was gravitating in a rebellious libertarian conservative direction that eschewed party labels.

Goldwater's concise essay, "The Conscience of a Conservative," framed things so neatly for me in those teenage years and certainly made more sense than Karl Marx's "Communist Manifesto" that was mandatory reading in many college history and political science classes. Goldwater's little book was never on the class reading list.

So to get some balance, I joined Young Americans for Freedom and subscribed to publications of the Intercollegiate Studies Institute while in college and started a personal political and career journey that interspersed journalism and politics.

Goldwater's little book, just 127 pages, was a profound awakening for me as I struggled to understand the core values of American liberty and economic creativity, my new country's approach to the world. "The root difference between the conservatives and the liberals of today," Goldwater writes in 1960,

> is that conservatives take account of the whole man, while the liberals tend to look only at the material side of man's nature. The conservative believes that man is, in part, an economic, an animal creature, but that he is also a spiritual creature with spiritual needs and spiritual desires. What is more, these needs and desires reflect the superior side of man's nature, and thus take precedence over his economic wants.
>
> Conservatism therefore looks upon the enhancement of man's spiritual nature as the primary concern of political philosophy.
>
> Liberals, on the other hand, in the name of a concern for 'human beings,' regard the satisfaction of economic wants as the dominant mission of society. They are, moreover, in a hurry. So that their characteristic approach is to harness the society's political and economic forces into a collective effort to compel "progress." In this approach, I believe they fight against nature.

This is strong stuff that forced me to look further and ask questions about the difference between conservatives and liberals. Goldwater's little book lays down the challenge squarely: "Surely, the first obligation of a political thinker is to understand the nature of man. The conservative does not claim special powers of perception on this point, but he does claim a familiarity with the accumulated wisdom and experience of history, and he is not too proud to learn from the great minds of the past."

And the clincher—Goldwater concludes:

The first thing [the conservative] has learned about man is that each member of the species is a unique creature. Man's most sacred possession is his individual soul—which has an immortal side, but also a mortal one.

The mortal side establishes his absolute differentness from every other human being. Only a philosophy that takes into account the essential differences between men, and, accordingly, makes provision for developing the different potentialities of each man can claim to be in accord with nature.

We have heard much in the time about "the common man." It is a concept that pays little attention to the history of a nation that grew great through the initiatives and ambition of uncommon men. The conservative knows that to regard man as part of an undifferentiated mass is to consign him to ultimate slavery.

Barry Goldwater was a good-looking, jut-jawed Arizona businessman and Air Force reserve pilot who built a department store with his brother, Robert, and got involved in local politics as a Phoenix city councilman in 1949. Goldwater's early political mentor Steve Shadegg and chief fund-raiser Harry Rosenzweig, a Phoenix jewelry store owner, quickly recognized they had an attractive, eloquent political star on their hands.

Shadegg and Rosenzweig reached out for help to William Baroody, founder of the American Enterprise Institute in Washington,

U.S. Senate Republican leader Everett McKinley Dirksen of Illinois, and Willie Bioff, a former union organizer and Mafia don retired in Phoenix to help groom Goldwater to run for the U.S. Senate in 1952 against incumbent Democratic Sen. Ernest W. McFarland.

Goldwater swept into Congress as part of the Dwight Eisenhower political wave that toppled Democrats under Harry Truman by defeating Adlai Stevenson for president in 1952.

Goldwater became an immediate national voice on fiscal and labor matters and developed a strong political alliance at the national level on fiscal, foreign affairs, and national defense issues with conservative anti-Communist senators of both parties such as Harry F. Byrd of Virginia, Richard Russell of Georgia, John Stennis of Mississippi, Karl Mundt of South Dakota, and Joseph McCarthy of Wisconsin.

After Goldwater's re-election in 1958, campaign adviser Steve Shadegg reached out to William Baroody (founder of the American Enterprise Institute in Washington), Harry V. Jaffa of Claremont College near Los Angeles, California libertarian activist Karl Hess, and Catholic Orthodox rebels William F. Buckley Jr. and Brent Bozell, founders of conservative National Review magazine, to start organizing a Draft Goldwater movement for the White House.

Brent Bozell, in fact, actually drafted Goldwater's pivotal Conscience of a Conservative that lit a match to the burgeoning new conservative political movement in the early 1960s, culminating in Goldwater's presidential nomination at the 1964 Republican national convention following the assassination of President John F. Kennedy the previous November.

Jaffa and Hess wrote Goldwater's memorable line in accepting the 1964 GOP presidential nomination, in which he galvanized both the hard right John Birch Society delegates and stuck a finger in the eye of party moderates led by Nelson Rockefeller, William Scranton and George Romney.

"Extremism in the defense of liberty is no vice; moderation in the pursuit of justice is no virtue," Goldwater said to thunderous cheers at the convention. This was a defining statement for me and many in the budding Reagan movement, as it brought together Churchillian upbringing in favor of global freedom from oppression and a new political agenda committed to economic liberty for all and moral virtue for society at large.

As Goldwater went down to resounding defeat in 1964 at the hands of Lyndon Johnson, JFK's vice president from Texas and Democratic successor as president, Ronald Reagan became the spokesman for the new movement of young conservatives with his support of Goldwater in a nationally televised address that became known as "the speech."

I was then a college sophomore in Virginia, editor of the student newspaper, and fully in pursuit of a conservative agenda that made more sense than things most of my professors were pushing in my history and political science classes.

For me, departure from the Democratic Party after Kennedy's death started with LBJ's humongous national social welfare programs that doubled federal government spending overnight. They almost ruined our economy.

I joined the Air Force after being drafted my last year in college and was fully in favor of our anti-Communist efforts in Vietnam; although, I thought the Johnson administration's prosecution of the war was abysmal and demoralizing to our country. But the left-wing crazies against the war and Communist fellow travelers, like the Berrigan brothers and Jane Fonda, kept me and most Americans with the failed Johnson and Nixon policies regarding Vietnam.

Hey, it was us against them, freedom versus tyranny, and I was going with freedom for the people of Southeast Asia and all the world. No regrets.

Another key defining moment for me was Reagan's mesmerizing TV appeal on October 27, 1964, in behalf of Barry Goldwater's presidential bid, known by Reaganites thereafter as "the speech." "I

have spent most of my life as a Democrat," Reagan said in his televised fireside chat with the nation.

I recently have seen fit to follow another course. I believe
that the issues confronting us cross party lines.

Now one side in this campaign has been telling us that
the issues of this election are the maintenance of peace and
prosperity. The line has been used, "We've never had it so
good."

But I have an uncomfortable feeling that the prosperity
isn't something upon which we can base our hopes for the
future. No nation in history has survived a tax burden that
reached a third of its national income. Today, 37 cents out
of every dollar earned in this country is the tax collector's
share, and yet, our government continues to spend 17 million dollars a day more than the government takes in.

Ronald Reagan had the attention of American conservatives and
a national public hungry for an alternative to the liberal status quo.
The speech became a national political battle cry. Reagan said: "This
idea that government is beholden to the people, that it has no other
source of power except the sovereign people, is still the newest and
most unique idea in all the long history of man's relation to man.
This is the issue of this election: Whether we believe in our capacity
for self-government or whether we abandon the American Revolution and confess that a little intellectual elite in a far-distant capital
can plan our lives for us better than we can plan them ourselves."

You could hear people saying before TV screens across America,
"Yes, sir, freedom, choice, getting behemoth government power
under control and more accountable to the people, controlling
spending and growth of taxes. Thank you very much. Sign me up."
It was a clarion call for a second American revolution.

Reagan said:

You and I are told increasingly that we have to choose between a left or a right. There is only an up or down: Up to man's age-old dream—the ultimate in individual freedom consistent with law and order—or down to the ant heap of totalitarianism.

And regardless of their sincerity, their humanitarian motives, those who would trade our freedom for security have embarked on this downward course. In this vote-harvesting time, they use terms like the Great Society, or, as we were told a few days ago by the president, we must accept "a greater government activity in the affairs of the people." But they have been a little more explicit in the past and among themselves.

Reagan spoke of us having "a rendezvous with destiny" if we wanted to maintain our freedoms and asked us to step up to the plate. He said the most important words in the U.S. Constitution were, "We, the People." On that day, with millions of other Americans, I became a devoted Reaganite.

I got an Army draft notice in 1966, my senior year at Old Dominion College in Norfolk, Virginia, but talked my way into the Air Force instead. After basic training at Lackland Air Force Base in San Antonio, Texas, I was sent to Williams Air Force Base near Phoenix, Arizona, the largest undergraduate pilot training base, where I was editor of the base newspaper, the Jet Gazette, and speechwriter for the wing commander. It was exciting to see America's finest fighter pilots come and go.

The frequent graduation dinner ceremonies included many top guns, such as Air Force General Daniel "Chappie" James, Tuskegee airman of "Black Man and Robin" fame with Gen. Robin Olds, another heroic war ace, who together flew the F-4C Phantom 105 combat missions over North Vietnam. General James' son was a student pilot while I was at Willie.

After four years of military duty, Eugene C. Pulliam, titan conservative publisher of The Arizona Republic, hired me as staff editorial writer and make-up person for the editorial pages. He also hired me to handle letters to the editor, and I had my own weekly column for three years. Then I went to Washington as press secretary for U.S. Rep. John B. Conlan, newly elected Republican congressman from Arizona in January 1973—my foray to the other side of the road from the news media.

Friend John Coyne, a marvelous writer for National Review and Arizona State University professor when I lived in Tempe, became speechwriter for Vice President Spiro T. Agnew, and I often visited Agnew's suite and fellow speechwriters Suzy Cox and Vic Gold in the Old Executive Office Building until Agnew resigned under bribery allegations, followed by President Richard Nixon's resignation amid the Watergate scandal.

These were heady years for a young congressional aide and great training about how Washington works.

John Conlan was defeated in a 1976 bid for the U.S. Senate, and Eldon Rudd, 20-year former FBI special agent and Marine aviator in World War II, also Republican, was elected to succeed him in the U.S. House of Representatives.

Rudd asked me to join his staff as administrative assistant and press aide in Washington. In his second term, then-House Republican leader John Rhodes of Arizona arranged for Rudd to join the House Appropriations Committee, where I became his staff assistant on all federal government spending issues, and on the House Budget Committee.

We used our position to help write a record of government mismanagement and spending waste in most of the LBJ Great Society programs, and Ronald Reagan continued his political march to the White House with a promise to the American people that he would turn things around—cut national government spending and taxes and improve our national security. He was able to get the tax cuts, which spurred a huge economic boost for the United States in the 1990s after they kicked in.

But Reagan was unable to do much to curtail government growth, despite Herculean efforts of his administration. It's difficult to turn an ocean liner around in choppy seas in a few minutes. And presidents who followed fell into the old trap of feeding the shark-infested waters of Capitol Hill and Washington's K-Street lobbyist-law firm corridor.

The politicians know the permanent government and lobbyists for vested interests will always win, because they will always be there, making lots of money, and feeding their clients at U.S. taxpayers' expense.

The nation's news media, unfortunately, does not do a good job telling that story fully. It's a scandal, but the news organizations get sucked into the social swirl and black-tie dinners—hobnobbing with those who are fleecing American taxpayers, loving their self-importance, and the world goes on as usual. It's disheartening and disappointing but a further reason to hope that the new generation of reporters and media-savvy communicators will take the torch and make a difference.

Reagan had eight years as president and will probably go down in history as one of the best American leaders. The aftermath in terms of government growth and spending has not been pretty. But there are chapters of the continuing story yet to be written.

The fight for liberty and opportunity for people throughout the world continues. I have seen too many wonderfully bright and astute young people with clear moral vision in my journalism classes to say the battle is lost.

They are the future, and the future looks bright when one turns off what the late Vice President Spiro Agnew once called "the nattering nabobs of negativism" in the sycophantic big-government liberal media.

CHAPTER FOUR

CREATING THE NEW RIGHT

*'Twas a woman who drove me to drink, and I never had the
courtesy to thank her for it.*

—W.C. Fields

P AUL WEYRICH, founder of the conservative New Right in the early
1970s, came up with the vision to form a large array of new political groups and conservative policy think tanks that would counter
what he saw as a liberal-left pro-Democratic political juggernaut in
Washington and throughout the country.

Weyrich formed the Heritage Foundation as a new Washington think tank, a counter to the liberal Brookings Institution and
the Free Congress Foundation, to organize a conservative agenda in
opposition to controlling Democrats and their support groups.

With Edwin J. Feulner and Margo D.B. Carlisle, Weyrich helped
form conservative staff operations within both houses of Congress
called the House Republican Study Committee and Senate Steering Committee, which were intended to formulate a political action
agenda to the right of the official minority Republican congressional leadership groups considered by conservative members of Congress and their supporters around the country to be too go-along,
get-along and ineffective as a true opposition to the liberal-left
Democratic majority on Capitol Hill.

Weyrich, a true political genius, also got together with Texas political direct mail fund-raiser Richard Viguerie, young libertarian activist John "Terry" Dolan, and a brilliant Catholic pro-family activist, Connaught Coyne Marshner, to formulate the idea for a grassroots network of conservative political activists to put pressure on local, state and congressional politicians and officeholders in every state, with donations to be raised from the grassroots and grants from wealthy supporters in every state.

The group Weyrich formed to put together the entire panoply of New Right political action met every Friday morning for several hours in his Capitol Hill office near the Supreme Court and was called the Kingston Group.

Leaders of Heritage, the House and Senate conservative staff groups, and representatives of outside support groups—the U.S. Chamber of Commerce, Associated General Contractors, National Right to Work Committee, Terry Dolan's National Conservative Political Action Committee (NCPAC), and National Right to Life Committee—convened each Friday to discuss and plan legislative and political strategy and action for the coming weeks.

One week, when a plan for a national grassroots conservative group was being batted around after Ronald Reagan's 1976 presidential primary run against President Gerald Ford, someone asked, "What will we call it?" Conversation stopped.

Paul Weyrich responded, "We'll call it the Moral Majority." There was stunned silence. "I like it," Feulner said. There was visible excitement all round the room. Everyone wanted to know who could be recruited to head the operation.

The Reverend Jerry Falwell of Lynchburg, Virginia, an evangelical Baptist preacher, had a huge following through his Old Time Gospel Hour. Weyrich opened up discussions with Falwell, who agreed to get the Moral Majority going as a Christian-oriented political organization. Another seat was added for the new Moral Majority's representative at weekly Kingston meetings.

Weyrich, now wheelchair bound after multiple back surgeries, is an Eastern Orthodox Melkite Catholic who suffers fools not gladly. But he remains a significant force and keen strategic visionary who has always thought and operated as a general of the army.

He and Feulner, former staff aide for President Nixon's Defense Secretary Melvin Laird, and others, got funding to sustain the New Right groups from such multibillionaire donors as Joseph Coors of the Coors beer company in Colorado, Richard Mellon Scaife of the Pittsburgh Mellon family, superglue inventor William Krieble of Connecticut, and direct mail fund-raising wizard Richard Viguerie.

I had taken a detour from journalism and my job at The Arizona Republic as a young man in January 1973 to move back east to become press secretary on Capitol Hill for newly elected U.S. Congressman John B. Conlan, an Arizona Republican, who as state Senate judiciary committee chairman cleverly carved the new congressional district in north Phoenix and Scottsdale and a quarter of Arizona to the Utah border.

Republicans ruled the dominant population in north Phoenix and Scottsdale, while most of the rest of the new congressional district was rural towns and communities mostly dominated by conservative Democrats. Conlan won easily in 1972 and again in 1974.

Forty-three new Republican House members were elected in November 1972 as Richard Nixon was re-elected for a second term as president. Conlan, former press secretary for Billy Graham's Christian ministries, got himself elected president of the House Republican freshman class.

So Conlan assigned me as his and the House GOP freshman class's representative each Friday at the Kingston meetings, giving me an inside seat on the history about to occur.

However, Conlan got ambitious and ran for the U.S. Senate against fellow Republican Representative Sam Steiger (a friend of Barry Goldwater) when Arizona Senator Paul Fannin, former Arizona governor, retired. Steiger won the primary but had attacked Conlan so nastily and had so turned off voters that Democrat Dennis De-Concini from Tucson won the general election and stayed in the U.S. Senate for three six-year terms before being succeeded by Jon Kyl.

I continued to attend Kingston meetings—after I left Conlan in 1976—as first executive director of the American Legislative Exchange Council (ALEC) that year and then as administrative assistant and appropriations committee staffer on Capitol Hill for Congressman Eldon Rudd, Conlan's Republican successor, until November 1980. At this point, I joined President-elect Ronald Reagan's transition team at the National Science Foundation and worked in his administration for a year at the U.S. Departments of Health and Human Services and Education before joining the prepublication group that started The Washington Times.Original attendees of the weekly Kingston Group strategy meetings from 1973 onward were Feulner and Philip Truluck (then of the House Republican Study Committee); Margo D.B. Carlisle of the Senate Steering Committee; Kathleen Teague (whose husband at the time was administrative assistant for U.S. Rep. Jack Kemp, New York Republican); Jerry James, Frank J. Walton and P. Thomas Cantrell (from the Heritage Foundation); Weyrich's Family Institute director Connaught Marshner; direct mail pioneer Richard Viguerie; Richard Thompson (administrative assistant for U.S. Sen. Jim McClure, Idaho Republican); Warren Richardson (chief lobbyist for Associated General Contractors); Terry Dolan (founder of the National Conservative Political Action Committee [NCPAC]); Reed Larsen of the National Right-to-Work Committee; Reed Irvine of Accuracy in Media; Lawrence Pratt and John Snyder of Gun Owners of America; and representatives of the National Right-to-Life Committee and a slew of other Washington special interest groups.

Weyrich was a conservative true believer, previously a news reporter and press secretary for U.S. Senator Gordon Allott, Colorado Republican, who co-sponsored the 1964 civil rights bill. It was a meeting regarding this civil rights bill that gave Weyrich the idea for the New Right network that he started.

Allott had sent Weyrich to attend a civil rights bill strategy meeting in 1964, mostly attended by Democrats and leftists. Weyrich told me when I first met him that the meeting had opened his eyes to the way the left's political operators, labor union people, and media supporters such as Washington Post columnist Carl Rowan networked to get things done for "agit-prop"—agitation and propaganda.

Weyrich told me he had decided to replicate their operation on the political right, and he did.

One major result after just three years of the Kingston Group's networking in Washington and pushing the conservative agenda out to the states through ALEC and other grassroots groups funded by Coors, Scaife, Viguerie and others was Ronald Reagan's 1976 primary run for the Republican presidential nomination against Gerald Ford and Reagan's ultimate victory four years later as president.

After I returned to news reporting at The Washington Times in 1982, Weyrich often called to put me onto stories he believed would help keep the right wing ethical and honest to the true principles that he advanced. These were stories that could be perceived as anti–right wing, in a sense.

But Weyrich, as a former reporter himself from Colorado, believed that the house had to be cleaned from the inside, preferably by news organizations that shared the same values he held dear—not The New York Times or other liberal-left media organizations that reveled in hit-jobs against conservatives and the right in behalf of their liberal-left agenda.

So Weyrich worked Robert Bartley, longtime editorial page editor of the Wall Street Journal; Robert Merry, who was a Journal reporter on Capitol Hill who moved to the Congressional Quarterly, where he is now president and publisher; and other influential writers such as Jeffrey Bell and Frank van der Linden.

Stories Weyrich directed me to over the years include:

—A story about the Heritage Foundation's then-Executive Vice President Burton Yale Pines dragging the conservative think tank against a view that the breakup of the Soviet Union was inevitable. In reality, Weyrich, superglue inventor Robert Krieble, and U.S. Sen. Robert Kasten—Wisconsin Republican—had gone over to the Soviet Union at great peril during the Mikhail Gorbachev era, before the fall of the Berlin Wall, to train Boris Yeltsin and his troops in American-style politics.

Kasten had perfected a grassroots political organizing and communication system that was called the Kasten Plan, which he taught to Boris Yeltsin and his political team in Russia so that Yeltsin could be elected in Moscow and topple Mikhail Gorbachev.

Krieble became my main source on the story, which was laughably denied by his own press flak in a letter to the editor published by The Times after the story was published. We don't reveal our confidential sources, so I had to take the hit at the time. But Krieble called me after his flak hosed me down in a letter-to-the-editor to encourage me to keep my head up, saying the staffer had acted on his own and didn't know about our confidential relationship.

—Weyrich also pointed me to the story about Terry Dolan's homosexuality and sickness with AIDS, which scandalized conservatives at the time. Dolan, founder of the National Conservative Political Action Committee (NCPAC), was a libertarian and liked homosexual leather bars. He was a very clever conservative political tactician and organizer but, like many people, lived a double life. I wrote the story, sadly, as coverage of Dolan's hugely attended memorial service at a Catholic church in Washington. I got a lot of heat from friends and sources who thought the revelations were inappropriate and in bad taste. But it was the truth.

—Also, there was the story about Sen. Edward M. Kennedy, Massachusetts Democrat, having sex under a restaurant table on

Capitol Hill with a female textile lobbyist. Although, Weyrich did not actually give me that story directly. He appeared before the Senate Armed Services Committee in early 1989 to oppose President George H.W. Bush's nomination of Sen. John G. Tower, Texas Republican and former chairman of that committee, to be Secretary of Defense.

Weyrich argued that Tower was an opponent of the Strategic Defense Initiative and "an alcoholic and a womanizer." It was the latter comment that attracted the media's attention.

My editors laughed. "Who on Capitol Hill is not an alcoholic and womanizer?" Wes Pruden asked. "I bet you could count them on one hand."

My national editor at the time, Fran Coombs, told me to do a "clip job" story with one exclusive. That meant, go to the paper's library and ask them to search all the clippings from other newspapers about sexual peccadilloes of members of Congress, going back to the famous 1974 story of House Ways and Means Committee Chairman Wayne Hayes of Ohio and stripper Fannie Fox and the famous Tidal Basin plunge.

"Do a clip job story about alcoholism and sexual antics of members of Congress, but anchor it with an exclusive story, which we can call our own," Coombs instructed. "We'll put it on Page One."

I only had three days to get the story done. Paul Rodriguez advised me to troll the bars and restaurants on Capitol Hill, where Senators Edward M. Kennedy and Christopher Dodd were notorious for getting drunk and hitting on young women.

So I went first to La Colline, near Washington's Union Station, and the only story there was that Kennedy and Dodd got very drunk one night and, as they left, smashed a lot of framed, autographed pictures of members of Congress and other luminaries who they did not like that were hanging on the restaurant walls.

The La Colline manager who told me the story suggested I walk up the street to La Brasserie, another restaurant near Union Station on Massachusetts Avenue, actually two side-by-side row houses, where he said Kennedy and Dodd hung out a lot, got drunk often, and hit on women. So off I went.

Being from Britain and still having the accent, I was able to sit at the bar and pretend I was a visitor, which I was. (I had never been to the restaurant before.) "Is this where the incident with Senator Kennedy happened?" I asked the bartender.

"What incident?"

"The sex incident, it's been in the British tabs," I fibbed to get him to talk.

"Are you from England?"

"Yes. I'm visiting. Is this where the Kennedy incident happened?"

"Yes, it is," the bartender responded. "Ingrid, there, waited on him when it happened," he said, pointing to a tall, leggy, attractive, blonde waitress. I waited for a couple to leave Ingrid's section and took the table, but she clocked off, and I had another waitress who was also gorgeous—Carla, a double for actress Deborah Winger. I expressed disappointment that Ingrid was not my server because I wanted to hear the Kennedy story.

"Are you a reporter?" Carla asked.

I couldn't lie. "Yes."

"Who do you write for?"

I told her The Washington Times. She said she didn't want to talk about the incident there but immediately invited me to meet her for coffee the next morning on the other side of the Capitol. We met at a McDonald's on Independence Avenue near the Library of Congress and Trover Book shop.

Carla told me straight-up that Kennedy had sexually harassed her, and the management of La Brasserie had told her to forget it.

She told me that Kennedy and Dodd got drunk one night in an

upstairs private dining room at the restaurant, and a tiny, beautiful Asian waitress asked them if they wanted dessert. Their special was raspberries with cream or ice cream and a liqueur. Dodd made an inappropriate comment to the waitress, and she fled in horror. So Carla took over the duty of waiting on the two drunken senators.

She said she went in, and Kennedy got up from the table, picked her up bodily, tossed her across the table into Dodd's lap, and then ran around the table and began making indecent comments and trying to kiss her.

Carla said she pulled herself away, ran out, and complained to the manager but was told to forget it. "They're good, powerful customers," the manager told her. So this was her payback, telling me the story and hopefully getting some justice for herself and colleagues who had to put up with this behavior for so long.

So what was the Kennedy story? According to Carla, confirmed later by Ingrid, Kennedy came to La Brasserie for lunch shortly after Senate passage of a major textile bill in September 1988. His date was a blonde textile lobbyist, Elaine. They spent more than an hour in an upstairs, private dining room in the row house on the right and had two bottles of wine while they enjoyed crab cakes and another dish, dessert and coffee.

I knew the details because Kennedy went to La Brasserie so often that he just signed the checks and paid at the end of the month when they sent him a bill. Carla gave me a copy of his signed check for the lunchtime visit with Elaine, which spelled out all their food and drink and the time they arrived and left. Documentation is a reporter's gold.

The coffee station was at the bottom of the stairs. Ingrid went into the private dining room to see if Kennedy and Elaine wanted a coffee refill. No one was there. She assumed they had left and that Kennedy had just signed the check and left it on the table as usual.

But as she turned to walk out of the private dining room's

swinging French doors, she heard noises. She turned and looked where the noises were coming from, and discovered Elaine and Teddy beneath the table.

Carla was at the coffee station downstairs and said Ingrid came rushing down with a red face and told her what was happening. A few minutes later, both said, Kennedy and Elaine came down the stairs flushed, both still straightening themselves up—their hands putting their hair and clothes in place.

I had my exclusive anchor story for the piece to show the hypocrisy of alcoholics and womanizers in Congress.

Fran Coombs told me to call Kennedy's office for comment. After some protests from his press secretary that he didn't want to even give the request any credence, he eventually called me back to say, after talking to Kennedy, "We will have no comment, it's a private matter."

Story confirmed. It ran on Page One in March 1989. Just days later, Ted Kennedy and our editor, Arnaud de Borchgrave were at a black-tie affair at the Canadian Embassy in Washington, where the story was a hot conversation topic. Kennedy was chuckling and seemed proud to acknowledge the story was true, Arnaud told me.

A comment about sources: They are anyone, anywhere with direct information and documentation. They are preferably on the record or can be on background "not for attribution" or completely off the record.

What does this mean?

On the record means a reporter can attribute anything and everything to the source, quoting by name and title.

Some brave souls in politics and government service are willing to do that and not go off the record. I have had many sources like that over the years who worked in government. Christopher Manion, a Senate Foreign Relations Committee advisor to Senator Jesse Helms of North Carolina, never went off the record. But I would quote him selectively as an anonymous source, on occasion, so as not to blow his cover, and because I wanted to keep other media guessing who our sources were.

Off the record means you have to find another way to source and verify information or tips before you can use them.

Background means you can use the information, if you're satisfied with it, and verify, so long as you do not attribute it to the source by name or title. This and off the record are very unsatisfactory for a reporter because the source might have an agenda and the reporter must validate the information before using it. This takes a lot of work, but sources are the cream of a reporter's work, so you work with them on their ground rules and do the necessary reporting to validate the story with other sources and documentation.

I always go for paper that documents what a source says and allows me to quote the documents instead of the person if he or she doesn't want to be a named source.

For the Kennedy story, Carla told me Kennedy was such a frequent customer at LaBrasserie that he just signed his daily bills and didn't pay them until the end of the month after the restaurant sent a total monthly bill to his Senate office.

So I asked her for a copy of the check signed by Kennedy for the nooner lunch liaison he had with Elaine when he was caught having sex under the table, and she provided it.

CBS News anchor Dan Rather's career was ruined by a stupid, badly sourced, erroneous story about George Bush's National Guard service. A story that was pushed by a producer who had political motivation against Bush and a poisonous source who provided doctored documents that were false.

The case of Scooter Libby, former chief of staff for Vice President Richard Cheney, was another case of bad, undocumented sourcing by news organizations. It became clear as the story unfolded that Libby was given declassified documents about CIA operative Valerie Plame, wife of Bush critic Ambassador Joseph C. Wilson, but it was actually Deputy Defense Secretary Richard Armitage who actually got the information to Chicago Sun-Times columnist Robert Novak and other media.

Both President Bush and Vice President Cheney had the power to declassify the intelligence documents provided to them at will, under prior presidential executive order, and apparently did so before Armitage blew Plame's CIA role to the press. So people in the Bush administration did nothing illegal. And Novak and others in the media gladly received the leaks.

You can be sure the same would have happened if Karl Rove, President Bush's political director in the White House, released any information. The president would have declassified it beforehand so the release would be legal.

All the huffing and puffing about illegal releases of classified information is likely much ado about nothing, because the people in power in government and the press play this game all the time. The politicians want to get the information out. The receiving news organizations want it like panting dogs in heat.

So the leaks occur, and news media recipients run with the story. Call people in the media whores because, in one sense, it's not an inappropriate term.

What is inappropriate, to me, is all the teeth-gnashing and finger-pointing by news organizations who don't get the leaks but try to make a big story out of how inappropriate the leaks were. Give me a break. Everyone in the media would take a government leak if they were lucky enough to be on the receiving end.

Washington Post reporter Dana Priest was awarded a Pulitzer Prize in 2006 for her story based on leaked classified documents about a supposed network of U.S. prisons worldwide to house captured terrorist suspects. So why all the media barking when they're not the recipients? It's such a farce.

Get the story and run with it. If you don't get the story, shut up and go for the next one. News is a competitive business just like any other. No one owes us anything. We have to earn it.

Christopher Manion, who worked in Congress advising senators for decades, has a good way of summing it up: "In Washington, anything is ethical if it is not illegal. Lust for power is what drives Washington, but no one mentions lust for power, because virtually everybody has it. They'll attack greed instead. After all, only people in the private sector are greedy, right?" In 1986, Elliott Abrams, a neoconservative national security expert who disliked Senate Foreign Relations Committee Chairman Jesse Helms, accused Helms' aide Christopher Manion of leaking information from a classified hearing. Manion was cleared and Abrams was convicted a year later of lying to Congress.

Actually, according to Manion, New York Times columnist William Safire had telephoned him asking him to leak the classified information, but Manion hung up on him. "You don't like the rules, give up your clearances," Manion told me, while acknowledging that leaking "is the mother's milk of behind-the-lines Washington warfare.

"Leaking is a career-builder for journalists and people on Capitol Hill. One staffer who's had clearances since the 1960s insists that the only way you can attack incompetent bureaucrats is through leaking. That's the way he justifies it."

Some distinguished veteran government leaders regularly leak information to selected reporters to educate the public about policy power plays and differences. They do this through what they like to call "background briefings" where information is generally attributed to "a senior government official" or some such anonymous reference.

The late Chief Justice William H. Rehnquist was fond of backgrounding reporters on cases before the Supreme Court and differences or struggles among fellow justices, and Rehnquist for many years regularly met for private breakfasts or lunch with Frank J. Murray, The Washington Times' superb Supreme Court and White House reporter.

CHAPTER FIVE

MY FBI GODFATHER

*Never give in—never, never, never, never, in nothing great
or small, large or petty, never give in except to convictions of
honour and good sense. Never yield to force; never yield to
the apparently overwhelming might of the enemy.*
—Winston Churchill at Harrow, October 29, 1941

E LDON RUDD was a 20-year veteran FBI special agent before he
got into politics in Phoenix-Maricopa County, Arizona, in 1970—a
man who never gave in and stood for honor and good sense. As a congressman representing the northeast quarter of Arizona for a decade,
he was one of those unsung heroes in government who brought
water to the arid Southwest as a member of the House Appropriations Committee and earmarked funding for the multibillion-
dollar Central Arizona Project.

Rudd's good deeds, mostly overshadowed by negative stuff that
gets media attention, helped make news throughout his life on the
front lines of the Cold War and Fidel Castro's mischief as an agent
of Soviet expansionism from Cuba throughout South and Central
America. He worked behind the scenes and took no credit for most
of the things he accomplished as the FBI agent who interrogated
Puerto Rican nationalists who shot up the U.S. House of Representatives in 1953 and was the last American to see Nicaraguan

strongman Anastasio Somoza alive before Marxist insurgents killed him with a car bomb.

I first met Rudd in my capacity as a young member of the editorial board of The Arizona Republic in Phoenix, as he started his campaign for a seat on the Maricopa County Board of Supervisors. He told the editorial board that he grew up in Camp Verde, near Prescott, Arizona, was fluent in Spanish, served as a Marine fighter pilot during World War II, and got his law degree at the University of Arizona in Tucson before joining the FBI in 1950. An impressive background.

He was intensely patriotic and anti-Communist, expressing vigorous support for better relations with Mexico because he said Arizona was on the border of a growing tidal wave of resentment and Marxist expansionism in our hemisphere being fueled by Cuban dictator Castro and his upline Soviet financiers. Rudd expressed strong support for what our country was doing in behalf of freedom from Communist control and oppression in Vietnam.

Having just come out of four years as base newspaper reporter and editor at Williams Air Force Base near Phoenix, the country's largest undergraduate pilot training base at the time, I immediately liked this man. He was stiff and uncomfortable with the media, but I liked his total honesty and evident good values that shone through in the discussion.

Rudd was the only FBI agent fluent in Spanish in the Washington, D.C. district field office when Puerto Rican nationalist terrorists somehow got into the U.S. House of Representatives balcony with guns in 1953 and shot up the House floor before being captured. So he was assigned to interrogate them and find out all he could about the people behind this savage terrorist attack right in our own U.S. Capitol, where, fortunately, no one was injured or killed.

The terrorists spilled their guts to Rudd. FBI Director J. Edgar Hoover was so pleased with his report that he called Rudd to his office to commend him personally, saying, "Rudd, you have your next choice of assignment." When the time came a few years later, Rudd took Hoover up on his promise and asked to become legal attaché at the U.S. embassy in Mexico City.

The legal attaché in each of our embassies throughout the world is a specially trained FBI agent who serves as our country's liaison with law enforcement and intelligence agencies of the host country. In the case of unfriendly countries, the intelligence or spying function is more pronounced. Rudd served in Mexico City from 1960 to 1970, a crucial decade for pro-Communist revolutionary activity throughout Central and South America spawned by Cuba's Marxist dictator, Fidel Castro, with help from the Soviet Union.

I left The Arizona Republic in January 1973 to go to Washington as press secretary and legislative assistant for newly elected Arizona Congressman John B. Conlan, who served two terms and then decided to run for the Senate against Congressman Sam Steiger, who was U.S. Sen. Barry Goldwater's choice. After that Republican primary bloodbath, Dennis DeConcini, the Democratic candidate won the Senate seat. Rudd ran for Conlan's House seat and won handily. He asked me to join him as his administrative assistant or chief-of-staff in Washington and then in 1979, after being re-elected, moved me over to the House Appropriations Committee as his staff assistant.

Rudd was ignored by the media, totally committed to constituent service. He worked quietly for things he believed in without seeking personal credit, a stealth politician in many ways—quite tall and handsome, very genuine while bluing his grey hair, and somewhat stiff in public discussion. He was very upset when John Kolbe, a political columnist for The Phoenix Gazette, then the afternoon Pulliam newspaper, said Eldon had "the charisma of a broomstick." Except, when he lapsed into Spanish, one saw a big difference in his demeanor and body language, animated and lots of charisma.

Congressman Charles Rangel, New York Democrat, made fun of Eldon for wearing white suits and shoes. On a Capitol elevator one day, Rangel looked at Eldon and said, "Hello, Colonel Sand-ers." Eldon just stared back, telling me later he resisted the urge to respond, "Hey, baby"—famous greeting of Rangel's Harlem prede-cessor, Adam Clayton Powell—"you usin' food stamps?" Eldon had good relations with Rangel, Louis Stokes from Cleveland, Ohio, and other decorated military veteran members of the Black Caucus from World War II and Korea. Rangel got a Purple Heart and a Bronze Star as an Army soldier in Korea.

But Eldon resented Rangel always pushing the race card and failed policies to throw more federal dollars at welfare programs. As a member of the House Appropriations and Budget Committees, Eldon worked to build a record to show that billions of taxpayer dol-lars spent on food stamps and other welfare programs were wasted, didn't help inner-cities to cut the number of single women with babies without fathers, drug trafficking, prostitution, HIV-AIDS, and other social blight.

During his FBI years as legal attaché at the U.S. embassy in Mexico City for a decade, Rudd was like a sheriff circuit rider because as our country's intelligence eyes and ears in the Mexican capitol, he also flew around in a Cessna aircraft on a rotating basis to U.S. consulates in other Central American countries—Guatemala, Honduras, El Salvador, Nicaragua, and Costa Rica, where he kept close tabs on intelligence regarding Panama and, at that time, the U.S.-operated Panama Canal.

When President John F. Kennedy was shot in Dallas on Novem-ber 22, 1963, after Lee Harvey Oswald was apprehended by Dallas police at a theater 80 minutes later, the Dallas FBI office contacted Rudd in Mexico City and asked him to round up all information he could immediately get on Oswald and fly a file to Dallas. Oswald, an employee of the Texas Schoolbook Depository in Dallas from where the shots that killed Kennedy were fired, was a member of the pro-Castro Fair Play for Cuba Committee and had visited Cuba and Mexico numerous times.

Rudd quickly collected all information available about Oswald and his activities from Mexican authorities and personally flew the file to Dallas in a small prop-plane as Air Force One took Kennedy's body with Jacqueline Kennedy and newly sworn-in President Lyndon B. Johnson to Washington. Rudd only made it out of Dallas's Love Field for the return flight to Mexico City minutes before the border was sealed and his return prevented. Years later, Congressman Louis Stokes, Ohio Democrat and chairman of the House Select Committee on Assassinations, asked Rudd to testify about what he knew.

I was in the Capitol elevator with Eldon in 1977 when Stokes broached the issue. "You'll have to subpoena me," Rudd said. "I signed a confidentiality agreement when I left the FBI not to talk about any of our activities or investigations in any forum." Stokes, also a member of the Appropriations Committee, and Rudd liked each other, and they talked further on the House floor about possible ways Eldon might help the committee, which ultimately concluded in 1979 that Oswald probably acted with at least one other person to kill President Kennedy.

Eldon told me personally that he thought at least one other person might have been involved as an accomplice with Oswald, but no one yet knows who. He said he believed that Oswald was the lone shooter who fired the four rifle shots from the sixth floor of the Texas Book Depository that killed John F. Kennedy and that there was no other shooter. He said the 10-month Warren Commission inquiry concluded in September 1964, and all forensic evidence and contemporaneous amateur film footage of JFK's motorcade at the spot in Dealey Plaza, led to this conclusion, supported in discussions with other FBI people at the time and afterward.

FBI special agents and ex-agents are a tight-knit fraternal group, like Marines, and stay in touch with each other through a formal association. In retirement, many of them go on to top security jobs for big American corporations or form their own consulting companies to help government agencies and companies, here and abroad, with security and law enforcement liaison.

That proved beneficial in November 1979, when Iranian militants stormed the U.S. embassy in Teheran and snatched 65 American hostages, including a 22-year-old embassy guard, Marine Sergeant James M. Lopez from Globe, Arizona, in Eldon's district. As soon as we learned that Sergeant Lopez was one of the hostages, Eldon called his parents and promised to do everything he could to help get information from the State Department and elsewhere, and he told Ruth Ziebarth, his chief caseworker in Washington, to make this a No. 1 priority on her "tickle system."

Eldon had a marvelous way of keeping the staff accountable with a tickle system, before today's modern computer systems, which was mainly his own index card system. Every time he asked us to do something, he logged it. We better have an answer or status report when something came up on his tickle system. He'd ask what the status was but would never shout or get upset if we couldn't say; we just got that look and a nice rebuke to pay better attention to deadlines.

Sergeant Lopez's situation was a high priority for Eldon. He often called Lopez's parents in Globe, visited them on trips to the district, and they called to coordinate information they were getting from the Defense and State Departments, which were controlled by President Jimmy Carter's people. Ruth called the Carter State Department throughout the year following the snatching asking for updates. But as a Republican office, as comedian Rodney Dangerfield always complained, we got no respect.

So one day, Eldon took things into his own hands. The Lopez's called one day and said they were coming back to Washington at State Department invitation for a briefing with other hostage families. They kept Eldon informed of the details and once in Washington told him of the exact time of the briefing. He called me into his office, gave me his car key, and asked me to drive over to the Capitol, where a vote was under way, and pick him up to go downtown.

"Park near the C Street entrance to the State Department," he told me. We walked in and he told a greeter, "Congressman Eldon Rudd, Arizona, I'm here for the briefing." They were surprised, but an escort quickly arrived and asked us to follow him to the elevator.

As we got on, Eldon looked down at me and tapped his ear. I didn't know what he meant. There was no conversation, and the elevator stopped. We got off, and the escort asked us to follow him to the briefing room. "No, I've got stiff knees and need to stand here for a minute and work it out," Eldon said, kicking his legs out and doing knee bends. "Come back in a minute." The man walked off.

"What's going on?" I asked. "What was this all about?" I said, tapping on my ear with my finger.

"Didn't you see all those people downstairs, and also the guy who rode up with us, with plastic pieces in their ears? We're staying right here." Eldon knew what was going on. The man came back to get us, but Eldon said he still wasn't ready.

Suddenly the elevator door opened, and off walked President Jimmy Carter with Secretary of State Cyrus Vance right behind him for the meeting with hostage family members. Eldon strode right up to him and held out his hand.

"Mr. President, Eldon Rudd, Arizona," he said. President Carter stopped with a wide smile, eyes bulging, looking up at tall Eldon, and they shook hands. I was standing next to Eldon, and a White House photographer accompanying Carter and Vance started snapping pictures. Eldon kept squeezing and pumping Carter's hand quite hard, not letting go, and they exchanged a few other comments before Vance pulled Carter away by the shoulders, and they walked off for the briefing.

I said to Eldon, "What was that all about?"

He stopped and looked down at me. "You know how these people have treated us, frozen us out and not given us information. I just wanted to shake the president's hand so hard that he peed his pants." It was just a little payback, a gesture to let the president know his administration's partisan lack of cooperation during the hostage situation was not appreciated. And with that, we went into the briefing.

That was Eldon Rudd to a tee. A man who had lived through turbulent years during the Communist revolutionary menace in Central and South America as our legal attaché in Mexico City and wanted bold action on the part of our political leaders.

When Ché Guevera, Castro's revolutionary leader, was shot in a firefight in Bolivia forests in October 1967, word went from Washington to Eldon at the U.S. embassy in Mexico City that Guevara's death needed to be confirmed so revolutionary terrorists throughout the region and friendly governments didn't think he was still out there.

Eldon flew himself down to Bolivia, was escorted by authorities to Guevara's corpse, removed a finger or two and wrapped them, and flew back to Mexico City where Guevara had previously been arrested and fingerprinted. It was Guevara's fingerprints; his death was confirmed. All in a day's work for a patriotic FBI special agent serving as our country's legal attaché in Mexico City.

Eldon was one of few Americans to see Nicaragua dictator Anastasio Somoza Debayle alive, before he was car-bombed in Paraguay in September 1980. They had met for the last time, one-on-one, at a meeting only shortly before. Unfortunately, our country supported and coddled anti-democratic dictators, including Somoza, but Eldon regarded these relationships necessary and essential, as a Castro Soviet-backed Communist revolution was under way in our hemisphere. Like all our presidents since Nixon, he was committed to policies to destroy the Soviet empire and international communism as a priority for our country.

Rudd appreciated Somoza's commitment to the United States' stand against Castro's Soviet-funded revolutionary and terrorist activities throughout our hemisphere. And Somoza appreciated Eldon's intelligence role as legal attaché in Mexico City in keeping information flowing between countries of the region and the United States. Rudd was delighted with the role of The Washington Times in supporting the Nicaraguan Contras against the Marxist Sandinistas.

Rudd was a strong opponent of the Panama Canal treaty struck by President Jimmy Carter in 1977 to turn over control of the strategic U.S.-built waterway after 73 years to the regime of Panama's dictator Omar Torrijos. Rudd told Thomas Boney, his able legislative director, that he wanted to attach a legislative rider to the treaty approval by the U.S. Senate to ensure financial protection for the United States and to make sure the canal kept operating solvently and efficiently for world companies dependent on trade and goods manufactured abroad.

The treaty gave the canal away. There was also a strategic worry. What if Panama allied with a U.S. enemy and closed it?

Boney got together with staff of the Senate Foreign Relations Committee and House Legislative Counsel to craft a rider, with help from Sen. Jesse Helms, North Carolina Republican. It was decided the General Accounting Office, now called the Government Accountability Office, should be required to oversee the canal's operations and report to Congress on a continuing basis after it was turned over to Panama. At least we would know if it was operating properly, without cost to American taxpayers, short of the need for the United States to take over the canal militarily in the event of a major strategic crisis.

The Rudd Amendment was adopted as a rider to a congressional resolution approving the Panama Canal treaty. It was all we could do, but the amendment was quiet testimony to Rudd's insistent commitment to keep the upper hand for American interests and world commerce even in a bad political situation.

During Ronald Reagan's 1980 presidential race against Jimmy Carter, Rudd was Reagan's ultimate source of the so-called Carter debate papers that David Stockman used to help prepare Reagan for the national TV debates in which he decimated Carter.

Again, it was Rudd's FBI ties that were the crucial link. Carter's White House staff had all agencies of the federal government feeding information to a group housed in the Old Executive Office Building, next to the White House, about Reagan's and Carter's positions, public statements, and record on all issues from A to Z.

The stuff was being boiled down and assembled in three-ring binders with help from Democratic National Committee opposition research operatives. The Carter people wanted a complete side-by-side comparison so Carter could be trained in a "murder board" before the debates to take on the Great Communicator.

In short, this was use of taxpayer money at the White House for a campaign re-election purpose. Reagan friendly ex-FBI agents working security there at night learned of the project and were offended that this was happening in the White House. They decided to even the playing field and get a copy of the "debate papers" to Ronald Reagan.

Eldon's ex-FBI friends let him know of their discovery and asked him to be the conduit. He agreed. Someone got the large stack of copied papers to an ex-FBI friend of Eldon's at Arizona State University. Eldon picked up the copied Carter debate papers on a weekend trip to the district. When I picked him up on Sunday afternoon as usual at Dulles Airport near Washington, he was carrying a Basha's shopping bag with a box inside as he came off the shuttle to the main terminal.

"I want you to clear the decks tomorrow," he told me on the drive into Washington. "I've got a special project for you, and you'll have to go off campus. I'll tell you more tomorrow." I was used to Eldon keeping things close to the vest.

On that Monday morning in late summer 1980, Eldon was more private than usual. He was in his office early on the first floor of the Longworth House Office Building, door closed, and said he wanted no interruptions. About 10:30, he walked out of his office and flagged me in, closed the door, and motioned for me to sit down in front of his desk as he took a telephone call.

It was a call that would change history, and I will never forget this moment.

"Governor, how are you?" Rudd asked. There were comments from the other end as I sat there wondering who he was talking to. Eldon pointed to a picture on his wall, and then I realized it was Ronald Reagan on the other end of the phone. "Governor, I have some information I need to send you right away. Who is your most trusted person, and what address do I send it to?"

As Reagan responded, Eldon wrote the information on a notepad on his desk. There were some more pleasantries, and he hung up. He tore off the note he had written, stood up, and handed it to me. Then he reached under his desk and handed me the Basha's bag with the box of papers. "Take this," he said. "Take the rest of the day off. Go somewhere and wrap this securely (no government materials); send it insured and everything else to this address."

Eldon's handwritten note from the conversation with Governor Reagan had Edwin Meese III as recipient, then the address for Reagan for President headquarters in Sacramento, California. I was on my way and shipped the box as directed to Meese in Sacramento within a few hours. The rest was history.

Eldon Rudd was a most unusual man in Congress, whom I grew to love for his true faith and commitment to our hemisphere's security and all its people's betterment as well as liberation of the oppressed in totalitarian countries everywhere on our globe. He was a devout traditional Catholic who went to Mass regularly and was totally committed to liberty, economic opportunity to all, and defeating evil in all its forms. Eldon made a huge impression and stamped me forever during my five years with him. What a wonderful man and human spirit.

I loved his values and true commitment to human life. He was vehemently anti-abortion. I will never forget one particular debate in the U.S. House of Representatives when he stood up in response to liberals' arguments about "a woman's right to choose." He said to a stunned House—and got a lot of flak from liberal-left pro-abortion types—"Yes, women have a right to choose what to do with their own bodies. But if they mess around and get pregnant, there's another body who deserves life and protection for a full life. No one has a right to snuff out another life for their own permissive convenience."

It was one of my proudest moments when I heard him deliver those remarks in 1979, because I saw the sincerity in his eyes and the commitment in his voice, and he took on the feminist pro-abortion movement frontally in a stunning way with reasoned arguments based on his faith in behalf of life, not for the convenience of secular humanist ideology and a hedonist culture.

He was always there after I left his staff in 1981 and moved on. He helped me source the Clinton at Oxford story in 1992 by connecting me to a former U.S. deputy legal attaché at our embassy in London and retired Scotland Yard and British intelligence officials who were employed when Clinton was dodging the draft in 1968 as a student in England and traveled to Russia under questionable circumstances. These questionable circumstances came out late in the 1992 campaign after President George H.W. Bush's people leaked Clinton's passport file from the State Department.

I was able to hit the ground running in England in September 1992, thanks to Eldon's help. I spent several weeks at Oxford and at the wonderful British newspaper museum in Colindale, a London suburb, reading all the stories to find any reference to Clinton. There was nothing. Our story confirmed that Clinton was not a serious Rhodes scholar student, the only one of his Oxford class not to finish required papers, sit for exams, or get his degree. He was a draft-dodger, pure and simple—but still elected governor of Arkansas for 12 years and ultimately president for two terms.

Even as Rudd's chief aide and House Appropriations Committee assistant for four year, I did not know until John Rhodes publicly disclosed in his eulogy at Eldon's funeral mass in Scottsdale in February 2002 that Rudd served as Rhodes' intelligence agent within the Republican conference throughout his tenure as Republican minority leader.

Rhodes disclosed that he and Eldon met each afternoon in the minority leader's office in the Capitol, starting in 1977, and Eldon briefed him on activities and positions of Republican House members—probably some Democrats as well. The former FBI intelligence agent par excellence quietly put his talents to good use to help his party leader. What a story that never saw itself in print until now.

I was sitting there at my dear friend's funeral mass at Our Lady of Perpetual Help Catholic Church in Scottsdale, Arizona, which was full and overflowing. Former Vice President Dan Quayle—a House colleague of Eldon's—and his wife Marilyn were there, along with Judy Eisenhower—closest chief aide to Senator Barry Goldwater for many years. Also in attendance was every Arizona politician and staff member from memory going back decades and a multitude of business leaders, who all greeted Ann Rudd, Eldon's widow, a lovely, cheery lady, with obvious affection and gratitude. It brought tears to many eyes seeing the outpouring of affection for the lady who selflessly supported her man in his public duty over so many years.

And suddenly it all came together for me about the genius and true patriotism of this man and our political system. Would that we had more such good men and women in public service at the local, state, and national levels. Most of our public servants are good people and loyal servants of their constituents. A small number who demean our political system are there to gain and enrich themselves instead of providing honest service to their communities and the people. Those of us in the media have to spend inordinate time exposing these bad guys.

And would that so many of my colleagues in the media not be ideological toadies for big-government collectivists and their fellow travelers, but honest reporters who tell stories completely and honestly as they unfold, without pushing an ideological agenda.

Eldon Rudd spent his life quietly gathering information as an FBI agent and using it with others of like mind, in every way possible, to help push the peg forward for the good of the order. From the confessions Eldon elicited from the Puerto Rican shooters in the House in 1953, to 10 years as an intelligence agent in Central America during turbulent times, to his decade in the House as congressman, it was all for the promotion of freedom and economic opportunity against totalitarian enemies and a socialist mindset that crushes freedom and innovation.

For Eldon Rudd, true to his Marine and FBI training, everything was on a "need to know" basis. He didn't show his cards, but rather, he moved with stealth to achieve the objectives he and others believed to be in the common interest.

As I sat there at his funeral mass, I thought to myself and lapsed into silent prayer: "I knew your heart, because you told me. It was such a privilege. You were such a good man. Thank you for all you did. We are so much better off because of what you did. Thank you, Eldon. Thank you, God. Embrace your true and valued servant in his eternal rest."

CHAPTER SIX

SKUNK AT GERALDINE
FERRARO'S PARTY

For the next 90 minutes, I answered every question imagin-
able into the forest of microphones in front of me. I didn't
think about anything except hearing the press out and
answering their questions until they got tired. I tried to call
on everyone at least once, but one young man from The
Washington Times, an ultraconservative newspaper owned
by Sun Myung Moon, kept popping up no matter who I
pointed to…attempting to grab the spotlight.

—Geraldine A. Ferraro, "Ferraro: My Story"

T HE JULY 1994 Democratic National Convention was the Geraldine Ferraro celebration.

I didn't choose to be the media skunk at the party when Democratic presidential nominee Walter F. Mondale chose the congresswoman from New York as his vice presidential running mate—the
first woman named to run on a national presidential political
ticket—in opposing Ronald Reagan's second term bid for the White
House.

What national reporter with years covering Capitol Hill and
prior service there wanted to be the one to break a story about financial wrongdoing by the first woman vice presidential candidate and

her real estate developer husband in Manhattan—especially when most of my media colleagues were applauding and glorifying the subject of the story?

But I charged ahead with the Ferraro story, supported by my editors, as I believed it unseemly for media colleagues to resist covering the financial and other corruption we had uncovered. Too often, reporters and news organizations openly wear their liberal biases and prejudices very obviously on their sleeves with no hint of impartiality or fairness.

Writers such as Bernard Goldberg, 30 years with CBS News, who wrote "Bias: A CBS Insider Exposes How the Media Distort the News," is absolutely on the mark when he compares veteran anchor Dan Rather to Tony Soprano and explains how Rather pushed him out of the network in 1996 after he wrote an op-ed piece for the Wall Street Journal supporting a flat tax and disclosing "the liberal bias that permeated the national press" in opposition to this tax reform. Goldberg writes: "The Dan was concerned. I violated the code of *omerta*, the sacred code of silence that both wise guys and news guys live and die by."

On the day Ferraro accepted the nomination at the Democratic National Convention in San Francisco, we reported that she and husband John Zaccaro had covered up a major campaign finance violation involving an illegal $150,000 loan to her initial successful 1978 House campaign in Queens, N.Y.

The story set off a firestorm of financial ethics reporting by competing big news organizations other than The Times throughout the summer of '84—Wall Street Journal, Los Angeles Times, Miami Herald—that derailed the Mondale-Ferraro campaign to unseat President Ronald Reagan and Vice President George H.W. Bush.

It also marked the beginning of my 20 years on the national scandal beat for The Washington Times—a role I wasn't seeking but virtually fell into my lap because the Reagan Justice Department had just months before indicted and later imprisoned a little-known maverick Republican congressman from Idaho, George V. Hansen, for failing to disclose on his yearly House financial ethics reports nice profits on four silver commodity transactions by his wife, Connie.

Hansen was the ranking Republican on the Domestic Monetary Policy Subcommittee of the House Banking Committee, and the government charged Connie was getting investment advice on the silver transactions from Texas billionaire Nelson Bunker Hunt. Hansen didn't report his wife's income because of a financial separation he had received under Idaho law so his wife, nicknamed "Tin-cup Connie," could raise money independently to pay off Hansen's past congressional campaign debts.

The arrangement was approved by the House Administration Committee and set up a big separation of powers controversy between Congress and trigger-happy prosecutors in the Reagan Justice Department who went after Hansen.

It was a great story. The government's federal indictment of Hansen highlighted the importance of congressional financial disclosure requirements to inform the public of possible conflicts of interest and how he might have avoided those requirements for illicit purposes. The U.S. Supreme Court later ruled the prosecution improper and threw out Hansen's conviction.

But my editors thought there must be other members of Congress who had not reported incomes of their spouses and assigned me in June 1984 to start going through the House financial ethics reports of all 437 members, going back several years, to point up the selective prosecution of Hansen.

Geraldine Ferraro was 13th on my growing list of House members who had not reported finances of their spouse when Walter Mondale chose her as his vice presidential running mate. As I listened to TV reaction coverage of the Ferraro pick, while having breakfast before going to work, the announcer said her husband, John Zaccaro, and family were with her at the Democratic convention. A lightbulb went off in my head.

Zaccaro? I had just seen that name somewhere. Her name is Ferraro. All I had done for weeks was pore through House members' financial ethics disclosure reports. I grabbed the House Ethics Committee's published volumes of prior reports, and, bingo, there it was. On ethics forms going back to 1978, Ferraro reported she was secretary/treasurer of a New York corporation called P. Zaccaro Inc.

A quick check with Washington Times library researchers Clark Eberly and John Haydon, indefatigable champions over the years in ferreting out facts, found P. Zaccaro Inc. in Standard & Poors or another business reference. The company was listed as a privately held real estate development firm in lower Manhattan, and they gave me the address and telephone number.

It was early morning eastern time when I called. A man with a thick New York accent answered.

"Hullo, is John there?" I asked.

"Who is this?"

My mind was racing. I didn't want him to know I was a reporter. "George Archibald from Washington. John's the president of the company, right? I need to reach him."

"What's this about?" the man asked.

"Business."

"He's in Frisco at the convention. Who is this again? You'll have to call him through the campaign."

My heart was pounding. For years as a New York congresswoman, Ferraro had not reported her husband's finances while serving as corporate secretary/treasurer of their family-owned real estate development company. This appeared at least as worthy of prosecution as George Hansen's failure to report his wife's silver transactions.

It turned out that Ferraro benefited from all her husband's company income, was a company financial officer, and was required under House ethics rules to report all that information for public conflict of interest scrutiny, just as Hansen was. Editors told me to call all possible sources and turn and burn on the story because they were touting it for Page One.

I promptly hit pay dirt with Paul Kamenar, an attorney and good source on campaign finance issues at the Washington Legal Foundation, who said the Federal Election Commission had zapped Ferraro and her husband following her initial 1978 House campaign for an illegal $150,000 campaign loan from Zaccaro.

The FEC's Democratic counsel, William Oldaker, had approved a funny payback on paper—involving reappraisal and supposed sale of a parking lot that Zaccaro and Ferraro had purchased with partner Manny Lerman shortly before—to cure the problem.

The three partners had initially each put in $25,000 to buy the lot and secured a bank loan for the remaining purchase price. The reappraisal tripled the lot's value and Manny bought out John's and Geraldine's shares on paper so they got the $150,000 needed to cure the improper campaign loan and satisfy the FEC.

We ran that story on the day after Ferraro became the Democratic vice presidential candidate. The next day, we followed with details of Ferraro not reporting Zaccaro's income and the couple's real estate development finances, comparing the situation with George and Connie Hansen. The story did not ignite an immediate media frenzy. Quite the opposite. If looks of my media colleagues in the congressional press galleries could have killed, I'd have been long gone. How dare I ruin their celebration of Geraldine's nomination?

But the Wall Street Journal, USA Today, Time magazine, and other big news organizations assigned their own reporters to look into Ferraro's possible financial ethics problems. The Washington Post, New York Times, and national TV networks ignored the story for several days until it became quite hot.

Because Ferraro, Zacarro and Lerman knew the property reappraisal and sale were a phony paper deal, they didn't think to pay federal and state capital gains taxes on the supposed profit. As the story unfolded and kept getting bigger, Ferraro and Zaccaro had to issue a $55,000 check to the Internal Revenue Service for unpaid back capital gains taxes. The stories played out incrementally for weeks as we hounded out details.

My editors sent me up to New York City to check out the Ferraro-Zaccaro real estate business. Their office building was in a seedy neighborhood under a freeway in Lower Manhattan. As the cab pulled up, I saw magazines spilling out of garbage dumpsters outside the building and scattered on streets and sidewalks under the freeway. The spoiled magazines, apparently tossed out from press runs, included photographs in full color of young naked boys sexually aroused.

One of P. Zacarro's tenants in their building was one of the biggest pornography empires in the country, owners of the Doc Johnson sex shops that trafficked child homosexual pornography magazines printed in their building.

We found the filthiest child porn magazines imaginable and were the first to report this to the country.

Ferraro and the Democratic campaign denied knowing P. Zaccaro had a tenant who produced such pornography. How could they have missed it? They went through the front door of their office building when pornographic magazines were blowing around everywhere from garbage dumpsters outside the building.

Through further reporting, we revealed P. Zaccaro's connection to the global Doc Johnson sex shop cartel linked to organized crime. The lid blew off.

By August, Ferraro called a big, carefully staged, press conference in Queens, New York, in a last-ditch effort to get the scandal behind her and salvage what was left of her vice presidential candidacy.

She appeared before a sea of microphones to give the impression of being a besieged woman and carefully allowed selected reporters only one question to prevent those with detailed knowledge from breaking new ground or holding her accountable for untrue statements and political spin.

"For the next twenty minutes, I answered every question imaginable into the forest of microphones in front of me," Ferraro writes in her book, "Ferraro: My Story."

> I didn't think about anything except hearing the press out and answering their questions until they got tired of asking.
>
> I tried to call on everybody at least once, but one young man from the Washington Times [yours truly], an ultraconservative paper owned by Sun Myung Moon, kept popping up no matter who I pointed to. "Let me get to everybody once, and I'll come back to you," I said to him. But still he kept jumping up and down, attempting to grab the spotlight.

Well, it wasn't an effort to grab the spotlight but rather to get her to tell the truth and stop political spin in the face of legitimate questions. That's how the Washington press corps treated Reagan-Bush. That's how they've treated Bush-Cheney.

There's definitely a double standard in the press because they are mostly ideologically attuned to the liberal Democratic point of view, opposed to conservatives and Republicans, and it shows all the time.

Reporters from many news organizations at the Ferraro press conference booed questions and even ended the press conference by giving Ferraro a huge round of applause. I thought this highly unprofessional and revealing of their bias.

I was pleased to let them be establishment-kissers. It was my task to play a different role and a privilege to do so. It was not my hope, as a result of breaking the Ferraro story, to be on the scandal beat for more than a decade afterward. But my editors were pleased with our scoops and our driving the story of the 1984 presidential year, and they graciously awarded me my first of four Pulitzer Prize nominations during my 23 years at The Times.

Ten years later, I was in Beijing, China, covering the 1995 United Nations Fourth World Conference on Women, and Gerry Ferraro was co-chair of the U.S. delegation along with First Lady Hillary Clinton and Secretary of State Madeline Albright. We were there for three weeks and saw each other every day in daily U.S. press briefings.

I had a private moment one day to tell Ferraro in Beijing that one of my great regrets as a reporter was inevitable pain imposed on a politician's or public official's family members when scandal stories unfold.

"I'm sorry for any pain imposed upon your lovely mother or children by anything I had to write or report," I told her.

She has lovely big blue eyes and looked right at me as I said this. "Don't worry about my mom or family," she replied. "We're tough." We shook hands and moved on. That chapter was behind us.

CHAPTER SEVEN

MICHAEL DEAVER CONVICTED

*Unlike most other Washington hit-and-run casualties, I was
aware of the actual source of the early criticism—The Washington Times. A young man named George Archibald...
who styled himself a Reagan "purist."*

—Michael K. Deaver, "Behind the Scenes"

ARNAUD DE BORCHGRAVE, editor in chief of The Washington
Times from 1985 to 1991, had a queen-size pull-down bed and
shower in his mezzanine office overlooking the newspaper's expan-
sive newsroom. He often worked late and slept there overnight. Late
janitors and early workers would see him in his silk pajamas and
slippers wandering around.

Many of us wondered why he stayed night after night at the
newspaper next to the National Arboretum on New York Avenue
in northeast Washington while Alexandra, his gorgeous and angelic
photographer wife, was at home alone twenty minutes across town.

De Borchgrave was quite committed to making the newspaper a
force to reckon with and kept the pressure on all of us to make that
happen.

Each morning early, sometimes still in his pajamas, Arnaud was
feared for his handwritten notes to editors and reporters on large
5-by-8-inch yellow index cards that he would toss down from the
mezzanine into the newsroom below.

The notecards, which we called "yellow rain," might commend a particular story, ask why a particular story failed to note this or that, or suggest follow-up for the next day's paper with details and source suggestions that surprised and helped the best reporters.

No one stayed ahead of Arnaud, a stellar, worldwide reporter in his own right for many decades, which was the beauty of his success as leader and editor—the best I had the privilege to work with in almost a quarter century at the newspaper.

De Borchgrave had been Newsweek magazine's energetic top foreign correspondent for 30 years, went to the battlefront and accompanied troops in Korea and Vietnam, broke huge stories, and was friend of world monarchs and political and military leaders.

He could get Jordan's King Hussein on the telephone or ex-President Richard Nixon, who visited him at the Times. Arnaud was, and still is, a reporter's reporter as the paper's editor-at-large and for United Press International wire service, also owned by The Washington Times Corporation.

Arnaud personally threw himself into our reporting to help us break immense stories at The Times during the 1980s and '90s. I was the personal beneficiary of his help on many occasions over the years. We kept The Washington Post on its toes, and Post Editor Benjamin Bradlee came to The Times on one occasion and acknowledged how Arnaud led that effort with less than five percent of the resources of The Post.

Arnaud sent me a yellow-raindrop after the long run with the Ferraro story. He attached a March 3, 1986, Time magazine cover story about former top Reagan aide Michael Deaver's new career as a high-powered Washington lobbyist, asking me to read it and come see him.

Deaver had left the White House as President Reagan's longtime events advance man and image maker to make money off his over 30-year connection to the president and Nancy Reagan, going back to Reagan's first days as governor of California in the 1970s.

The Time magazine cover photograph showed Deaver in the back seat of a chauffeur-driven car at the bottom of Capitol Hill with the U.S. Capitol dome outside the side window, scarf around his neck, car telephone to his ear, with the cover headline: "Who's this man calling?" The subhead: "Influence peddling in Washington—lobbyist Michael Deaver."

The story told how Ronald Reagan's former valet, bag carrier, and advance man (while Reagan was California governor) became the president's chief White House image maker in Washington and had now formed his own lobbying company to parlay his long association with Reagan and continuing access to the president into big bucks for himself.

The story reported that Deaver was making millions of dollars through lobbying contracts with big corporations and foreign governments and had swanky expensive offices in a high-rise building near the Watergate in Washington's Georgetown section overlooking picturesque monuments across the Potomac River.

It's the old story, going back to the Warren Harding administration's Teapot Dome oil scandal of the 1920s and continues even today with the recent Jack Abramoff Indian casino lobbying scandal—greedy people at the height of government power who grew tired of working for noble political ideals and goals, ultimately deciding to cash in for themselves.

When I went to see Arnaud, he told me to call Richard V. Allen, Reagan's first White House National Security Council chief, for a meeting. Allen was representing several corporate and foreign government clients as a lobbyist in Washington. Arnaud said he would call Allen in my behalf to make sure he'd see me.

Allen was the Gipper's national security adviser when he ran for president in 1976 and 1980, but Deaver had forced him out of the White House by telling the Reagans Allen had accepted gratuities from a Japanese newsman for whom Allen was a source.

Allen had resigned in embarrassment in 1982 after the New

York Times tagged him for receiving $1,000 in cash and three wrist-watches from a Japanese newsman. The gifts were the newsman's way of thanking Allen for sourcing him on important stories. Allen didn't want to insult the reporter and put the gifts in a bank safety box. Deaver somehow found out and leaked the story to the New York Times.

It was payback time.

"We tagged Ferraro, a Democrat, and now it's time to tag a big Republican who worked for Reagan for balance," Arnaud told me. "Just call Dick Allen, and see what he has." He wrote Allen's direct office telephone number on a yellow-rain card and handed it to me.

Allen had helped source many of Arnaud's stories over the years, so there was a bond of mutual trust and friendship tested over many decades.

Allen took my call and told me to come right over to his office. As I sat down, he told me straight up that he knew Deaver was the leaker to The New York Times regarding the gifts given to him by the Japanese newsman because Deaver vocally urged Allen's resignation as soon as the story broke.

Deaver and Nancy Reagan were very close, and for some reason, Nancy was often out of sorts with her husband's most trusted long-time conservative advisers—Edwin Meese, Judge William Clark, Allen, and press-political adviser Lyn Nofziger. Deaver became Nancy's agent and informant as they both waged countering battles against the president's hard-core conservative confidantes.

The war between moderates and conservatives on Ronald Reagan's staff had started years before when he was a gubernatorial candidate and governor of California. Deaver was partner in a California public relations firm with Peter Hannaford, a clever policy-oriented man and writer. Deaver went on the road with Reagan as events organizer, valet, and liaison with local media, while Hannaford was policy thinker with Meese and wordsmith when Reagan was governor.

A brilliant conservative thinker and writer, Hannaford was highly regarded in conservative circles, along with Meese, Clark and Nofziger as "keepers of the flame" on policy and ideological matters, while Deaver with Richard Darman and James Baker often tried to push Reagan into more moderate-liberal pragmatic policy stands, particularly on social cultural issues.

Deaver demurred from many religious right positions and was more comfortable with the liberal Hollywood movie crowd and gays.

Conservative leaders Paul Weyrich, Edwin Feulner on the outside, and the Meese-Clark-Nofziger troika in the White House viewed the Deaver-Darman-Baker team as "the squish troika." Battles abounded throughout Reagan's presidency, until Deaver ultimately left to cash in with his new lobbying business.

Reagan's conservative troika and Hannaford openly told me that they viewed Deaver as a traitor because, as Allen and others told me, "He didn't want Reagan to be Reagan."

Many of Reagan's close White House aides told me that Deaver often went behind their backs to undermine them as he could. This was a reason for deep resentment.

Deaver all but admitted in his book, "Behind the Scenes," that he played this role. In efforts to be a more powerful power broker when Reagan was governor of California, Deaver acknowledged that he learned in travels alone with Reagan as they flew around the state and country for the governor's speeches that Nancy was the route to Reagan's heart. Deaver admitted that he set about pragmatically to forge a closer alliance with Nancy.

As I read the paperback draft manuscript of Deaver's book, sent out in 1987 to potential book reviewers by his publisher, William Morrow and Company, Inc., of New York, Deaver's Federal District Court trial for perjury following my series of stories was underway. My editors gave me the draft, told me to give it a quick read, and "see if there is any news in here."

As I read the draft book-review manuscript sent to our book review editor, Colin Walters, I remember feeling a sense of deep dismay over Deaver's callous account of how he decided to play Reagan's heartstrings to his own advantage through Nancy Reagan in order to gain pre-emininent power among Reagan's inner circle of most trusted advisers.

In the draft manuscript, Deaver tells a revealing anecdote about when he and Reagan flew alone together. He says that as the plane took off each time, Reagan would grip the arms of the seat, put his head back, and close his eyes until the plane was safely in the air.

Deaver writes that he asked Reagan after takeoff one time whether he was afraid of flying. No, Reagan replied. He was simply saying a prayer on each takeoff to ask the Lord to take care of Nancy and the children while he was away.

Deaver explains that this was when he realized that Nancy was the key to Reagan's heart, and that thereafter, he cultivated a closer relationship with Nancy in order to get the president's ear through her.

When Deaver's book was ultimately published, its jacket had a picture prominently showing Nancy Reagan kissing Deaver on the check or whispering in his ear as he and Reagan prepared to board a presidential helicopter—Deaver with a full file of papers under his arm—as Reagan patted cocker spaniel, Rex.

I wrote the story about Deaver's admission in the book-review draft of his book that he worked through Nancy to undermine Reagan's conservative advisers. The paper banner it on the front-page. At the time, Deaver was on trial for perjury in U.S. District Court, having lied five times before a federal grand jury and a congressional investigating committee that were investigating his profiteering as a Washington lobbyist after leaving the White House.

The investigation of court-appointed Independent Counsel Whitney North Seymour Jr., was prompted by my stories, so there was no love lost between Deaver, his attorney Randall Turk, and me.

Seymour's investigation and ultimate perjury charges against Deaver closely tracked months of my stories.

I was covering Deaver's perjury trial when my story about his book was published. The story leads with Deaver's boast that he discovered Nancy to be the key to Reagan's heart and soul and that he set about to capitalize on the situation. Deaver had rewritten that section for final publication, after our story went to press.

Meese, Allen and Nofziger told me that Nancy Reagan hit the roof when our story appeared, and she insisted that Deaver rewrite and tone down his account before publication. The rewrite goes as follows:

Reagan rarely talked about himself during our hours on the road or in the air. But after six months or so, I noticed that every time we took off in a private jet, he would stare out the window.

Finally, I asked him, "Are you saying a prayer?" He said, "Yes, but how could you tell?" I said, "I thought I saw your lips moving. What are you praying about?" "For Nancy," he said. I troubled the thought no further. But I knew what he meant: If anything happened to him, he wanted Nancy to be all right, and to be there for the children.

When I had sat down with Dick Allen months before, he said Deaver was a manipulative suck-up artist. They were bitter enemies.

Quite honestly, this works to a reporter's advantage in getting a story when two powerful Washington people are going against each other like Napoleon versus Wellington in mortal combat.

But such antagonism and conflict makes careful reporting and thorough, very careful fact-checking and multiple sourcing and documentation all the more essential.

Powerful people at war who spill the goods on each other often exaggerate and always spin things their own way. It's our job as reporters to meticulously sort out truth from fiction and fact from exaggeration as well as to detect outright falsehood. This is the daily gruel of reporting in Washington and anywhere.

Allen told me that Deaver had done several things to build a quick multimillion-dollar business for himself that were a violation of the federal ethics in government laws:

—One federal ethics violation was, knowing the government was about to replace the aged Air Force One aircraft used by the president, Deaver tried to get a lobbying contract with Boeing on grounds he could give them a leg up on the contract. He had traveled everywhere with the president on Air Force One and could map a new technically modern cabin structure as few others could. And to secure Boeing as a client, Deaver had gone to Office of Management and Budget Director James C. Miller to press for more B-1 bombers, built by Boeing, in President Reagan's fiscal 1987 budget, which was going to cut the B-1 program.

The administration did not add more B-1s, but Deaver had made his point to Boeing through the Miller meeting that he still had real access at the upper reaches of government and that they should hire him for the Air Force One lobbying contract, which Boeing did.

—Another federal ethics violation was that Deaver led the White House advance team for President Reagan's March 1985 summit on acid rain and other issues with Canadian Prime Minister Brian Mulroney in Ottawa, and while there Deaver laid the groundwork for a lobbying contract for himself with the Canadian government to represent them on the acid rain issue after he left the White House.

This, again, was a blatant conflict of interest that violated the intent of federal ethics laws.

After my meeting with Dick Allen, I called OMB press spokesman Ed Dale, a former New York Times reporter, and asked whether Deaver had met with Director Miller. I had covered budget issues for The Times years before when David Stockman was OMB director and had a good respectful relationship with Dale.

He confirmed that Deaver had recently come to the New Executive Office Building to meet with Miller. I asked whether the B-1 bomber issue was raised, and Ed said he didn't know but would check with Miller and get back to me.

Miller was a strong Reagan-oriented conservative allied with Meese, Clark and other hard-liners in the White House. He knew how Deaver had worked to undercut them. So it was no surprise when Ed Dale called back and said Miller confirmed that Deaver had, indeed, raised the B-1 issue in their meeting and proposed procurement of more planes be put in the forthcoming budget.

Bingo.

On the acid rain issue, I knew that veteran U.S. Representative John Dingell, Michigan Democrat and chairman of the House Energy and Commerce Committee, was a big opponent of Canada's position that smokestacks of Detroit automakers were responsible for the problem.

Hardly surprising, as Dingell represented the Detroit area and his wife was an executive for General Motors. So I called the staff director of Dingell's investigations and oversight subcommittee, Michael Barrett, to get his take on Deaver's role.

Sure enough, Barrett said he knew that Deaver already had the Canadian government as a client and his firm was working the acid rain issue in their behalf.

Double bingo.

I went to the Foreign Agents registration records at the Justice

Department and verified that Deaver was Ottawa's lobbyist for $100,000 in 1986. By Deaver's own account in an interview, his first-year billings for all lobbying clients were around $4 million.

Pretty good profit for someone who was a career political and government flack for 20 years and worked his way up to the White House with an income of no more than $100,000 a year.

In the interview with Deaver himself, as he knew I was a hard charger working for President Reagan's self-proclaimed favorite newspaper, it was apparent he would be on edge and cagy. I knew a woman in his office who had previously worked as a Reagan appointee at the Department of Health and Human Services and got an interview through her. I said we wanted to do a comprehensive feature story following the Time magazine piece and bring a photographer.

My editors thought I should take a feature writer with me so we could get Deaver to open up about his long relationship with the Reagans and so forth before I started peppering him with hard questions about possible ethics violations. So Lucy Keyser, a very low-key, amiable and gifted reporter and writer went with me.

It was classic good cop-bad cop.

We went to Deaver's Georgetown office that had a panoramic view of the Potomac River and Washington skyline. With tapes running, Lucy opened up with questions to get Deaver talking about how far back he went with the Reagans, and he started preening and gushing his self-importance. The photographer was all over the office snapping pictures of Deaver from every angle.

So the photographer could finish his job, we asked Deaver to stand in front of his window for some final pictures before we resumed the interview. He agreed but suddenly asked the photographer, "What kind of lens are you using? Is that a telephoto lens?" Yes, the photographer said. "No telephoto lens; they distort," Deaver said, and made the photographer change the lens.

After he went back to his desk, I decided it was my turn to bear in on questions about his clients and possible ethics issues. I asked him whether Boeing and the Canadian government were his clients and what issues he was representing them on. He snapped that he was not going to talk about specific clients. "That's none of your business. I'm not going to discuss clients," he said.

Lucy jumped back in with some softball questions to settle him down. Then I tried to press him some more, but he got irritated and abruptly ended the interview.

But we had what we went for, although Deaver now knew we were preparing to blow him out of the water, at least on the Boeing and Canadian acid rain lobbying, because federal law prohibits former government officials from lobbying the government on any matters that they were involved in when they were in the government, for at least two years after leaving a federal post.

The law is meant to stop government officials from turning their service into personal profit, but it never has. Washington is full of people who once served in government agencies and Congress and who cash in big-time afterward as lobbyists with public relations and law firms that hire them as "rainmakers" to bring in high-paying corporate and union clients or foreign governments seeking favor from the United States.

They call Washington's K Street "whore alley," because so many law and PR firms with scores of lobbyists have offices there. Deaver drove a Jaguar XJ6 and had his office in tony Georgetown to push a first-class image.

The federal lobbying ban is lifetime if a government official's role was substantive on a particular matter, which was the case for Deaver on the new Air Force One plans, as he had started to help the Pentagon procurement people map a new cabin structure while he was still at the White House. And on the acid rain issue, he had advanced and participated in President Reagan's two-day meeting with Canadian Prime Minister Mulroney, where that was Canada's top agenda item.

After my meeting with Dick Allen, I spoke with our Canadian ambassador in Ottawa in 1985, Paul Robinson. He told me in an interview that he learned from Canadian officials that Deaver had initiated talks about a lobbying contract with the Canadian government when he advanced and participated in the Reagan-Mulroney summit, before leaving the White House, which was against the law.

When our stories rolled, we reported that fact.

As I reported the story from early 1986 into 1987, and was in regular contact with the White House press office, I was told by a good source that John G. Roberts Jr., deputy White House counsel for President Reagan, had sent a memo to White House Counsel Fred Fielding advising that the president should "distance himself" from the controversy over whether Deaver had violated ethics laws as a lobbyist.

I was unable to verify the account or get a copy of Roberts' memo at the time, so I was unable to write a story. But the documents were released after President Reagan's death.

John Roberts, now Chief Justice of the United States, wrote as deputy White House counsel on April 7, 1986, that President Reagan should "avoid any expression of approval of Mr. Deaver's activities," as Congress was beginning an investigation of Deaver and a reported $18 million offer by Saatchi & Saatchi to buy Deaver's year-old lobbying firm.

Roberts wrote in his White House memo—before Deaver was convicted of lying to Congress and a grand jury investigating whether his lobbying of former associates in the White House violated ethics laws—that even if Deaver broke no laws, "a sizeable portion of the public nonetheless regards the sheer lucrativeness of his trip through the revolving door as at least distasteful."

But seeing what was coming, Deaver called a friendly Washington Post reporter who covered the White House and was with the press corps covering a presidential trip to California.

Deaver's aim was to give The Post a heads-up on what he knew was unfolding, in hopes the friendly Post reporter would give him a break and run with his version about the Boeing representation and blunt our blow.

Deaver was smart as a whip. My questions were informed and direct. Despite Lucy's marvelous efforts to cajole in our interview, he knew there would be blood in the water when we did our story.

I was at home at 8:30 p.m. when Josette Shiner called me and said the first edition of the Post had a front-page story about Deaver lobbying for more B-1 bombers in behalf of Boeing. The story had basic facts but little context and quoted Deaver as saying it was all on the up-and-up.

"We need your story right away for our first edition," Josette told me. "You have an hour."

Lucky for us, the Post's first "bulldog" edition always hit the street several hours earlier than The Times, so for years, Times editors could see how "the other paper" was playing the day's news with some time to spare to make final decisions on our front-page play and the whole package.

The aim was always to beat The Post in every area, because we were Seabiscuit, they were War Admiral, and—as National Editor Francis B. Coombs. Jr. used to say—journalism is war.

Josette read me the Post story over the phone. It didn't have OMB's confirmation that Deaver had personally lobbied Reagan budget director Jim Miller on the B-1 issue in behalf of Boeing, which I had confirmed and had Ed Dale's great verifying quotes in my notebook.

So I scrambled with a story that luckily was much more hard-hitting and complete than The Post's and also went on Page One.

From then on, we had to stay ahead of The Post on the Deaver story, so Deaver's damage-control strategy backfired.

The next day, my editors asked, "What you got for tomorrow?" We didn't know if the Post would come back with another story. Probably not, because theirs was a handout from Deaver to blunt us, and they didn't have anyone working on the extensive story as we were.

And, frankly, we didn't care whether The Post would follow up. We were ready to rock-and-roll with other stories. If they wanted to make this a race, we were confident that we were set to blow them away.

The adrenalin was running, and off we went.

We told the acid rain story and how Deaver had started brokering a lucrative deal with the Canadians while still working for Ronald Reagan at the White House.

We reported that he had hired a top official from the U.S. Trade Representative's office to help build his client base among foreign businesses and governments trading with the United States.

Another of our exclusive stories reported that Deaver was getting President Reagan's daily schedule and using this knowledge to impress prospective and current clients. He was sending a courier to the Old Executive Office Building next to the White House every day to pick up a copy of the president's personal detailed minute-by-minute daily schedule prepared by Frederick J. Ryan Jr., the president's scheduling director and later White House chief of staff.

Ryan had worked for Deaver at the White House. Deaver was good at using former subordinates to get information he needed, and exert official government pressure, to increase his own influence and business income. He was a classic Washington story.

Deaver's knowledge of all the president's moves and who he was meeting, discussions he was having, and issues involved was a gold mine of information for Deaver in plotting ways to gather lucrative clients and impress upon them how important he was with an inside track on all the president's moves and actions.

I had a White House press pass, so when I learned Deaver was getting the schedule, I went to the courier pickup office in the basement of the Old EOB—entrance down the steps off 17th Street, N.W., at the intersection of Pennsylvania Avenue, and sat on a bench until Deaver's courier arrived.

They had a sign-in and sign-out register, so I looked over prior days, and sure enough, couriers for Deaver arrived late afternoon and early morning for packages from Ryan's and other White House offices every day.

I watched a courier in Spandex bicycle gear with his helmet come in and ask for a package for Michael K. Deaver and Associates. He got it and left.

I walked over to the sign-out register, and it showed the big brown White House envelope was from Ryan's office. It was the president's daily schedule. The front-page Washington Times story hit like a ton of bricks and was immediately picked up by the wire services, made the nightly TV news, and that was the end of Deaver getting the president's daily schedule.

Soon after our first wave of stories, Whitney North Seymour, a patrician Republican attorney from New York, was appointed at the request of the U.S. Justice Department to investigate Deaver for possible ethics violations.

We wrote stories about Deaver hiring top officials at his lobbying firm from the U.S. Trade Representative's Office to help him lure foreign clients and keep one step away from personal ethics act violations. He got millions of dollars worth of contracts to represent foreign government and company clients.

Representing foreign governments and companies is perhaps the biggest money-making industry for professional lobbyists, lawyers and public relations people in Washington. That's why the city almost came to a standstill when the Dubai ports deal blew up in early 2006, and the public upchucked over the possibility that an Arab country-owned company would take over management of American seaports and all the cargo going in and out.

But going back years, corporate America has been hand in glove with any country that would produce cheap products for us.

And our Pentagon and military services, with companies like Northrop Grumman, Martin Marietta, and other warplane and missile manufacturers have sold fighter aircraft and weapons of mass destruction to foreign governments through our country's military sales program—Jordan, Egypt, Saudi Arabia, Israel, Iraq, Iran, Libya, Morocco, Turkey, Greece, Germany, any country that wanted them.

Pilots and mechanics from these countries were trained at U.S. Air Force bases in Arizona. I witnessed this firsthand as an Air Force enlisted man for four years at Williams Air Force Base near Phoenix from 1967 until 1971.

Many of these people hated us, and we used to joke about the possibility of having a Middle Eastern war over the Arizona desert at the Gila Bend Gunnery Range because the Arabs and Israelis gave each other the finger from their planes and cursed each other over the radio as they practiced dropping their ordinance and firing missiles from their American-built warplanes.

Deaver turned his lobbying firm into a big moneymaker for himself as a foreign agent, as so many Washington people do. We wrote stories of his possible ethics abuses that helped provide a roadmap for Seymour's inquiry and covered his probe as well.

Deaver was ultimately convicted on five counts of lying during the independent counsel's investigation and convicted in the federal jury trial in Washington. He got no jail time but was sentenced to many years of probation and community service.

I was privileged to receive another Pulitzer Prize nomination for this series of stories and an index citation in Deaver's book, "Behind the Scenes."

In the promotional draft version sent by William Morrow and Company publishers to book editors, Deaver calls me the source of his legal problems. In the final published version, Deaver writes: "Unlike most other Washington hit-and-run casualties, I was aware of the actual source of the early criticism—The Washington Times. A young man named George Archibald, a deputy assistant secretary in the U.S. Education Department, had been told to look for another job. His superiors disagreed with certain of his views. His name was then unknown to me, but the exit of anyone who styled himself a Reagan 'purist' was often blamed on the attendant lords, the closet moderates, Deaver, Baker, or Richard Darman."

Deaver also acknowledges his role in Dick Allen's firing and the departure of others from the White House while he was there. "As the former White House Enforcer, the keeper of the moral code, I can hardly blame those who found in my difficulty a reason for gloating," he writes.

He blames part of his difficulty on his belief that "I made too many enemies, including members of the management of the Moonie paper, The Washington Times."

He does not point out that his own longtime former boss, Ronald Reagan, had publicly said on many occasions that The Times was his favorite newspaper. It must have been a particularly bitter pill for Deaver to realize that all our stories about him were being read each day by the president.

About the interview that Lucy Keyser and I conducted, Deaver writes in his book: "The conversation with Archibald, and a fellow reporter, was a rambling one. But loaded with questions carefully pointed. I felt they were based on gossip, and tissues of fact, that could have been dropped only by sources close to the new White House staff. My continuing relationship with the Reagans, to the point of being called in for occasional advice, was seen as an irritant there."

After the jury's unanimous guilty verdict on five perjury counts, as Deaver and his attorney, Randall J. Turk, walked past me in the courtroom, his brother Bill turned to me as he passed and blurted out, "Are you happy now?"

Deaver until he died in 2007 was a highly paid lobbying executive in Washington as vice chairman of Edelman International, showing again that even career government political people who break the law and are convicted felons often land back on their feet and keep going.

He was a clever man, and any person is entitled after much stress in public service to make at least one big mistake and to recover as best he can. Deaver certainly recovered.

He and I saw each other and talked briefly at the Postal Service's celebratory unveiling of the Reagan postage stamp on February 10, 2005. He was very cordial. That's the way it is in Washington. You burn someone as a reporter one day, and as my colleague Paul Rodriguez always told me, they'll be right back talking to you afterward.

On both sides, newsmakers and reporters, we move on from yesterday's battles and scars. The intersection of politics and media has one essential road rule: Burning bridges is not a good strategy on either side. Both savvy political newsmakers and those of us in the news business know that.

CHAPTER EIGHT

TACKLING ANTI-ZIONISM

Imputing diabolism to Hitler can be a strategy of pretending that his was a peculiar aberration. This allows us to evade the gross fact that communism has proved a far more potent and persistent evil than Nazism, which was a brief flare-up by comparison.

—Joseph Sobran, in an April 1985 column

A FIRESTORM IN 1990 over nationally syndicated columnist Joseph Sobran's comments belittling Adolph Hitler's diabolical extermination of six million European Jews in comparison to Josef Stalin's extermination of 20 million-plus in the Soviet purge and gulags—plus a slew of Sobran's other columns questioning America's fervent alliance with Israel and asserting his anti-Zionist views—caught me in the middle of a big ideological fight at The Washington Times.

The fight involved the growing power of neoconservative intellectuals in Washington and New York, who fervently backed Israel and wanted U.S. foreign policy directed against the Palestinians and their Arab state supporters, versus some, including my own national editor at the time, Francis B. Coombs Jr., who backed Sobran's views.

Wesley Pruden Jr., editor in chief, was always a strong supporter of Israel and did not like Sobran's anti-Zionist stand. John Podhoretz, who was then editor of Insight magazine (another publication of The Washington Times Corporation), now a columnist for The New York Post, also fervently opposed Sobran.

Podhoretz is son of Norman Podhoretz, founder of Commentary (a Jewish magazine), and Midge Decter, Jewish. Both are fervent Zionists and supporters of Israel.

Joe Sobran was a clear thinker and gifted writer among regular syndicated newspaper columnists—not that I liked everything he wrote. I loved his clear libertarian attacks against the ever-growing behemoth state. But when he wrote about the Nazis and Israel, I saw prejudice in his tone and arguments and realized there would ultimately be a huge blow-up.

Sobran was a senior editor for National Review magazine, founded by conservative icon William F. Buckley Jr. Sobran shared anti-Zionist views voiced by Patrick Buchanan, former Nixon speechwriter, who said as a presidential candidate, "There are only two groups that are beating the drums for war in the Middle East—the Israeli Defense Ministry and its amen corner in the United States."

This was a glove clearly laid down by Buchanan against pro-Israel interest groups, politicians, academics, entertainers, and media elites who put Israel's position first in efforts to reach a settlement of the decades-long Middle East crisis and a Palestinian hopes for a separate state.

In his columns, Sobran echoes Buchanan's line—questioning our country's determined alliance with Israel—and defends President Ronald Reagan's controversial April 1985 visit to Bitburg, Germany, to honor German soldiers buried there.

Sobran and Buchanan voiced the Hitler-Stalin comparison to minimize the Nazi Holocaust, which was obviously a huge insult to Jews and Christians who historically suffered under many totalitarian socialist regimes.

Sobran terms Hitler's extermination of six million-plus Jews from the invaded countries of Europe "a brief flare-up." Stalin's atrocities, by the numbers, were worse, but genocide is genocide. I didn't get Sobran's efforts to minimize Hitler's horrible crimes against humanity versus Stalin's.

Sobran in a later column writes: "[It] strikes me as misleading to speak of Hitler's crimes as 'the Holocaust.' This has been a century of holocausts. There is no 'the' holocaust. We are kidding ourselves if we talk as if there were anything 'unique' about what the Nazis did." Sobran's conclusion is, "[We] have no right to denounce 'the Holocaust' as long as we shut our eyes to the [Communist] holocaust in progress."

So Hitler's extermination of six million people was not as bad as Stalin's annihilation of 20 million-plus?

The feathers hit the fan. The neoconservatives and Bill Buckley decided that they wouldn't put up with this unfeeling use of a calculator to minimize or rationalize tremendous horrible human rights atrocities by Hitler and his Nazi regime.

My American-born father told me how he and Allied troops and medical corps during World War II saw firsthand the trail of Hitler's horrible atrocities and how Hitler mobilized his own country and all occupied countries and their peoples for the purpose of exterminating Jewish men, women and children.

Why would anyone minimize these horrifying acts compared to another tyrant's worse atrocities—Josef Stalin or any other dictator who murdered multimillions over three decades? Atrocities against people and their human rights anywhere, no matter how big, are evil assaults against all humanity.

Twelve American presidents from both parties and their diplomacy and the United States Congress have consistently supported the state of Israel. Particularly in the wake of freeing Iraq from Saddam Hussein and an ensuing ethnic civil war there, election of Hamas in Palestine, and Iran's arms buildup and destabilizing role to spread terror against the United States and the West generally.

But the Sobran flare-up was handed to me by my editors. Fran

Coombs, then national editor, let me know he was definitely on Sobran's side but had a problem with John Podhoretz, who was trying to marshal opposition to Sobran.

The neoconservatives wanted Sobran's head and were pushing very hard to get Bill Buckley on their side. Sobran was a senior editor for National Review and was supported by William A. Rusher, NR's original publisher, and others. So the story was a donnybrook in the making.

Fran Coombs told me to go to Podhoretz to get his take on the story, so I did.

It was a Friday afternoon when people were taking off early, and when I walked into Podhoretz's Insight office upstairs on the second floor of The Washington Times building, his secretary had gone. His office door was open, and I heard him talking on the phone, so I sat down in the reception area until he was finished.

He said to the person on the other end, "I've got it handled. I know who the reporter is. Don't worry; I'll make sure he covers it properly."

My ears perked up. Who was he talking to? As the conversation wound down—I was only hearing Pod's side of it—it became apparent he was talking to his mother, Midge Decter.

So they were trying to wire my story.

I met with Podhoretz after he hung up, and he gave me a line of negative stuff against Sobran. I went back and reported to Fran Coombs.

"Screw the neocons," Coombs said.

Feeling caught between warring factions within the paper and without, I decided to cover the story as honestly as possible and not be pigeonholed by ideological zealots on either side but rather let the chips fall where they may.

Bill Buckley and National Review had gone out of their way starting in 1971 to run a series of articles against nativist and racist anti-Semitic groups that had formed in the fifties through seventies and called themselves conservative.

It was Buckley's view that National Review needed to inform its readers and the media at large about what the founding intellectuals of modern American conservatism thought about certain groups and movements that had stuck their noses into the conservative tent but were actually bigoted racist neo-Nazi hate groups against blacks and Jews.

One target of National Review's "purification" of the conservative movement was against a group called Liberty Lobby, its head Willis A. Carto, and their newspaper called Spotlight, which consistently featured nativist, anti-black and anti-Jewish diatribes.

Carto was a big ally of 1950s Southern segregationist leaders, heads of white citizens' councils, and wrote his concerns about "mongrelization" of the races because of intermarriage.

According to a National Review investigative piece by C.H. Simonds in September 1971, validated in subsequent federal court libel cases through 1986, Carto stated in a letter to fellow anti-black racist Earnest Sevier Cox in 1955 that "only a few Americans are concerned about the inevitable niggerfication of America."

My national editor Fran Coombs, who moved up the ladder to run the paper thanks to Wes Pruden, used the same phrase about "niggerfication" of our country, as did Assistant National Editor Robert Stacy McCain—a Coombs surrogate in the newsroom and culture page editor of all things, much to my horror.

Carto also wrote in 1955 to fellow racist Norris Holt: "Hitler's defeat was the defeat of Europe, and America. How could we have been so blind? The blame, it seems, must be laid at the door of the international Jews."

Buckley had drawn a line in the sand and said this kind of racist bigotry and anti-Semitism must be expunged from the conservative movement. He was joined in that effort by fellow columnist and National Review contributor James Jackson Kilpatrick (editorial page editor of the Richmond News-Leader in the '60s), who in those days authored a book titled "The Southern Case for School Segregation."

The result was a huge blow-up between Buckley and Carto and drawn out federal slander lawsuit in U.S. district courts in Washington.

I had covered the story and marveled as Buckley would sit in the courtroom during breaks and pump out his syndicated columns on his laptop, several times a week, in no more than 30 minutes.

The lawsuits went on until a judge and jury ultimately sided with Buckley and National Review against Carto in 1986.

It was an all-black jury except one white juror, and Carto hired ultra-left lawyer Mark Lane, who brought a nice-looking, capable black female Harvard law student with him to court every day. They piled issues of National Review before them in the courtroom.

The strategy soon became apparent. It was to paint Buckley, the scion of American conservatism, as a racist—despite mountains of evidence published by Carto himself that it was Carto who was an anti-Semitic, anti-black, racist bigot and organizer of legions of like-minded followers throughout America, which later included Timothy McVeigh and Terry Nicholls of Oklahoma bombing fame.

Buckley was on the stand for cross-examination. Lane approached and turned to his paralegal as she reached into stacks of National Review copies piled before her on the table and handed him a magazine, which he in turn handed to Buckley.

The issue had a large caricature of Harlem's flamboyant Democratic Congressman Adam Clayton Powell on the cover, right after he was expelled from the U.S. House of Representatives for corruption in 1967. Lane asked Buckley to read the cover headline to the jury. Buckley protested to U.S. District Judge Norma Holloway Johnson. Who told him to answer the question.

Buckley plaintively read the headline: "The jig is up, baby."

Lane walked over and turned to the jury, spitting out Buckley's reading of the headline as a question. "The jig…is up…baby?" he shouted, emphasizing "jig."

Then Lane again turned to his paralegal, who handed him a book. Lane took it and walked to Buckley on the witness stand, handing him the book.

"This is a dictionary, Mr. Buckley, do you recognize it?"

Buckley took it and looked. "Yes, I wrote the foreword to this dictionary."

Lane asked Buckley to open the dictionary to the word "jig" and read the definition to the jury. Buckley again turned plaintively to Judge Johnson and said, "Your honor"—but the judge cut him off.

"Answer the question, Mr. Buckley."

Buckley looked at the dictionary. "Jig, a dance, a gavotte," he read.

Lane cut him off. "Mr. Buckley, that's not the first definition of the word 'jig' in this dictionary. Read the definition from the beginning."

Judge Johnson said, "Answer the question, Mr. Buckley."

Buckley read, "Jig, short for jigaboo, black person, Negro, nigger."

You could have heard a pin drop in the courtroom.

Buckley protested under further questioning that Adam Clayton Powell had always called people "baby" and that he had danced for years to avoid the law and ethics requirements—therefore the cleverly written headline: "The jig is up, baby."

But Lane had made his point with the mostly black jury that the National Review cover was some sort of subliminal racist message, and Buckley, although mostly an absent editor with others putting out the magazine every two weeks, was responsible.

The jury was obviously repulsed by Carto's neo-Nazi racism and anti-Semitism, but Lane's line of attack against Buckley made its mark. The jury found for Buckley in the end but awarded just one dollar in damages. A Pyrrhic victory indeed.

With that backdrop, the Joe Sobran story took on greater meaning for the wider conservative movement. Sobran's nativism, in his columns, turned on red lights.

In one Sobran column in early 1985, he writes: "Along with those who care deeply about what Hitler did to the Jews, there are the Elmer Gantrys who inevitably attach themselves to every legitimate cause. In the '60s, we were manipulated by people who used the memory of slave ships to extort moral deference and expressions of white guilt, which were parlayed into political power and—the bottom line— money. The same thing is now being done with Hitler's mass murders. If you don't condemn them in the prescribed ritual ways, the guilt-mongers will find a way to lump you with Hitler himself." And Sobran irreverently adds that The New York Times, founded and run by Jews, ought to change its name to "Holocaust Update."

Did Sobran think years later that Timothy McVeigh, Terry Nicholls and their Oklahoma City bombing partners in crime were Elmer Gantrys?

I had to cover the story fairly and fully as always and did my best to do so. The neocons went against Sobran hammer and tongs, and Buckley ultimately fired him as a senior editor at National Review.

But as I covered the story, I found Sobran to be a very open and gentle guy in person, eloquent, with a terrific wit and profound sense of the foundational values that came from Thomas Jefferson, James Madison, and Alexander Hamilton, up through Barry Goldwater and Ronald Reagan in the '60s through the '80s: limited government at the federal level, with an emphasis on national defense and security; personal liberty for our citizens; and economic opportunity for all through free enterprise for businesses, large and small, and taxes as low as they can be.

I just could not understand his nativist views that Bill Buckley, icon of America's modern conservative movement, and others considered racist and anti-Semitic. Similarly, I could not understand the enthusiasm of my own national editor, Fran Coombs, for Sobran's nativist views.

It was a very difficult and stressful period covering this story. John Podhoretz, a brilliant neoconservative intellect and writer, in my view, was most obnoxious and arrogant—who, like Coombs, looked down his nose at people, particularly women, and was an insensitive bully and a control freak.

Many of Sobran's views on issues not involving race, Zionism and immigration resonated with many Americans, which made covering the story of his firing from National Review for anti-Semitic writings quite difficult to navigate.

I could see why Buckley and thoughtful intellects on the conservative side liked Sobran, despite his racial and anti-Jewish prejudice. Some of Sobran's pithy comments on public issues and the state of the American polity include the following:

—"Politicians never accuse you of 'greed' for wanting other people's money—only for wanting to keep your own money."
—"In one century we went from teaching Latin and Greek in high school to offering remedial English in college."
—"I find myself surrounded by teenagers with body-piercing and exposed navels, gabbing on cell phones and listening to hip-hop. Maybe I'm missing something here. But I just don't feel the least bit threatened by immigrants."
—"If the welfare state is here to welcome them, the solution is to get rid of it, as should have been done long ago. Overpopulation is a problem for socialist systems, not for free societies. In fact, the welfare system may be more destructive [to] the immigrants' families than to the natives."
—"After tens of millions of [abortion] 'procedures,' has America lost anything? Another Edison, perhaps? A Gershwin? A Babe Ruth? A Duke Ellington?...As it is, we will never know what abortion has cost us all."

—"Freedom is coming to mean little more than the right to ask permission."

—"Most Americans aren't the sort of citizens the Founding Fathers expected; they are contented serfs. Far from being active critics of government, they assume that its might makes it right."

—"The most fundamental purpose of government is defense, not empire."

—"War nearly always serves as an occasion for serious expansions of state power and the destruction of legal protections."

—"War is just one more big government program."

CHAPTER NINE

STICKY STORIES THAT STUCK

Political hacks, media advisors and the like, whether they're Republican or Democratic, spend millions of dollars attempting to convince voters that their particular candidates possess wonderful characteristics. It should come as no shock to members of the U.S. Senate or the U.S. House of Representatives that many citizens throughout the country—citizens who vote, work, pay their taxes and obey the law—believe a large conglomeration of thieves, perverts, drug users and liars meets in Washington, D.C.

—Private Investigator Billy A. Franklin,
"Tough Enough"

———————————

A MILD-MANNERED Richmond obstetrician and surgeon, Dr. Lewis H. Williams, hired Virginia Beach investigator Billy A. Franklin in May 1988 to investigate stories that former Virginia Gov. Charles S. Robb, husband of President Lyndon B. Johnson's daughter, Linda Byrd, had attended boat parties with prostitutes and drug traffickers associated with organized crime figures, where cocaine was snorted on a regular basis.

Robb was then Democratic candidate for the U.S. Senate in Virginia, and Williams, active in Republican politics, was supporting his opponent, Maurice Dawkins.

That summer, reporter Rose Ellen O'Connor of the Virginian-Pilot in Norfolk broke a series of stories detailing Robb's social indiscretions and dalliance with young party girls. Robb was in full denial mode, but the stories were the talk of the state.

The Washington Times' Editor in Chief Arnaud de Borchgrave sent me a yellow-rain note to telephone Helen Marie Taylor, a wealthy widow from Texas then living on her horse and cattle farm in Orange, Virginia, who had called him to inquire if we wanted to advance the story.

I called Mrs. Taylor to express interest but told her I wasn't interested in rehashing stories already broken. I wanted something new and big, if there was anything more.

She said in our first telephone conversation, "There's a bigger story involving a law enforcement investigation of organized crime that was compromised by Robb's administration when he was governor in an effort to cover-up Robb's secret party life and infidelity."

Whoa. I asked her how I could confirm that. She responded that conservative political friends had informed her that private investigator Billy Franklin at Virginia Beach had some details that he might share. She gave me his telephone number, with a plea for me to follow up.

Taylor was known to me as a political activist and wealthy contributor to conservative causes—a regular participant in yearly Conservative Political Action Conferences in Washington organized by the American Conservative Union, Human Events, and Young America's Foundation.

I had no idea at the time, but learned years later, that Franklin, a private detective who ran Franklin Security Systems in Virginia Beach, Virginia, was hired by Taylor and Republican political activists to put together information against Robb and feed it to the media.

Franklin acknowledged this in his own book, "Tough Enough." I just followed the story, and it turned out to be a great one regarding Robb's adultery and sexual dalliance as governor of Virginia, his administration's interference and efforts to quash ongoing criminal investigations, and Robb's attempted cover-up of prior malfeasance as a U.S. senator that got him called before a federal grand jury and almost indicted for abetting illegal wiretapping and obstruction of justice.

I telephoned Franklin, who said he was willing to cooperate and invited me to drive down to his office in Virginia Beach, where he set me up with a lot of sources. Franklin told me that John Sherwood of the Virginian-Pilot had chased the investigation cover-up story but to no avail.

Franklin introduced me to several retired Virginia state police who had participated in an undercover operation code-named Operation Seagull, a joint criminal investigation by the Virginia state police Bureau of Criminal Investigation (BCI), Virginia Beach police department, and ultimately the FBI. The operation started in 1979 to probe organized crime, gambling, prostitution, and drug-trafficking operations in the Hampton Roads area of Virginia, particularly activities of Virginia Beach real estate tycoon Edward G. Garcia Jr. and his associate Bruce L. Thompson (a business partner of New York mob boss Anthony "Tony G" Gargulio of the Gambino crime family), who had homes on Staten Island and Virginia Beach.

"Bruce Thompson is the one who set Robb up with women at boat parties where cocaine flowed freely," one undercover agent named George told me. The parties occurred continuously when Robb was governor of Virginia from 1982 to 1986, when he often stayed at the governor's beachfront cottage on the National Guard compound at Camp Pendleton, he said.

"Bruce set Chuck up with Tai Collins, a former Miss Virginia USA, with whom he had a puppy-dog affair," Franklin told me.

Both Tai Collins and Becky Harris, her employer at a Virginia Beach lingerie shop and Miss Virginia USA chaperone, confirmed Franklin's account.

George showed me official identification and other proof of his involvement in Operation Seagull, but we agreed that I would only use his first name.

He had been a pilot in undercover capacity, who actually got in with Eddie Garcia and became pilot of the hotel owner's private plane.

Garcia asked George one day in 1982 to fly Robb to Virginia Beach for an evening grand opening of Garcia's newly purchased Radisson Hotel next to the Virginia Beach convention center.

Robb was always willing to go to Virginia Beach, where he could party with women and drug-using friends, according to Franklin, Collins, Harris and others who attended and witnessed the many boat parties when Robb was Virginia's governor.

Robb married Lynda Byrd Johnson, daughter of the late President Lyndon B. Johnson, and would sneak out of the governor's cottage at Camp Pendleton in Virginia Beach in the wee hours of the morning to go partying with the Virginia Beach drug crowd—and all this was under surveillance of a federal-state-local undercover police investigation that Robb was unaware of.

He was being filmed, tape-recorded and watched by undercover police investigators, and their reports were going to the Virginia state police's Bureau of Criminal Investigation near Richmond and to the FBI.

But George said he thought he had to run it up the flagpole with state police superiors when Eddie Garcia asked him to fly Robb on his private plane to Richmond for the Radisson Hotel opening, because he was an undercover police officer and Virginia law prohibited a law enforcement investigation of the governor without the attorney general's okay.

Robert Berryman and Jay Cochran, then heads of the Virginia state police's BCI at the time, both appointed by Robb, told George not to fly the governor.

So pilot George, the undercover operative, told Garcia he had a mechanical problem with the plane. Garcia then asked Larry Watson, a high-rolling gambling partner, to fly Robb in his own private seven-seat plane, Garcia told me in an interview.

But unknown to Garcia, Watson also was an undercover police agent buried in the crime enterprise as part of Operation Seagull. Watson secretly taped the conversions with Garcia and sent the tapes up to those running the state and federal law enforcement sting operation against illegal gambling, interstate drug trafficking, and interstate prostitution trafficking.

This caused Cochran to get together personally with Virginia Attorney General Gerald Balisles, himself later governor of Virginia, who nixed the flight to prevent Robb showing up again in reports of the undercover crime probe.

This is where obstruction of justice and interference with the undercover Operation Seagull came to the attention of federal authorities. I wrote the story on October 7, 1988, under the headline: "Robb's busy social life limited crime probe, agents say." The story prompted U.S. Attorney Robert Wiechering to open a criminal obstruction of justice inquiry.

Our story reports that, first, undercover investigators started getting orders from Robb-appointed state police superiors not to include Robb's name in their reports when he appeared at any restaurant, hotel, nightclub, boat marina, or offshore private boat party that was under surveillance by police. Ultimately, police had to close down surveillances because Robb kept popping up everywhere with Thompson and his party friends.

David K. McCloud, Robb's chief of staff and then chairman of his Senate campaign, acknowledged to me in an interview that Balisles tipped off Robb about the undercover operation, "The governor was advised through official channels that there was an undercover investigation and that there was a plane, which had been arranged to take him to Virginia Beach for purposes of attending a function." McCloud told me. "That official source was the attorney general of Virginia."

This was outright obstruction of justice.

McCloud said Governor Robb was told that "because of the investigation, he should not—he should just be aware of that and he should stay away from it, and he did do that. He did not go on the plane."

But Robb did tell his friend Bruce Thompson, who worked for Eddie Garcia, what he was told by Attorney General Balisles, which blew the cover off the undercover pilot and gambling investigators, thus compromising the entire operation and their safety, the undercover agents told me.

Two days after my story broke, it took an interesting turn.

Virginia Gov. L. Douglas Wilder, who was lieutenant governor under Robb and the first black elected to those offices, had just returned from an overseas trip and was talking on his car telephone with Hampton Roads developer Daniel Hoffler, who was bringing Wilder up to date on the latest stories.

Robb and Wilder were bitter rivals. Hoffler, a top Robb supporter, served as Wilder's finance chairman for his successful gubernatorial campaign.

Wilder and Hoffler talked about my October 7 story—not knowing that the car telephone call was intercepted and illegally recorded by an amateur radio buff, Ricky Dunnington, who with his twin brother Bobby owned The Raven restaurant—both close friends of Bruce Thompson.

The Dunningtons monitored police calls with radio scanners, because they had a lot of scams going on. Ricky recognized Wilder's voice, taped the call, and gave a copy of the tape to Bruce Thompson—who provided it to David McCloud, chief of staff to Senator Chuck Robb in his U.S. Senate office in Washington.

Here's where things got dicey. McCloud, a federal employee, had another Senate staffer, also a paid federal employee in the Russell Senate office building on Capitol Hill, transcribe the tape—at taxpayers' expense—and then leaked a transcript to The Washington Post in June 1991 in an apparent effort to embarrass Wilder after the Robb infidelity-cocaine parties story had re-emerged on NBC-TV's "Expos" program a few months before.

The Post's Donald P. Baker wrote the stories about the leaked transcript. On the tape, Wilder is heard chortling with "a high-pitched cackle" about Robb's problems with stories about parties involving prostitutes and cocaine, telling Hoffler that Robb had been "reduced to nothing," Baker reports.

"Wilder told Hoffler…that the stories said state police 'had to shut down their investigations of drugs and gambling in Virginia Beach because Robb repeatedly appeared where they were involved in an investigation. It's very, very sticky,'" Baker reports.

"'[Q]uite frankly, Robb is finished,' Wilder said. 'He's finished because it [his behavior at the beach] can't stand any kind of muster, and I'm quite certain he knows it.' As a result, Wilder said, Robb's endorsement of him would be 'suspect.' Wilder added, 'I don't want his endorsement, don't need his endorsement.'"

Billy Franklin's work had paid off again a few months prior as NBC-TV's show "Expos" decided to resurrect stories about Robb's peccadilloes midway through his second Senate term. In a 2-1/2-hour taped interview for the program, they grilled Robb about cocaine use at the Virginia Beach parties, about women named Frankie and Jamie and a hot tub incident, and former Miss Virginia USA Tai Collins.

Robb was caught totally off guard and mumbled almost incoherently. Having previously denied knowing Collins, he admitted having her in his room at New York City's Hotel Pierre, where she gave him a "nude massage." The admission catapulted Collins, a lovely tall blonde from Roanoke, Virginia, into Playboy as "The Woman Senator Charles Robb Couldn't Resist," probably giving Robb some PR boost among vigorous men.

But Robb and his staff, paranoid and panicking over the impending "Expos" show, a huge mistake politicians make, released the 2-1/2-hour videotape of the NBC interview to the press beforehand, thus fueling other media stories to an even wider audience.

In the "Expos" show, a car dealer named Gary Pope told about one 1983 party, "This girl was down on her knees...doing cocaine right in front of Governor Robb."

The later stories about the illegal taping of Wilder's call backfired on Robb as the public was more offended by misuse of his Senate office for political dirty tricks than Wilder's apparent glee over Robb's girly and drug troubles. The tape incident also roiled federal prosecutors into action.

Robb's U.S. Senate chief of staff David McCloud, state political director Bobby Watson, and press secretary Steve Johnson were hauled before grand juries and copped pleas to various crimes bringing fines and prison sentences. The Dunnington brother pleaded guilty to one count of illegal wiretapping. Bruce Thompson was indicted as a conspirator and convicted. Robb himself was hauled before a federal grand jury in Norfolk but not indicted.

Robb suffered irreparable damage but survived a Senate challenge in 1994 by Marine Lieutenant Colonel Oliver North after Robb's Republican colleague.

U.S. Senator John Warner of Virginia left the GOP reservation by endorsing third-party Republican moderate Marshall Coleman in the race against North, as an independent. However, six years later in 2000, popular Republican former Governor George Allen challenged Robb and handily sent him into political retirement.

As stories came my way in the mid- to late eighties after the Geraldine Ferraro story, they turned more and more away from financial stories and investigating efforts of political people in Washington to be self-gainers—although this is an endless story in Washington that needs to be covered vigorously and fully, now as ever before. It became clear to me as I covered the Ferraro and Deaver stories that there was an underlying common denominator that troubled me as a reporter.

It was Virginia Beach detective Billy Franklin who brought it home to me with his comments that Mr. and Mrs. America throughout the country are losing faith in our system. They work hard, often two adult workers in each family. They pay their taxes and vote to send people to local, state and federal government positions, people who they believe share their values and work ethic—people who they believe truly appreciate their commitment to hard work, their religious beliefs, their communities, and their families and who are sympathetic to their ever-present stress.

But are our elected officials at all levels truly committed to what they say during election campaigns? Many Americans don't believe so. Billy Franklin puts it rather bluntly when he says in his book "Tough Enough" that many people, regardless of political party, "believe a large conglomeration of thieves, perverts, drug users and liars meets in Washington, D.C."

As a reporter, I've seen my share of perverts and liars. But it has been my distinct privilege and honor, whenever possible, as a newspaper reporter, to take them out.

Here's another example: Quentin Claiborne Crommelin, who at age 44 pleaded guilty in Arlington, Virginia, to sexually assaulting a young intern from the Senate Foreign Relations Committee staff. The headline under a story by Charlotte Hays, one of our very gifted feature writers over the years, says it perfectly: "The story of a sex offender who was also one of the Hill's most powerful conservatives."

Crommelin, a decorated Vietnam veteran, worked for Sen. Jesse Helms, North Carolina Republican, as a legislative aide and adviser on defense and national security matters. He was from a wealthy

Alabama family. Both his father and uncle were Annapolis graduates and Navy admirals. They had a Navy frigate, the U.S.S. Crommelin named after them. Somehow, Quentin didn't make it to Annapolis and, after military service in Vietnam, ended up on Capitol Hill in Washington as one of many clever aides to Jesse Helms.

He was good-looking, blond haired, had lots of Southern charm, and really liked the lovely ladies in the office, the younger the better it seemed.

Charlotte Hays' story leads with Crommelin's line to the much younger lady he seduced and was trying to force to perform an immoral act on him. "Do it for your country," the victim quoted him as saying.

What was it about these handsome, perverted political men who always wanted a woman to service them instead of being lovely, romantic, good men and faithful to their spouse?

Or in Crommelin's case, Hays reports, he would break down sobbing before friends after six gin and tonics because he wanted to marry his teenage second cousin in Alabama, saying he was in love with her and "a good wife was what he really wanted in life."

Senator Helms, in a conversation we had, reminisced about what a brilliant staff assistant Crommelin was to the late Senator James Allen of Alabama during the Panama Canal treaty debates and then for him. "But obviously he had a screw loose as well," Helms told me.

I knew a lot of the Helms staff people as sources, and after my series of Chuck Robb stories in 1988, was approached by several ladies who worked for Helms about a serious problem, as they saw it, with Crommelin, who they said had raped a young woman in 1983 and was still a stalker of young women and an abusive sexual pervert.

I went to lunch with one lady on the Helms staff who regaled me with tales of pure horror about this man, particularly the attempted rape of a beautiful, 20-year-old, leggy, blonde intern named Lisa.

Crommelin immediately zeroed in on Lisa, the Helms staffer told me, would take her to dinners on the patio of La Brasserie on Capitol Hill, wrote a law school recommendation for her college boyfriend.

In Charlotte Hays' story, Lisa acknowledges this account:

"Quentin made me feel I was very intelligent and he could teach me so much. He had that peculiar brand of Southern gentility that goes with lots of land and ancestors who have fought in every war since the Revolution. Both my boy-friend and I were impressed."

[Hays reports] At the time, she was sharing an apartment with her boyfriend and several other young conservatives—an arrangement that didn't seem to deter Crommelin.

Crommelin left Capitol Hill in July 1988 to practice law and asked Lisa to become his secretary. She didn't realize that he was a sexual predator and had her in his sights. She accepted his offer and left college for a year.

Crommelin took her on trips with him, made romantic advances and continued making moves on her. Lisa said she was reluctant to quit her job and admit she was wrong to work for him but suddenly did so on October 30, 1988.

He asked for a final meeting to wrap up business affairs and took her on a wild car ride through the Virginia countryside, parked near Dulles Airport, and tried to force her to [have sex with him]...and while in a state of complete panic for her safety, drove her back to his apartment in Arlington and again tried to force her...

Lisa escaped with her boyfriend's help and found an attorney who helped her file attempted sodomy and abduction charges. Ultimately, the prosecutor agreed to accept a guilty plea to aggravated sexual battery, resulting in a 10-year suspended prison sentence and an agreement by Crommelin to enter a program for treatment of psychosexual disorders.

Lisa's attorney, Lee Satterfield, said the prosecutor told him Crommelin agreed to the felony guilty plea so long as the words [describing the attempted sex act]...did not appear in the charge. To the end, it seems, Quentin Claiborne Crommelin Jr., failed Southern gentleman, remained determined to cling to the shreds of his dignity.

Another sticky story was the death in 1986 of John Terry Dolan, brilliant, young conservative political genius who died at age 36 of AIDS.

Dolan founded the National Conservative Political Action Committee (NCPAC)—pronounced nick-pack—which devised a brilliant political and fundraising strategy that propelled Republicans to take over control of the U.S. Senate in 1980 as Ronald Reagan was elected president.

The Senate election victory propelled by Dolan and NCPAC, with help from the Christian Coalition and efficient state Republican campaigns, was astonishing, because it gave Reagan the essential help he needed to get his tax-cut package and federal government spending reorganization through Congress in 1981.

Republicans took 12 Senate seats from Democrats in the 1980 elections, achieving 53–46 control. There was a Democratic comeback in 1986, with 54–46 control, until 2000 when Republicans narrowly regained the Senate majority.

But it was the 1980 election where Terry and NCPAC won their political spurs by raising many tens of millions of dollars for Republican candidates. In their key races,

Republican James Abdnor knocked off veteran Democratic incumbent and 1972 presidential candidate George McGovern in South Dakota; Bob Kasten beat Gaylord Nelson in Wisconsin; Charles Grassley took out John C. Culver in Iowa. Also, Republicans Dan Quayle knocked off Birch Bayh in Indiana, and Steve Symms edged Frank Church in Idaho.

Other Republican Senate pick-ups in 1980 were Jeremiah Denton in Alabama, Frank Murkowski in Alaska, Paula Hawkins in Florida, Mack Mattingly in Georgia, Warren Rudman in New Hampshire, John East in North Carolina, and Slade Gorton in Washington.

Dolan was a take-no-prisoners political operative like Karl Rove, President George W. Bush's White House political director. In fact, as college students in 1972, Rove and Dolan ran against each other for national chairman of College Republicans when Rove was at the University of Utah.

Lee Atwater—late legendary political adviser to Ronald Reagan, George Bush I, and many congressional candidates—was Rove's Southern regional coordinator, and they traveled the campuses together collecting delegates in a mustard-brown Ford Pinto. Rove won the hard-fought contest at age 22.

Dolan went on to form NCPAC. Also in his early twenties, Terry was a political brother in a very orthodox Catholic group of people who founded and funded the conservative New Right organizations in the early seventies—Paul M. Weyrich, Edwin J. Feulner Jr., Richard Viguerie, Phyllis Schlafly, and others. Their aim was a political sea change.

Dolan forged a partnership with Viguerie, who had Barry Goldwater's 1964 presidential mailing list and was building a big direct mail fund-raising business for conservative political causes and candidates.

Dolan had a politically smart sense for the jugular in going after liberal candidates in 1978, telling reporters, "We can elect Mickey Mouse to the Senate. People will vote against the liberal candidate and not remember why."

In a NCPAC fundraising letter prepared by Viguerie's company in 1978, Dolan said: "The union bosses will have their troops out on election day digging up derelicts, vagrants and anyone else who will take a dollar to cast a vote…[AFL-CIO president] George Meany's henchmen will just drive them to the polls like a herd of blind cattle.... We must stop these villains from seizing total and final control of our elections."

But Dolan was secretly a closeted gay man with strong party-ing instincts who socialized with other gay men and, it turned out, frequented homosexual leather bars and discotheques. The word got around and caused a huge explosion among his political confreres on the right, with Paul Weyrich leading the charge to excommuni-cate him from their ranks. Weyrich called me and urged me to write a story before Terry died.

I telephoned Terry at his office. Brent Bozell, a close associ-ate, took the call. I asked him if Terry had AIDS. Brent demurred, acknowledging that Terry was sick at his home near Dupont Circle in Washington and telling me the name of Terry's doctor, who I found was an advertiser in the Washington Blade offering services to HIV-AIDS patients.

I did not get a return call from Terry. But NCPAC threw an anniversary party on a Potomac River restaurant boat at the Wash-ington marina off Maine Avenue to which I was invited.

Bo Hi Pak, a founder of the Times who knew Terry from the 1978 Tongsun Park Koreagate lobbying scandal and hearings before Minnesota congressman Donald Fraser's House investigating com-mittee, was there. Terry had supported the Koreans and the Rev. Sun Myung Moon's Unification Church when under attack by Fra-ser, and Moon's CAUSA International anti-Communist group gave $775,000 to Dolan's Conservative Alliance to help the political sea change he and NCPAC were advancing.

At the party, Terry's face looked heavily made up with cosmetics. He seemed uncomfortable, not his cheery self, but made the rounds of guests. I took a moment to tell him I needed to talk at his conve-nience, as soon as possible, for a story because of all the rumors that were swirling. "Don't worry, we'll get together," he said. But I didn't get a call.

The illness progressed rapidly after the boat party, and Dolan soon died.

It was one of the toughest stories for me, because I had known Terry for many years before I joined The Washington Times. He and his close colleagues at NCPAC, Craig Shirley and Brent Bozell, had helped me source many stories over the years. I was active in College Republicans six years before him, drafted, but by 1972 out of the military.

I had to write the story honestly and fully about his illness and cause of death as part of my coverage of a huge memorial service that was held for him at a church near Catholic University. Hundreds of Washington's top conservative political activists and leaders were there—Patrick Buchanan, Weyrich, Feulner, Viguerie, along with Terry's bereaved family and NCPAC colleagues. It broke my heart to have to write the story, but this was an important chapter about a huge cultural and social division within the conservative pro-family movement. We had to tell it.

Tony Dolan, Terry's brother and chief Reagan speechwriter in the White House, spent $6,000 for a full-page ad in The Washington Post after Terry died, stating that Terry had repented, confessed to a Catholic priest, and died in the state of grace according to the church's teachings. "The decidedly unrepentant homosexuals had tried to make [Terry] Dolan 'one of them,'" a Catholic friend who attended Terry's memorial mass later observed.

Two years later, Ellen Hume of the Wall Street Journal wrote a devastating piece in March 1988 for Regardie's magazine and the Journal about what she called the "Lavender Bund" on the right. The piece was headlined: "Fear and Self-Loathing on the Far Right."

It started in 1976 when Mississippi Republican congressman Jon C. Hinson was accused of committing an obscene act at a homosexual hangout in Virginia.

Hinson, also married and strongly conservative, then survived a fire in a homosexual movie theater near the U.S. Capitol in southeast

D.C. He denied being homosexual, won re-election in 1980, but just three months later was arrested on charges of attempted oral sodomy in a House office building restroom. He resigned his seat in April 1981 and died of AIDS at age 53 in July 1995.

Similarly, in October 1980, Maryland congressman Bob Bauman, an organizer of Young Americans for Freedom (YAF) and the Draft Goldwater movement during my college days in the '60s—a married man with four children—admitted (when charged by prosecutors with oral sodomy of a teenager) that he secretly went to male strip clubs in Washington following House sessions.

Bauman was outed by a young male homosexual prostitute who said the Maryland congressman performed oral sodomy on him, and the story was splashed on the front pages of The Washington Post and in the gay press for months thereafter.

Bauman was a leading proponent of the conservative pro-family agenda carried by a bipartisan group of Republicans and southern Democrats in the House. He had been an active spear-carrier for the right for decades, served previously as telephone clerk in the House Republican cloakroom while he also orchestrated YAF activities with leading conservative activists on college campuses.

I remember as one of those activists when a freshman at Randolph-Macon College in Ashland, Virginia, being woken up one Tuesday morning, January 8, 1963, by my friend Kenneth Tomlinson from Galax. He said Bauman was on the hall phone and "needs bodies" in Washington to demonstrate outside the National Gallery of Art in favor of getting United Nations troops out of Katanga in Africa. This demonstration would occur as President and Mrs. Kennedy unveiled Leonardo da Vinci's famed Mona Lisa portrait, "La Gioconda," which had been loaned by the French government for an unprecedented U.S. museum tour. The French ambassador and other dignitaries would be there.

We were supporting Katanga insurgent leader Moise Tshombe and wheeled to Washington up U.S. Route 1 in a packed station wagon with ample quantities of booze. We almost got arrested at the Mellon Art Gallery when someone accidentally in his ebullience clipped U.S. Assistant Secretary of State G. Mennen "Soapy" Williams on the shoulder with a protest sign organized by Bauman, who talked police out of arresting us.

Bauman pleaded not guilty some 17 years later when charged with committing oral sodomy on the teenage boy, said he was an alcoholic, and sought treatment.

His lovely wife of many years left him, and he lost his conservative eastern Maryland seat to a Democrat and became an activist for homosexual causes.

Republican Wisconsin congressman Steve Gunderson was the next to fall. Elected to the U.S. House at age 29 in the 1980 Reagan sweep, he lived an open gay life in Washington social circles with several male partners while he was a Republican lawmaker.

But a homosexual rights activist confronted Gunderson and his partner at a gay bar in Washington, threw a drink in his face, and created a commotion about Gunderson being a hypocrite and supporter of Newt Gingrich's conservative pro-family "Contract With America."

The Washington Blade, D.C.'s widely distributed weekly tabloid for the homosexual community, had the story. The Blade networked the story to gay publications in Wisconsin and throughout the nation.

California congressman Robert Dornan, a hard-charging Catholic conservative and former military pilot called "B-1 Bob," got wind of the potential problem for the House Republican conference and outed Gunderson on the House floor in 1994.

Dornan was one of the most outspoken conservative members of Congress in my entire two decades covering Capitol Hill. I asked him about the outing of Gunderson. "Oh, you mean the Dairy Queen?" he said. "He's a complete disgrace to everything we stand for."

Gunderson himself acknowledged that his lifestyle was out of sync with the Republican Party's cultural worldview and politics. He told reporters, "They couldn't have a guy like me, quote 'legitimizing and mainstreaming the [gay rights] issue,' so as we've seen with the Bob Dornans of the world and people like that, I have become the target."

On the House floor after Dornan outed him, Gunderson asked his colleagues, "All I ask in return is that you don't intentionally make me any less worthy than you."

Gunderson wrote a pro-gay book with his partner at the time, Rob Morris, in 1996, "House and Home." He did not seek re-election that year and now has another partner, Jonathan Stevens. He remains an active gay rights activist and is president and CEO of the Council on Foundations in D.C., a nonprofit membership group for 2,000 grant-making foundations and corporations.

There were other highly placed veteran Republican gays in Congress—U.S. Congressman Jim Kolbe of Arizona, who recently retired after representing the big southern Tucson-area district that Democratic U.S. Representative Morris K. Udall represented for decades.

It is an unfolding story of continuing perversion in Washington, D.C., our nation's capital, that will unfortunately probably continue forever. As Lord Acton said, power corrupts and absolute power corrupts absolutely.

CHAPTER TEN

BARNEY FRANK'S "BOY TOY"

My strongest memory as national editor is the evening in
August 1989 when we hustled the Barney Frank call boy
scandal into the paper.

— Francis B. Coombs Jr.,
managing editor, The Washington Times

<hr>

MY REPORTING PARTNER Paul Rodriguez discovered a male
prostitution and credit card sex-for-hire ring after a February 1989
police raid at a house in an elite northwest Chevy Chase residential
neighborhood that bordered D.C. and Maryland.

Paul had read a brief item in the metro section of The Washington Post that reported the raid and wanted to know why 12 U.S.
Secret Service agents were involved in the bust with local D.C. met-
ropolitan police.

He thought of the Secret Service's White House protective
responsibilities for the president and vice president and rushed to
the house to check things out.

He found police officers piling boxes of documents on the porch
and sidewalk for transport as evidence. Because Paul was an ex-D.C.
undercover policeman, and a marvelous schmoozer, the officers let
him look around. The boxes contained bank and credit card slips of
clients. The name of the group operating the prostitution ring was

Professional Services, Inc., which seemed innocuous enough. However, Professional Services was a cover name for a male escort service that provided sex-for-hire.

The house in Chevy Chase served as the prostitution ring's telephone network operations base where operators answered phone calls from prospective clients (who found its ads in telephone yellow pages under escort services) and organized liaisons between clients and available prostitutes.

Those running the ring at the raided house also took in the day's receipts from prostitutes, mostly charged to Master Card, Visa and American Express cards, and deposited those receipts with their local bank.

After Paul came back to the newspaper with his initial find and put me onto a more extensive document search, we found that Professional Services was one of the D.C. area's leading homosexual prostitution rings, also operating in Virginia and Maryland.

We tracked the merchant identification of the group to a particular bank, whose officials told us that Professional Services was a subsidiary of Chambers Funeral Home, one of Washington's oldest and finest mortuaries.

Now we had to do the hard gumshoe work to investigate and develop the story. Paul told editors he wanted to go on night duty, checking local bars and hotels to scope out the operation and gather sources. I continued as the daytime document man who followed Paul's daily leads with help mostly from researchers Clark Eberly and John Haydon in the paper's library.

Paul quickly found that Henry Vinson, an embalmer at Chambers Funeral Home on Wisconsin Avenue in Washington, D.C., was chief pimp for Professional Services escorts. One of their most active prostitutes was a young man named Steven Gobie, who also went by the name Greg Davis.

Paul went to Chambers Funeral Home's headquarters to find Henry, who wasn't there, but Robert Chambers, grandson of the funeral home scion—another embalmer—came out. He was book-keeper for the prostitution ring and had used the funeral home as a cover for the "merchant identification" and credit card authority at the local bank used by Chambers.

"He was nervous," Paul said. "Very effeminate. I told him I could help them get law enforcement off their backs if he could provide us names of high-profile clients."

Chambers asked how he could do that. Paul said, "Let me see some credit card slips to see if I recognize any names."

Chambers took Paul into a file room with cabinets full of credit card receipts. Paul convinced Chambers to let him borrow hundreds of Master Card, Visa and American Express credit card slips signed by clients of Professional Services, so we could check client names against all our available databases and directories in our newspaper library.

Chambers produced a blue Samsonite woman's cosmetic case that we called "the football" for Paul to transport the stash of credit card slips back to the newspaper, and Paul filled it to the brim.

When he arrived back at The Times newsroom about noon in early March 1989, the newsroom was mostly empty.

Paul stood in the corner of the newsroom next to a water fountain as he came in from the parking lot and yelled to me across the newsroom to join him in Managing Editor Wes Pruden's vacant office off the newsroom floor.

I rushed over. It was lunchtime, and Wes wasn't there, but the office was open. We closed the door and all the window blinds and sat down.

"I got Chambers to loan us a ton of credit card vouchers so we can see who their clients are," Paul said.

He opened the cosmetic bag and gave me a handful of credit card slips. He grabbed a handful, and we both sat there looking for any big names of prostitute clients that might pop up.

After going through several dozen, I looked at one American Express credit card slip and blurted out, "Oh, look at this one."

It was a $200 charge to Professional Services on The Washington Times American Express Card assigned to Assistant Managing Editor Mark Tapscott. Mark had been our national editor after he served as communications director for Donald Devine, President Reagan's first director of the U.S. Office of Personnel Management, and came to The Times after Devine was brought down by his pro-Democratic deputy, Loretta Cornelius. I had covered that story.

"Oh," it Paul said as he looked at the Tapscott credit card slip. "We've gotta call Fran and Wes right away." The reference was to Fran Coombs, then national editor, and Wes Pruden, then managing editor of The Washington Times.

Paul got Wes' secretary, Marge Wells, on the phone to find them. The two editors rushed into Wes' office within an hour. This situation changed the whole dynamics of our sex-for-hire story and ultimately the dynamics at The Washington Times from thereon for an entire year.

The paper's administrative editor, Ted Agres, made a copy of Mark's credit card voucher and commenced an investigation of his entire expenses history, which found tens of thousands of dollars of spurious charges.

Mark was also the auto pages editor for The Times and drove a formula racecar with the paper's name on it, which was a huge advertising boon for the paper. He was apparently having an affair with a lady in the paper's advertising department who handled this account.

This was a very painful moment for me. Mark was married to lovely Kathleen. They lived near my family in Reston, Virginia, for several years. I had gone drinking with Mark on occasion after work when he was national editor and knew he had an eye for other women. But not guys?

I ultimately had to interview Mark for our first story, when our reporting was completed, one of the most difficult moments in my newspaper career.

We named Mark as a client of Professional Services and his use of the company credit card to procure their services and quoted him as denying homosexuality.

He later sued me and the newspaper for defamation because we linked him with the homosexual call boy Professional Services ring, even though we had the documentation.

The basis of his lawsuit opened him up in legal discovery by the newspaper's attorneys for interrogation about his own sexual proclivities and practices.

Tapscott's deposition by The Times' marvelous attorney, Allen Farber, was several hundred pages long. It went into every aspect of his sexual preferences and practices, as well as his misuse of the company credit card.

Fran Coombs waved me into his office one day and handed me the transcript of the deposition and said, "You cannot believe this. Here. Stay as long as you want and read this."

It was devastating and so disheartening.

Tapscott promptly folded and settled his lawsuit. He was made to write a check for $1 in damages, made out to The Washington Times. Wes Pruden came down to the newsroom with a note to the staff stating victory in the case and pinned both the note and Tapscott's $1 check on the newsroom's main bulletin board. It was a scalp the editors relished.

Tapscott married The Times advertising account lady with whom he had an affair after his wife divorced him. He went on to edit a financial newsletter, became managing editor of the Montgomery Journal in Maryland, then was media director at the Heritage Foundation for several years. He is now editorial page editor for the Washington Examiner.

This story had other horrible turns for me, but a reporter must follow a story where it goes, fully honest, no holds barred.

I later found two other former sources and friends in the Professional Services mess—Chip Dutcher, another former Devine associate at the U.S. Office of Personnel Management, who was later head of civil service appointments at the White House, and Paul Balach, an aide to then-Labor Secretary Elizabeth Dole, who I knew at the U.S. Education Department.

They both were gay. We had to report them both having procured credit card homosexual sex in the unfolding gay prostitution scandal story because of their sensitive, high-level government positions. It broke my heart.

It turned out that it was Balach's complaint about misuse of his own credit card by a Professional Services male prostitute with whom he had developed a relationship that led to the police bust of the Chevy Chase networking house and the Secret Service involvement as the primary law enforcement agency for credit card and financial fraud.

As we reported in The Times, the documents showed that a number of clients—lawyers, doctors, business executives, government officials, and even one of our own editors—used corporate credit cards to procure escort services. Also, a number of military officers from the United States and allied countries charged male escort services.

We were told by one former top-level Pentagon officer that top civilian and military intelligence officials were worried that "a nest of homosexuals" may have penetrated top levels of the Reagan administration and, in turn, been penetrated by Soviet-backed espionage agents posing as male prostitutes. We had credit card slips signed by senior Reagan officials in the White House and Cabinet agencies.

Dozens of credit card slips totaling tens of thousands of dollars were signed by a former ABC-TV news reporter named Craig Spence, then a highly paid lobbyist for the Japanese government in Washington.

As I made a separate pile of Spence's slips in Wes Pruden's office on the day Paul brought in "the football," they totaled several thousand dollars a month. I said to Paul, "There's no way anyone could have this much sex with prostitutes. He'd be doing nothing else."

Spence had covered the Vietnam War as an ABC-TV reporter, was a close friend of Ted Koppel, Eric Sevareid, and hundreds of Washington luminaries. It turned out Spence was hiring Professional Services male prostitutes to attend his lavish social parties and work the crowd to service guests. He had rooms wired with microphones and cameras and blackmailed guests caught participating in homosexual sex at his parties.

This scandal story reached right into the top social structure of Washington media elite—a huge challenge for me and Paul as reporters.

But, thankfully, our chief editor at the time, Arnaud de Borchgrave, formerly chief foreign correspondent for Newsweek magazine for three decades (having traveled to every major capital of the world and knowing top military, intelligence and political leaders in most countries), personally rolled up his sleeves and jumped in to help manage our coverage.

One afternoon, Arnaud led Paul and me on a memorable chase across Washington to Craig Spence's apartment complex on Massachusetts Avenue in Washington, near the British Embassy, in an effort to interview Spence, who was in his apartment at the time.

Arnaud talked to Spence from the lobby, but he wouldn't let us up. Arnaud got a pledge from Spence to call us later, which he didn't do.

National Editor Fran Coombs then called two other great reporters, Jerry Seper and Michael Hedges, to join the team and take over the Spence story. Paul and I had too many other leads to follow. Seper and Hedges broke the stories about Spence hiring male prostitutes for his house parties.

They found that Spence even hired an off duty Secret Service uniformed guard at the White House for security at his parties, who helped organize a midnight tour of the White House and Oval Office for Spence, his prostitutes, and his clients, while President and Mrs. Reagan were asleep in their official residence.

Seper and Hedges had tracked down Spence with the help of The Times' New York bureau reporter Liz Trotta, another Spence friend, and interviewed him before he ultimately killed himself in his tuxedo in one of New York City's most exclusive hotels. It was a bizarre story.

Steve Gobie, one of the Professional Services prostitutes, approached Paul Rodriguez to become our source, wanting to protect his own back as a convicted felon already on probation in Virginia for trafficking cocaine and sex with a minor. He told us two of his clients were an elementary school principal in Chevy Chase named Gabriel Massaro and Congressman Barney Frank of Massachusetts.

Gobie had a lot of documentation and good memory in our initial interviews. But Fran Coombs said we needed to get him polygraphed.

I called private investigator Billy Franklin in Virginia Beach, a polygraph expert and instructor who had helped me with the story about Virginia U.S. Senator Charles Robb's adultery and obstruction of justice involving an investigation of organized crime while Robb and his girlfriends attended cocaine boat parties when Robb was governor of Virginia in the early 1980s. Franklin recommended a private investigator in Fairfax, Virginia, Paul K. Minor, to do Steve Gobie's polygraph.

Minor also later did the polygraph of Anita Hill, who had made sexual harassment charges against Supreme Court nominee Clarence Thomas, and said she passed the test. It turned out she was lying.

But in Gobie's case, Minor said he failed the test when questioned about being the homosexual prostitute lover of elementary school principal Gabe Massaro and Massachusetts Congressman Barney Frank.

Billy Franklin asked us for the "control questions" Minor asked in the Gobie polygraph. When I provided them, Franklin, who trained polygraphers, said Minor's interrogation was inept, and the control questions were inadequate to account for Gobie's emotional state and profuse sweating.

The Washington Times had paid Minor $1,500 for the polygraph exam of Gobie, which he botched. We determined through our investigating that Gobie was honest in all respects regarding his homosexual relationship with Massaro and Frank.

It was my task to reach Massaro. School was out for the summer, and he was visiting family in Florida. Four calls and a visit to the school failed to reach him.

I went to the Chevy Chase Elementary School with a map of the building we made Gobie sit down and draw, as proof of his claim that the principal let him use a second-floor guidance counselor's office at night to turn tricks and network client meetings.

Gobie's map was completely accurate, showing the way to the office from various entrances into the school, the view from the counselor's office window, and fixtures on the wall, except some furniture in the guidance counselor's office had been moved around when I got there.

Gobie proved truthful as a source, as he had lots of phone records and credit card documentation to prove his relationship with Massaro and Frank. Additionally, we tested him in every way because of his reprehensible background. He gave us copies of letters Congressman Frank sent on House of Representatives stationary to Virginia probation officials after he was convicted of drug trafficking and sex with a minor.

Frank's letters asked that Gobie be allowed to cross from Virginia to the District of Columbia, so Gobie could be his driver and housekeeper. The real reason for the letters was that Frank wanted Gobie to live with him as his homosexual lover and "boy toy." Gobie was a prostitute user, too, and our reporting uncovered one of the hidden bad secrets of the underworld homosexual culture.

A tough issue arose as we continued our reporting. Paul was told by his prostitute sources that there was "another editor" at The Washington Times besides Mark Tapscott who was a client of Professional Services. The editor was described to Paul as an older man, balding, tanned, with a European accent.

"No way," I said to Paul when he told me the description and exclaimed, "Arnaud?" Paul told Fran Coombs, Assistant Managing Editor Tom Diaz, and Wes Pruden.

One late afternoon, while Paul and I were in Fran's office off the main newsroom floor writing a story on deadline, Diaz walked in behind us and handed Paul a manila folder. Paul was at the keyboard, and I was standing behind him as we wrote the story. "Hold this until we talk further, and I give you the go-ahead," Tom told Paul, then turned and left.

Paul dropped the folder on the floor. An 8 x 10, black-and-white photo of Arnaud spilled out.

"What's this?" I asked Paul.

"Nothing."

I felt blood rush to my head. "What do you mean nothing? That's a picture of Arnaud. Are you investigating Arnaud? Are you going to show this to your whore sources? Does Arnaud know what's going on?"

I was angry, because there was no love lost between Wes Pruden and Arnaud de Borchgrave. This was an act of complete disrespect and professional cowardice.

Someone at The Times had been feeding stuff about their rivalry to the Washington tabloid City Paper, which had run gossip items for weeks. We suspected a metro editor, John Wilson, of being a leak to City Paper Editor Jack Shafer. I could just see this getting to them and blowing our whole story out of the water, plus the dicey relationship between our top editors. Also, my personal loyalty was to Arnaud, who was a terrific supporter of our stories over the years and always rolled up his sleeves to help as he pushed us forward.

Wes Pruden, in contrast, was a terrific column writer but a reclusive, shy man who rarely mixed with reporters. He hardly ever came into the newsroom except to walk to daily editor's meetings at 4 p.m. or to pin a tart memo on the bulletin board. Hardly anyone in the newsroom had even met him.

"I'm off the team if you're investigating Arnaud behind my back," I exploded to Paul.

"Settle down. Let's get this story written."

"No, I'm off the team if this is going on."

Paul got up and went to get Fran, who came in fuming.

"Sit down and write the story," Coombs shouted.

"No, I'm off the team if there's a secret probe of Arnaud going on that he doesn't know about. This will get out and destroy us," I said.

Fran left and brought Tom Diaz, the No. 3 editor, who came in spitting and fuming.

"Where's your loyalty?" Tom said, jabbing his finger at my face.

"Don't you question my loyalty. Let me out of this room."

Tom kept yelling as Fran and Paul stood by.

"Step aside, and let me out of this room," I demanded.

By this time, people on the copy desk and others in the newsroom were looking toward Fran's office, wondering what was going on. Tom had his back to the door, blocking it, with his shirt sleeves rolled up, and playing the macho bully that he was.

"Let me out of this room," I yelled, and Tom finally stepped aside and let me out. I rushed toward my desk in the middle of the newsroom, shaking, and just crashed into my chair, my mind a total blur.

Paul came over to say he was sorry I had been left out of the loop. Fran came over shortly and told us to convene in Wes Pruden's office.

We went in. Tom Diaz was standing behind Wes, arms folded, looking stern. I sat in the chair in front of Wes' desk. Paul stood against the wall. It was after 5 p.m.

Wes started by saying he was "disappointed" with me for "letting your ego get in the way of the story." I was taken aback.

Paul then spoke up and said, "No, Wes, this is not George's fault. He's my partner. We should have told him what we were doing."

Wes stopped and looked at Paul, then me, and said, "Okay, here's what we're going to do. I want everybody here at 9 tomorrow morning, and we'll go to Arnaud and tell him what we have to do." And we were dismissed.

From home, I telephoned Arnaud that evening and told him everything that had occurred. When I finished the 90-minute commute to the paper from my home in Front Royal, Virginia, Wes and Josette Shiner had already met alone with Arnaud in his office. Arnaud apparently laughed when they told him they had to show his picture to the prostitute because he fit the description of "the other editor."

"Go ahead and show them; it's not me," he told Wes and Josette. The other Professional Services sex-for-hire client turned out not to be Arnaud at all but rather a member of the paper's outside editorial board who worked for the Center for Strategic and International Studies—also an older man who was balding, tanned, and spoke with a European accent.

I went back and looked again through the Professional Services' credit card vouchers that Paul had initially gotten from Robert Chambers, and sure enough, this CSIS guy's signed slips were there.

And sure enough, someone leaked the story of our blow-up to the City Paper, and Jack Shafer ran it in his weekly media gossip column. Tom Diaz was furious and wouldn't speak to me for weeks. But he and Wes got into some huge rows after this incident, and Wes summarily fired him one day for irreconcilable differences.

Arnaud and Wes patched things up, but there was no real trust between them after this. They just put up with each other because they had to.

Meanwhile, the Barney Frank part of the continuing call boy saga broke wide open in late August 1989. I was sitting in the newsroom making calls and checking facts when my phone rang.

"This is Gabe Massaro, principal at Chevy Chase Elementary School," the caller said. "You've been trying to reach me. How can I help you?" My heart was pounding. I jumped up and yelled to Paul as I put my hand over the phone, "It's Massaro!"

"We need to talk to you about an important matter; can we come over to the school and meet with you?"

He asked what it was about. I said it was for a story about him and the school, and we'd be there immediately if we could meet. "Yes," he said, "now's a good time because I start teacher meetings tomorrow, so come on over."

Paul and I ran for the car, and off we went. On the way from the paper, next to the National Arboretum in northeast Washington, to Chevy Chase—a 20-minute drive—we plotted our strategy.

Gobie previously had told us that he and Massaro attended a TV taping of the Phil Donohue show in Washington about the Nicaragua Contra-versus-Sandinista issue, and Gobie had asked a question when Donohue ran through the audience.

We had called Donahue's show and purchased a tape. Our Washington Times photographer, Joseph Silverman, shot black-and-white stills from the tape as Fran Coombs ran it in his office. There was Donohue—mike in hand—with Gobie standing and Massaro sitting in the seat next to him in the audience. We had those photos with us when we raced off to Chevy Chase Elementary School.

On the way, we decided to turn on our tape recorders in our jacket pockets before we entered the school and that we would show Massaro the Donohue show photo as soon as possible in the interview to make the connection between him and Gobie and get his explanation.

After pleasantries and excusing an intern from the interview at our request, Massaro questioned why we wanted to see him. Paul whipped out the photo from the Donohue show. "Who is this man; how do you know him?" Paul asked, pointing to Steve Gobie.

"Oh, that's my friend Steve," Massaro responded, and he started giving us a story about Steve being a troubled youth who he had worked to help while on probation for drug problems. He said Steve had become "like a member of our family." Massaro was married with children.

"But he's a male prostitute, surely you knew that?" Paul said. Massaro denied it.

Paul and I kept hitting him with factual details and questions for about 10 minutes. Suddenly Massaro saw we knew the truth. He suddenly broke down sobbing in his office and admitted everything about his homosexual relationship with Steve and how he had allowed Steve to use the school guidance counselor's office as a nighttime place to flop and carry on his prostitution activities.

He also admitted in response to questions that he knew Steve Gobie also was servicing Congressman Barney Frank of Massachusetts.

Massaro said he had dinner with Gobie and Frank at Frank's Capitol Hill apartment, as Gobie had told us, and verified the date and other details the prostitute had already provided to us.

This was definitely another most difficult and troubling interview I ever did as a reporter for The Times. As I sat there, I knew this man's career was over as soon as we wrote our story, but there was no time for contemplation—we had to get the rest of it.

We left the school at about 4:50 p.m. and raced across Washington to Capitol Hill as rush hour commenced. It was a scary ride, Paul driving, but we got there in about 20 minutes.

And as we got near the row house on Capitol Hill where Frank had a basement apartment, there he was, walking up the sidewalk on Pennsylvania Avenue, a half-block away, as we drove up.

Paul wheeled around to find a parking space, and we ran to

Frank's apartment door. He answered our knock with his shirt already off, getting ready to go somewhere for an evening event.

"Barney, we need to talk to you right away," Paul said. They knew each other well, and he invited us in as he went back to the bedroom to put on a shirt. We sat down in the sparsely furnished living room until Frank returned.

"What's up?" he asked. Paul plopped a tape recorder on the coffee table, and said, "This is on the record."

Frank responded, "Let's go."

Paul whipped out the Gobie-Massaro picture from the Donohue show and asked the same questions: do you know this guy, who is he, what is your relationship?

Frank looked stunned but answered directly, "Steve Gobie, a friend of mine." We said we knew Gobie was a male prostitute with a felony record of drug use and sexual abuse of a minor in Virginia.

Frank responded that he was "a gay closeted man" and that he met Gobie by responding to a personals ad in the Washington Blade, a gay newspaper, and had paid sex with Gobie, and then they became lovers.

We already had the ad, in which Gobie advertised himself for service: "Exceptionally good-looking, personable, muscular athlete is available. Hot bottom plus large endowment equals a great time. Greg. 333-3706."

Frank acknowledged that Gobie had lived with him for many months but denied knowing, as Gobie had told us, that Gobie had operated his prostitution operation from the congressman's apartment while Frank was on Capitol Hill as a House Judiciary Committee member. He also demurred on questions regarding what he had done officially with Virginia probation authorities, so Gobie could live with him.

A big downfall for Frank was that he had gone to Reps. William

Natcher, Kentucky Democrat, and John Myers, Indiana Republican—the two congressmen who oversaw the opulent House gymnasium with Olympic-size pool in the basement of the Rayburn House Office Building—to complain about freshman Rep. Dick Armey using the gym as a bedroom and bathroom in 1985 before Armey could afford to move his family to an apartment in Washington.

Armey, a Texas economics professor and ultimately House majority leader, used a cubicle with bed and phone in the gym to sleep for several months after he was sworn in as a freshman congressman because he was too poor to rent an apartment in Washington and also maintain his family home in Texas.

Armey had his clothes in his House office and, around 10 p.m. each day, would go down to the gym to shower and sleep after finishing his mail signing and other preparations for the next day in Congress.

One evening in 1988, around 11 p.m., Armey told me in an exclusive interview, he woke up to shouting and splashing in the pool and got up to see what was going on. Peering around the corner, he saw Barney Frank, naked, with a half dozen young naked men doing cannon balls in the pool and grabbing each other's genitals and other homosexual activity.

Steve Gobie had told Paul and me that he was one of Frank's play pals and often frolicked with him and Frank's gay friends as his guest in the House gym. So we had multiple sourcing from firsthand witnesses.

After our stories ran, the House Ethics Committee started probing and got into a knot over investigating the sex lives of members of Congress. It was a can of worms indeed. The Times blazed that story across the top of the paper on October 20, 1989, under the headline: "Sex forays in House gym probed."

Then-Managing Editor Wes Pruden headlined his column that day: "Why this House is a real 'house,'" and said straightforwardly: "So now we know why a large number of congressmen, liberal, conservative, Republican and Democrat alike, are arguing that a congressman's private life, no matter how sordid, is nobody's business but his own. It's no fair picking on Barney Frank this time. He may not be the only congressman running a whore house in the basement."

Pruden picked up a quote in our news story from a senior Democratic congressman who had told us, "It's not just Barney. I've heard stories about other members, too, who have been involved in sexual forays in the House gym. This could be serious."

"Indeed it could [serious]," Pruden wrote, "but if you imagine that congressmen are aghast because it's a bad idea to take hookers to the House gym, you just don't know anything about the wonderful folk of the 100th Congress. They just don't want to be caught with their pants down."

Gobie told us that he and Frank even located President George H.W. Bush's honorary gym locker in the House gym the size of a city block in the subbasement of the Rayburn House Office Building. It was the locker the elder Bush had when he was a Texas congressman, and Frank and Gobie opened and defiled it as a display of their animosity.

As I mentioned, Frank made a huge mistake when he filed his complaint against Armey with Natcher and Myers for breaking the gym rules after hours, because Armey knew what Frank was doing. Rep. Guy Vander Jagt of Michigan, chairman of the House Republican Congressional Campaign Committee, had read our first call boy stories and stopped Paul and me in the Rayburn House subway to the Capitol one morning to tell us we should talk to Dick Armey about Barney Frank.

I telephoned Armey's office for an appointment, and he saw me right away to tell me all he had witnessed of Barney with his naked chums in the pool. Armey referred to Frank in our meeting as "Barney Fag," years before his famous public use of the phrase caused a news furor for about a week.

Armey then said it was a slipup and apologized, but I knew better. It might have been a slipup, but "Barney Fag" had for a long time been part of Dick Armey's lexicon.

When our stories rolled, we reported the fact that Frank had written to Virginia probation authorities, in his capacity as a congressman and House Judiciary Committee subcommittee chairman, asking them to allow Gobie to come across the Potomac River from Virginia to the District of Columbia on grounds that he was trying to rehabilitate this young man and employ him as his driver and housekeeper.

Gobie gave us a lengthy interview on the steps of the U.S. Capitol telling us again for the record that the real reason for the letters was that Barney Frank wanted his boy toy for continued sexual pleasure after their first meeting and used his congressional office and position to obtain that for himself.

The stories rocked Congress and led to a House ethics inquiry into Frank's use of his official office to get Gobie off the criminal hook.

The House Ethics Committee recommended that Barney Frank be reprimanded for misusing his office, the lowest punishment, but Reps. William Dannemeyer, California Republican, and Newt Gingrich of Georgia, then House Republican whip, led an effort to upgrade the reprimand to a censure. They failed.

Frank and House Democratic Whip David Bonior of Michigan angrily promised that they would make Gingrich pay for his effort.

Bitterness over the Frank matter carried over to payback against Gingrich when Republicans later gained control of the House, and Gingrich became speaker in 1995. The ethics complaints filed against Gingrich by Democrats were definitely part of the Barney Frank payback.

The scandal didn't hurt Frank politically. His liberal Democratic Massachusetts district has lots of gays. He was re-elected in November 1980 by a larger margin than before and has been re-elected to the House 14 times since.

CHAPTER ELEVEN

CHURCHILL AND GINGRICH

*It has been said that democracy is the worst form of govern-
ment except all the others that have been tried... It's not
enough that we do our best; sometimes we have to do what's
required... The price of greatness is responsibility.*

—Winston Churchill

Mʏ ʜᴇʀᴏ ᴀs ᴀ ᴄʜɪʟᴅ growing up in World War II England was
our prime minister, Winston Churchill, who led us to victory against
Adolph Hitler. Our family listened every evening to Churchill on
the radio (we called it "the wireless"), so he was my early introduction to world history and politics and to America.

Churchill's mother was Jennie Jerome of Brooklyn, New York,
a gorgeous actress who married Lord Randolph Churchill. Winston Churchill's great grandfathers on his mother's side both fought
with the Continental Army against the British to gain American
independence.

Libbeus Ball, Churchill's great grandfather, was a Continental
Army major with George Washington at Valley Forge in 1778 and
helped fight the campaign that later vanquished Cornwallis and the
brutal redcoats.

Churchill, in his youth, was a newspaperman and soldier in
the Second Boer War in South Africa. He also fought and reported
in World War I. He wrote and painted throughout his life, in and

out of politics, and chronicled the epic history of English-speaking people in the 18th, 19th and 20th centuries. He also chronicled World War II in a marvelous six-volume history.

Churchill was an amazing man of action and words, a true hero, who deeply influenced my generation as much as anyone.

As a youth, I listened endlessly to recordings of Churchill's speeches. His memorable "never give in" speech at Harrow boys' school in 1941, a few years before my birth, rallied the English people in the face of Hitler's onslaught to conquer Europe and the world.

I loved Churchill's growling voice and jowly face, his ever-present cigar, the way he waved his hat, his command of language, and his unwavering optimism and call to courage that left no doubt: "Never give in—never, never, never, never—in nothing great or small, large or petty, never give in except to convictions of honor and good sense. Never yield to force, never yield to the apparently overwhelming might of the enemy."

Churchill told the story of the lead-up to World War II and the way the allies went up against Hitler, Mussolini and Hirohito fully, honestly and passionately as he saw it, with vision and faith—yet he often walked alone.

He was not a suck-up politician seeking consensus but rather as prime minister, and Conservative Party opposition leader after World War II, had the confidence of his monarchs, King George VI and Queen Elizabeth II, who valued him for his honesty and values. He was a true leader and magnet who defined himself by his own strength, erudition, wisdom, speaking and writing skills.

His understanding of history and political ability to rally the public were in his genes and unparalleled in his age.

Churchill saw centuries ahead. His enduring faith in mankind and its future, his towering sense of honor, compassion, openness to criticism, and curmudgeon sense of humor made an indelible mark on me. He was my hero in every sense of the word.

My father realized this as I was growing up, and regaled me with Churchill stories to keep me interested when I had to wash and wax his car on Saturday or Sunday afternoon.

There was the story of Churchill taking a leak in a well-appointed lavvy in the House of Commons as Labour leader Aneurin Bevan stepped up to the urinal and unzipped. Winston immediately turned aside to the corner, dad said, as the socialist leader pulled out his equipment.

Dad said Bevan chided Churchill, "Come along there, Winston boyo, we've all got the same thing, look you."

He said Winston growled back through his cigar, "I know you socialists. Soon as you see something big and successful, you want to nationalize it."

Such saucy stories told by my father made me laugh as a boy growing up and cemented my opposition to socialism and top-down centralized government. My love of Churchill ultimately led me to Goldwater-Reagan conservative libertarian political views with morality.

My mother, with her constancy and determined loyalty to her father and brother, my father, sister Valerie, our two cousins, Jennifer and Penelope, and all her women tennis and horse friends, made me think about the two women Labour Party members in the British House of Commons who gave Churchill a particularly hard time and were so different from our family in the way we perceived life and the role of government.

I later realized that Churchill was an early anti-feminist, although his wife, Clementine, was a major help and influence in his life.

One political buzzard constantly pecking Churchill's backside was hard-line socialist Liverpool backbencher Member of Parliament Bessie Braddock, a common, unattractive, heavy woman whose current incarnation in the United States Senate is probably Maryland Democrat Barbara Mikulski, although Bessie also had the smarts and chutzpah of Hillary Clinton.

Churchill was ambling through the corridors of parliament with his bodyguard one afternoon in spring 1946, as the war was ending—probably after a few whiskies and brandies—and MP Bessie Braddock was coming the other way toward him. Braddock shouted as they passed, "Mr. Churchill, you're drunk."

Churchill pulled the cigar out of his mouth and glowered, responding instantly, according to his bodyguard: "Yes, and you, madam, are ugly. But tomorrow, I shall be sober, and you will still be bloody ugly."

Churchill's major political nemesis in the British House of Commons was the Labour Party's Lady Nancy Astor, born in Danville, Virginia, and married to the 2nd Viscount Astor, my grandfather's most important horse owner when he was a leading jockey in England in the early 1900's and later trainer at Beverly House in Newmarket.

Churchill told Lady Astor that he felt a woman being in Parliament was like one intruding on him in the bathroom. She reprimanded him, "You're not handsome enough to have such fears."

Some time later, Lady Astor hosted a costume ball for which Churchill asked her what disguise she would recommend he wear. She told Churchill, "Why don't you come sober, Mr. Prime Minister?"

At the end of the war, Churchill and Lady Astor got into a furious argument during a social weekend retreat hosted by Churchill's cousin, the Duke of Marlborough at Blenheim Palace, Churchill's boyhood home in the Cotswolds.

After several days of rowing and drinking, Lady Astor impatiently yelled at Churchill, "Winston, if I were your wife, I'd put arsenic in your coffee," to which Churchill immediately responded, "Nancy, if I were your husband, I would drink it."

These stories repeated by my father were indelible examples of the rough and tumble game of politics, the ideological differences and personal rivalries among politicians, and the way they always go after each other to gain the high ground.

The stakes are incredibly high when politicians seek to decide how to use the revenues of our multitrillion-dollar tax system and redistribute the money as Congress, the president, state legislatures and governors want. It just takes 50 percent plus one in a democratic system to overrun all the rest. With a multitrillion-dollar national budget, which ain't chump change, all politicians whether Democrat or Republican, liberal or conservative, are after the money. They're perpetually like fleas on a dog.

The closest thing to a Churchill-type figure I encountered in three decades on Capitol Hill was Newt Gingrich, a former history professor and Republican congressman from Georgia who was House Republican whip before becoming House Speaker when the GOP won control of Congress in January 1995.

Gingrich was a young Turk Republican backbencher starting in the late 1970s. As House Republican whip for years leading up to the pivotal 1992 and 1994 congressional elections, he rallied a band of six dozen conservative House rebels to kick his party out of its minority lethargy and, with them, went to the public to rally an electoral majority to win control of Congress.

Gingrich was a savvy, tech-oriented politician who adroitly used C-SPAN to get the rebellion message out to the people. He organized Republicans each day to give one-minute speeches as the House convened to get out their message of the day and organized teams of congressmen to stay after the House went out of session to give more speeches to a wide television evening audience on issues in the news through a parliamentary gimmick called "special orders."

He also fed the press with stories about emerging scandals to soften up the Democrats and break their back. One story, among many, that Gingrich discussed with Paul Rodriguez and me was a little perk that congressmen had called the House bank.

Members of Congress got their pay every two weeks and could have it deposited in an account maintained by the House sergeant at arms in the U.S. Capitol. Each congressman got nifty checkbooks with their names and an ornate image of the U.S. Capitol to impress anyone who got a check, which was one of a thousand re-election ploys used by incumbent members of Congress.

But there was one other benefit Gingrich tipped us about: Congressmen could overdraw their House bank accounts with no penalty to the tune of tens of thousands of dollars, and their overdrafts became taxpayer-funded loans with no penalty and no interest.

Several members of Congress even used their overdraft privileges to buy lovely homes and vacation properties with bad checks, and the House sergeant at arms just kept a list of each congressman's overdrafts and covered them with taxpayer dollars.

Paul Rodriguez and I investigated this huge scam in 1990 and 1991. Congress had written itself a special law regarding its own yearly appropriation, then just over a billion dollars.

Unlike the Pentagon and other executive branch agencies whose appropriations on the books had to be drawn down monthly from the U.S. Treasury, with congressional oversight, Congress's annual appropriation for itself was deposited fully on the first day of the fiscal year into selected banks around the country.

The banks were owned by big contributors to the Democratic Party and Democratic candidates, such as Joe Allbritton's Riggs Bank in Washington. The favored banks got to use their share of the deposited congressional appropriation for loans that paid them huge interest profits. And they covered bank overdrafts of congressmen who used their House checking accounts as an interest-free piggy bank.

Some House members such as Democratic Rep. Stephen J. Solarz of New York racked up tens of thousands of dollars of overdrafts to buy real estate and purchase other luxuries.

It was a bipartisan scandal of huge proportions. Both Democrats and Republicans used the House bank for their own enrichment.

And thanks to Newt Gingrich's tip, we rode the story for several years.

When the story broke in late 1991, it was like a brick through a window. Media friends of the House Democratic leadership ran like beach bums with a bee sting, not knowing where to turn.

It was fun seeing them interview each other as they tried to figure out how to handle the story. The Democratic House Sergeant at Arms at the time, Jack Russ, who protected the bad-check writers in Congress, even tried to shoot himself to death in a park on Capitol Hill as we had found 325 members of the U.S. House of Representatives caught in the scandal.

The House Ethics Committee, evenly divided between Democrats and Republicans, made it a tough story to unravel incrementally because the panel immediately moved in after our initial stories to protect their fellow politicians from both parties.

The committee got House bank records from the sergeant at arms and compiled a secret list of congressional bad-check writers from 1988 to 1991. Two committee members, then-Congressmen Jon Kyl of Arizona and Jim Bunning of Kentucky, now both U.S. senators, leaked us information and names of check-kiters as they got it.

We had to operate this way because the ethics committee list was scrubbed of names to protect the culprits. The panel's staff came up with a secret numbering system to identify each congressman, and we had to break the code to finally learn the names.

Ultimately, Paul McNulty, then Republican counsel on the House Ethics Committee, had decided to help us and convinced Kyl and Bunning to source us. As a result of our reporting, we were able to force the panel to release the names of 303 House members who had written bad checks.

In the paper, we headlined the story as: "Rubbergate."

We published a graphic of the 50 worst offenders on October 3, 1991. Rep. Tommy Robinson of Arkansas, a Republican and the worst offender, had 996 bad checks, and Rep. Gary Ackerman, New York Democrat and the 50th on the list, had 111.

The 50 worst offenders included 40 Democrats and 10 Republicans. Even Gingrich was on the list with 22 rubber checks. He had been a major source on many stories over the years and not happy that our graphic pinned him, but facts are facts and the chips have to fall where they may.

The story was picked up by local papers, radio and TV stations all across the country and resonated with average folk who would have to pay bank fees of $25 for any bounced check because of insufficient funds.

All House members on the bad-check list faced outrage from angry constituents in their districts. The result was a political time bomb. In the 1992 House elections, with all 437 members up for re-election, there was a one-fourth turnover.

Voters elected 110 new faces for a 10-seat Republican gain, changing Democratic control from 268–167 to 258–176.

Republicans finished the job after we broke the House Post Office scandal that dominated news over the next two years, picking up 54 seats in the 1994 election to gain a 230–204 House majority for the first time in four decades.

We first broke that particularly egregious scandal in early 1992, involving young relatives of congressmen and their staff members, hired as patronage employees, who trafficked cocaine, marijuana and other drugs in Capitol Hill buildings and corridors.

The House Post Office scam involved powerful members of Congress using their huge yearly official expense accounts, amounting to more than a million dollars each, to purchase massive quantities of postage stamps that they laundered back into cash for their own personal pocket money.

When Jeff Trandahl, a Newt Gingrich staff aide, tipped us off about this scam, I thought to myself, "We've got to send some people to jail on this one. This is beyond the pale. Let's put these thieves and dope dealers behind bars.

"Journalism is war, indeed."

The culprits involved were so blatant that they snared House Speaker Thomas Foley, through his power-hungry wife, Heather, in an attempted police cover-up that blew everything open.

The drug part was fairly straightforward. Wendell Magruder, a 32-year-old Democratic patronage employee in the U.S. House of Representatives, used his position as a postal clerk in the Longworth House Office Building to coordinate a large drug ring on Capitol Hill. He used tens of thousands of dollars from his postal cash drawer to buy drugs from dealers and replaced the money as customers paid him.

Down the hall from Magruder's basement postal station was the House folding room, where dozens of other patronage employees worked round the clock to fold and mail congressmen's constituent newsletters and other taxpayer-funded free mail.

The work was mundane drudgery and employees there were among the House's biggest drug users. Hallways around the folding room bustled in trading of cocaine, crack and marijuana.

The scandal erupted when Magruder's cash shortages mounted in his postal drawer. His supervisor, Niki Risenhoover, daughter of a former Democratic congressman from Oklahoma, was one of Magruder's drug customers and covered his tracks as the cash shortages mounted above $16,000.

Yvonne Welborne, another postal clerk, found a bag of cocaine under a mat in her work area. She told Democratic-appointed House Postmaster Robert V. Rota, "who just turned his head the other way and nothing was done about the drugs," Mrs. Welborne told prosecutors in a sworn statement that we obtained.

Magruder went on the lam because of his mounting postal drawer cash shortages, and Capitol Hill police investigators were called in. Heather Foley, Speaker Thomas Foley's wife who served as his unpaid chief of staff, and House counsels Steven R. Ross and John T. Caulfield, who reported to Mrs. Foley, interceded to stop the police investigation and avoid scandal—according to police meeting records and memoranda we obtained at the time.

Heather Foley's attempted cover-up failed because good Capitol Police professionals wouldn't stand still for it and turned over their evidence to U.S. postal inspectors, who House Democratic leaders could not muscle and control.

Postal inspectors moved in coordination with U.S. Attorney Jay B. Stephens and his assistant, Thomas J. Motley. House office buildings under Democratic control became a crime scene. Federal indictments for embezzlement, conspiracy and drug trafficking quickly followed.

Rota, Risenhoover, Magruder and others went to jail. Rota and his minions were the small fish, but once behind bars, they sang for federal prosecutors and broke the rest of the scandal wide open.

It involved embezzlement and laundering of official tax dollars for personal gain by one of the biggest powers in Congress—U.S. Representative Dan K. Rostenkowski from Chicago, Illinois, chairman of the tax-writing House Ways and Means Committee—and also by several other Democratic House members.

The scam was fairly simple and devised after a group of House conservatives complained of an abuse by colleagues involving congratulatory letters for childbirths and high school graduations, birthday and Christmas cards that congressmen routinely sent out to constituents at taxpayer's expense. This was just another gimmick politicians used to ingratiate themselves with families in their districts and push up their name identification for votes in the next election.

Congressmen had their tax-paid staffs reading birth announcements, high school graduation lists, any awards for constituents reported by the newspapers in their districts, and then had them compile lists for letters the lawmakers could send giving their constituents a pat on the back.

Congressmen were using their free postage perk, called the "franking privilege" (the lawmaker's signature in lieu of a postage stamp in the top right-hand corner of the mailing), to send out literally hundreds of thousands of letters every month as a way to bolster their voter re-election advantage. The money to pay for staff time to compile the mailing lists, produce the letters, and mail them was all taxpayer dollars.

Complaining conservative House members that this was an abuse of taxpayer money caused panic in Congress. Neither Democrats nor Republicans wanted to end their "abuse of the franking privilege," as it was called.

So the House Administration Committee came up with a clever compromise: No longer could congressmen use the franking privilege for gratuitous congratulation mail for childbirths, graduations, birthday and Christmas cards—but they could buy stationery and postage stamps with their expense allowances for travel and so forth by reallocating amounts as they wanted.

So the decision was to allow members of Congress to take money out of one pot, put it into another, and continue the practice of sending out all the congratulation letters at public expense—except they had to use postage stamps bought with their official expense allowances.

Congressman Dan Rostenkowski had another problem in his corrupt Chicago district. He had to pay people to register voters and get people out to vote. They call it "walking around money." And after the House Administration Committee came up with the decision on the postage stamps for congratulatory mail, Rosty figured out a way to get his walking-around money.

He started buying lots of postage stamps with his official expense funds—100 perforated stamps to a sheet, $1,000 or $2,000 worth at a time. He had his administrative assistant put the mint-fresh, unused stamps in a big brown envelope when he went over to the House floor for a vote or other business. And he called Bob Rota, the House postmaster, to the floor, where they met.

"Here, I don't need these stamps. Give me a refund." The stamps had been purchased with taxpayer dollars from Rosty's official congressional expense allowances. But when he turned them in and got the cash, the money didn't go back into his official fund. It went into his pocket, no one the wiser.

The same with two Pennsylvania Democrats who Rota got in on the action, Austin Murphy and Joe Kolter. This happened on literally scores of occasions over the ensuing years. It was a huge embezzlement and money-laundering conspiracy at the expense of taxpayers.

Jeff Trandahl of Gingrich's staff told us about the scam, and a source of ours on Rota's staff confirmed it. I went back five years in the detailed House clerks' reports and added up postage purchases by Rostenkowski, Murphy and Kolter. The amounts were staggering.

We published a story with a graphic detailing hundreds of thousands of dollars of postage purchases and questioned how the lawmakers could possibly have sent out so much congratulatory mail. Of course, they hadn't. They had traded in the stamps and pocketed hundreds of thousands of dollars in cash refunds. We went back through thousands of pages of House expenditure records and documented the story.

After the stories broke, U.S. Attorney Jay Stephens empanelled a federal grand and Dan Rostenkowski, two Pennsylvania congressmen, and House Postmaster Robert Rota were all indicted, convicted of conspiracy and embezzlement and were sent to jail. Rostenkowski and 54 others from Democratic districts were defeated in the 1994 congressional elections—enough to give Republicans the House majority and elect Newt Gingrich as speaker.

Gingrich's political strategy had worked. A drumbeat of media publicity that he spawned about substantial congressional corruption on many levels, over a period of more than five years, got the message to the grassroots, hardworking public, who answered with their votes and changed political power in Congress.

In January 1994, with Bill Clinton as president, Republicans swept to majority rule of both houses of Congress for the first time in more than four decades.

The Senate swore in 54 Republicans and 46 Democrats. The House swore in 230 Republicans, 204 Democrats, and one socialist Independent who sided with Democrats.

Republicans retained their congressional majority for 12 years until Democrats won majorities in both houses in the 2006 elections.

CHAPTER TWELVE

COVERING BILL CLINTON

Nineteen sixty-eight was one of the most tumultuous and heartbreaking years in American history. Lyndon Johnson started the year expecting to hold his course in Vietnam, continue his Great Society assault on unemployment, poverty, and hunger, and pursue re-election. But his country was moving away from him. Though I was sympathetic to the zeitgeist, I didn't embrace the lifestyle or the radical rhetoric. My hair was short, I didn't even drink, and some of the music was too loud and harsh for my taste. I didn't hate LBJ; I just wanted to end the war, and I was afraid the culture clashes would undermine, not advance the cause.

—Former President Bill Clinton, "My Life"

━━━━━━━━━
━━━━━━━━━

IN HIS AUTOBIOGRAPHY, "My Life," Bill Clinton downplayed his left-oriented views as an anti-Vietnam War protester in the late 1960s, while acknowledging he "was sympathetic to the zeitgeist," which included anti-war marches in London outside the American Embassy at Grosvenor Square where Clinton and his fellow American Rhodes scholar chums at Oxford—Nelson "Strobe" Talbott, Frank Aller, Christopher Hitchens—chanted such things as "LBJ, LBJ, how many kids did you kill today?"

To avoid the military draft, the young man from Hope, Arkansas, ended up as a Rhodes scholar at Oxford University in England in

October 1968 with help from his liberal mentor, Democratic U.S. Sen. J. William Fulbright of Arkansas (powerful chairman of the Senate Foreign Relations Committee and leading opponent of the war), for whom Clinton worked in Washington following his undergraduate years at Georgetown University in Washington.

At Oxford, Clinton was anything but a serious student. He partied heavily, drinking quantities of beer and smoking pot with his roommates and friends at 46 Leckford Road. He also chased women, particularly several lesbian ladies who were his constant companions.

The former president and his radical Oxford friends constantly joined British Marxists for anti-Vietnam protests in the late '60s and early '70s.

Christopher Hitchens, dubbed "Oxford's Mao-Mao" by the campus newspaper, Cherwell, led an uproar with Clinton, Talbott, Aller, and other university students when British Foreign Secretary Lord Geoffrey Howe addressed the Oxford Union in 1970. They dropped a hangman's rope noose from the balcony as Howe defended British support of the anti-Communist military campaign in Southeast Asia.

According to professors and graduate students who knew him at the time, Clinton's objective was not to pursue his Oxford degree but rather to avoid the draft and help other American students avoid military service. Among them was Aller of Spokane, Washington, his closest friend at Oxford's University College, for whom he drafted several letters to help Aller evade military conscription.

Lincoln Allison, a politics lecturer at University College then, said he sat around with Clinton and Aller and other students in the middle commons rooms at Oxford, instead of doing academic work, "agonizing about their latest letter from their draft board, the war, and all the rest of it."

Sir Maurice Shock, Clinton's supervising tutor and later president of Oxford's Lincoln College, acknowledged to me when

I reported the story, corroborated by other professors and lecturers, that Clinton frequently skipped lectures, failed to submit required papers, and did not sit for required exams.

He was seeking a Bachelor of Philosophy in politics degree but ultimately failed to get a degree because he had not fulfilled most of his academic requirements. He was one of six American Rhodes scholars in his class not to get a degree. Oxford later awarded him an honorary degree after he became president.

Someone in President George H.W. Bush's State Department leaked Clinton's passport file to the media toward the end of the 1992 presidential campaign, showing that he had traveled by train across Europe, through Holland and Finland to the Soviet Union, during Oxford's 40-day Christmas and New Year break in December 1969 and January 1970.

The immediate question was how the cash-strapped lad from Hope scraped up thousands of dollars for the trip and Communist KGB sponsorship to get into Moscow, where he stayed at the exclusive National Hotel off Red Square.

The suspicion was voiced during the campaign that Clinton was groomed by the pro-Communist left during his Oxford years as an aspiring U.S. politician friendly to their causes, who they could count on to do their bidding.

The record was convoluted, and I came away feeling that Clinton simply gamed the system to evade the draft, was pro-liberal left, but never actually became a pro-Marxist ideologue along with Strobe Talbott, Christopher Hitchens, and some of his other Oxford chums.

Yet Clinton participated in anti-U.S. war protest demonstrations with leftist throngs in London, including British actress Vanessa Redgrave—a key financial angel of the British Communist Party. He also participated with pro-Viet Cong radicals outside the American Embassy at London's Grosvenor Square in the famed November 15, 1970, second Moratorium Against the War.

The prior year, he was a volunteer at the Vietnam Moratorium Committee in Washington to help organize nationwide rallies against the war in November 1969.

Before the 1969 Moratorium protests, Clinton went to Oslo, Norway, capital of pro-Communist anti-U.S. operations, for training by "peace movement" leaders at the Oslo Peace Institute. There he met Father Richard McSorley, a Jesuit professor friend and peace activist from his undergraduate days at Georgetown University, who recorded in a memoir that Clinton accompanied him on visits in Oslo to Norwegian peace groups and university groups.

Clinton and Father McSorley returned to England in time for the November 15, 1969, Moratorium demonstration of some 500,000 Britons and Americans outside the U.S. Embassy in London's Grosvenor Square, carrying coffins, flags and anti-U.S. protest signs against our defense of South Vietnam against Communist takeover.

Clinton's transcontinental trek to Moscow immediately following the November 1969 Moratorium protests was certainly sponsored by the Soviet regime itself, which was supporting and providing weapons to the Communist North Vietnamese government, including MIG-21 fighter aircraft and surface-to-air missiles to shoot down American fighter planes and bombers. But I never found any documentary proof that Clinton's trip was financed by the Soviet KGB or its surrogates in the pro-communist movement, as widely suspected in print and public discussion. However, it is interesting to note that the KGB controlled bookings in Moscow's luxurious National Hotel and only guests favored by the Soviet regime could stay there.

Clinton himself in his 957-page autobiography that includes a long section about the 1969–70 journey to Moscow never explains how he raised the money to pay for the trip or its real purpose beyond basic tourism.

Clinton's own account of the trip in his book is that he went first to Amsterdam for tourism with artist friend, Aimée Gautier, who Clinton says coaxed him at one point at the Dutch port city to have sex with a prostitute advertising her wares in a red-light district window. But "I declined," Clinton writes.

From Amsterdam, Aimée returned to England, and Clinton says he traveled alone by train to Copenhagen, Oslo and Stockholm, where he was busted by authorities for drugs:

At the border between Norway and Sweden, I was almost put out in the middle of nowhere, [he writes]. At a tiny railroad station, the guards searched the luggage of all the young people, looking for drugs. In my bag they found a lot of Contac pills, which I was taking to a friend in Moscow.

Contac was relatively new and for some reason wasn't yet on the Swedish government's list of approved drugs. I tried to explain that the pills were just for colds, widely available in American drugstores and without any addictive qualities. The guard confiscated the Contac pills, but at least I wasn't thrown out into the snowy desolation for drug trafficking, where I might have become an interesting piece of ice sculpture, perfectly preserved until the spring thaw.

While Clinton's story may describe the details of his long trek to the Soviet Union, he does not adequately explain the rhyme and reason for his expedition.

He goes on to say that he checked into Moscow's luxurious National Hotel on New Year's Day 1970. "It had a huge high-ceiling lobby, comfortable rooms, and a nice restaurant and bar. The only person I knew in Moscow was Nikki Alexis, who had given me the two friendship cards I loved when I went home from Oxford the previous summer."

Nikki, a native of Martinique in the West Indies and daughter of a diplomat for her country, was studying English, French and Russian at Patrice Lumumba University in Moscow.

Clinton said he teamed Nikki as a translator with three visiting

American businessmen from Virginia, who were in Moscow seeking Soviet government help to locate missing prisoner-of-war sons and other relatives perhaps held captive in North Vietnam.

Clinton had met the Virginia executives on a National Hotel elevator. Clinton wrote that he helped the American businessmen meet with both Soviet and North Vietnamese officials in Moscow.

Again, the looming question, never answered, is how the bearded lad from Hope could achieve such diplomacy for American parents of POWs in Moscow unless Soviet KGB masters perceived that he was an American anti-war activist and draft dodger already in their grip.

Also, after detailing all the touristy stuff about the long journey to Moscow, Clinton never explains how he paid for the trip as a practically penniless Oxford student with just a $2,760 yearly Rhodes Scholar stipend or how he got all the red carpet treatment and access to important Soviet bureaucratic officials.

There was obviously something important missing in Clinton's account, but by now we're all used to that. He's a born spin doctor; he makes Nixon look like a clumsy elementary school fibber. Clinton just never gave anyone the full and honest story about anything, whether Gennifer Flowers, Monica Lewinsky, you name it. The guy's one of the smoothest and best politicians in our lifetime but a pathological prevaricator and liar.

Strobe Talbott, Clinton's Oxford roommate, obtained and translated former Soviet Dictator Nikita Khrushchev's taped memoirs while at Oxford, and many of my sources believed that Talbott, another virulent Democratic activist protester against the Vietnam War, helped organize Clinton's entry into the Soviet Union as an anti-war guest of the Communist regime.

But this belief was not documented, and all those with firsthand knowledge of Clinton's arrangements clammed up when the trip became an issue at the end of the 1992 presidential campaign.

Described by everyone who knew him in his Oxford days as an affable bumpkin with political aspirations, the Soviet trip was an enigma. We had to know if he was being groomed as a possible Communist fellow traveler, or worse, an agent for the other side, and we had to turn over as many stones as possible to find out.

The Washington Times sent me to England in September 1992 to investigate firsthand Clinton's tenure at Oxford and his trans-European trip to Moscow. Despite extensive research of BBC photo and video archives and the British newspaper museum at Collinwood, a London suburb, I did not find a picture of Clinton waving a Viet Cong flag outside the American Embassy at Grosvenor Square in London as part of an anti-war rally, as my editors had hoped.

I found no quotes of Clinton excoriating American involvement in Vietnam along with leftist firebrands—with whom he lived and partied—in either Cherwell (the Oxford campus newspaper), regular British newspapers, or the plethora of pro-Marxist and left-wing newspapers and magazines of the day.

My trip to England resulted in an extensive front-page special report that was published on October 25, 1992, headlined: "Clinton at Oxford: 'Brideshead' visited in the war years."

Editor in Chief Wesley Pruden personally edited the piece. His masterful wordsmithing gave the story a lot of flourish and panache. Pruden graciously told me regarding my reporting, "It was all there, I just reorganized things a little."

But his special way with prose, his rewriting of the lead and the cadence throughout as a result of his editing gave the piece additional zing it needed to be a memorable and strong story.

In the piece, I conclude: "Like many things about Mr. Clinton's life and career, his Oxford years are a tangle of contradictions. He is remembered by some as an affable bumpkin who stood out among typically haughty Harvard-like Rhodes scholars, but others thought his Southern charm to be phony, a rube playing Rhett Butler."

Before my work on the Oxford story, Senior editors of The Washington Times had assigned me to help cover Clinton's White House quest in March 1992, after crack investigative reporter Jerry Seper already had spent several weeks in Arkansas to start the newspaper's background investigation of the obvious Democratic presidential primary frontrunner.

Jerry had telephoned Pruden to tell him he had too many story leads to follow and needed additional help. I was sent as Jerry's document man and to do my own additional reporting.

Seper was an undercover policeman in California before becoming a reporter for The Arizona Republic in Phoenix and then The Washington Times. His police background was invaluable because law enforcement people were willing to talk to him as a former law enforcement colleague frankly and source his stories.

Seper was able to hit the ground running when he first arrived in Arkansas before Easter 1992 to cover Clinton's presidential primary bid, by talking to sheriffs and their deputies throughout the state, state police troopers, and district attorneys.

Clinton had been governor for going on 12 years, and the cops and DAs knew everything about him—the womanizing, the Whitewater land development deal, brother Roger Clinton's cocaine trafficking with multimillionaire financier and Thoroughbred horse owner Dan Lasater (a Bill Clinton contributor). The cops and Clinton's political opponents in Arkansas provided slew of trails for us to follow as the early election campaign unfolded.

The immediate question facing us was how Clinton had achieved his ascendancy within the Democratic pack of 1992 presidential candidates so early in the primary season. He had briefly thrown his hat in the 1988 presidential primary ring but pulled out shortly after Gary Hart's adultery scandal with Donna Rice broke open, forcing Hart to withdraw.

Betsey Wright, Clinton's chief political adviser and guardian of his own "bimbo eruptions," had gone to him privately and told him frankly that he would have to drop out of the 1988 race as well and bide his time until '92. Wright knew Clinton had several current sexual liaisons under way and many past flings that could come back to haunt him.

She knew the tabloids and conservative-oriented publications would eat him alive and destroy his national political ambitions if the press cottoned on to his own flagrant womanizing and inability to keep his pants zipped. Wright cautioned Clinton, and he shortly dropped out of the Democratic primary race for the White House, saying he was deferring to Senator Dale Bumpers of Arkansas and set his sights ahead.

Our initial review of Clinton's presidential fund-raising for the 1992 race found that he had cleverly used his governor's office to tap into campaign cash bundling by law firms and big corporations that benefited from state economic development.

Clinton's campaign director, Bruce Lindsey, a Little Rock attorney, organized the cash bundling through a group of wealthy Clinton supporters who tapped scores of business executives and lawyers throughout Arkansas and the nation for maximum $1,000 or $2,000 contributions for the Clinton war chest, which had $4 million when we started our investigation.

As a young governor of Arkansas in 1978 to 1980, and from 1983 to 1992, Clinton quickly learned as all politicians do that lots of re-election campaign cash could be raised from well-heeled business executives and attorneys who made their money off government contracts and subsidies.

But to finance his White House ambition, Clinton took campaign fund-raising to a new level with creation of a billion dollar state economic development agency that he convinced the Arkansas state legislature to establish in 1985, primarily for port development along the Mississippi River that traversed Arkansas and neighboring states.

The agency called the Arkansas Development Finance Authority

(ADFA) brokered billions of dollars of state-guaranteed, tax-exempt bonds for industrial and port development up and down the Mississippi River: start-up costs for new businesses such as Arkansas Freightways (now a national trucking firm called American Freightways), construction of huge medical and university facilities, and so forth.

Law firms representing the bond underwriters and borrowers of the bond moneys earned hundreds of millions of dollars in fees, so when Clinton and Lindsey tapped them for political contributions, they ponied up in order to stay on the taxpayer-funded bond sales gravy train.

The ADFA bonds were sold to financial firms such as Stephens Inc., Arkansas' largest investment company, who served as underwriters for developing private companies. Law firms such as Hillary Clinton's Rose Law Firm in Little Rock and others did the legal work on both ends of the bond issues—for bond underwriters who managed the bond sales and companies that received the proceeds—and raked in tens of millions of dollars in fees over the six years from creation of ADFA until formation of the Clinton for President campaign in 1991.

Stephens Inc. raked in $3.8 million to $5 million in fees for 60 bond issues worth $1.8 billion from 1983 to 1991.

The Wright Lindsey & Jennings Law Firm of Little Rock, where Clinton was a partner before he became governor, pulled in $811,285 in fees. Kutak Rock & Campbell, another Little Rock firm that took Clinton's first ADFA head—Wooten Epes—as a partner, got $318,635 in fees as bond counsel for $51.5 million worth of hospital bond issues approved by Epes.

Hillary Clinton's Rose Law Firm got $109,450 in ADFA fees, as the Clintons listed her retirement plan at the firm, valued between $100,000 and $250,000, as their largest financial asset.

Clinton and Lindsey knew they'd hit pay dirt when 13 of 64 lawyers with the Friday Eldredge & Clarke Law Firm of Little Rock, which obtained just $24,755 in ADFA fees, immediately donated $10,500 to the Clinton campaign.

Executives for Stephens Inc. and its Worthen Bank, attorneys with all the law firms that got ADFA fees, and business executives who benefited from ADFA bond proceeds also contributed generously.

By spring 1992, Clinton had amassed a campaign war chest of $4 million-plus, more than any other Democratic presidential primary candidate. He marched through the Democratic primaries, was nominated as the Democratic presidential candidate in August, chose Sen. Al Gore of Tennessee as his vice presidential running mate, and they went on to beat President George H.W. Bush and Vice President Dan Quayle the following November.

But big problems loomed. During the lead-up to the presidential campaign and afterward, Jerry Seper had investigated a real estate investment deal that Bill and Hillary Clinton had made almost 14 years before with Jim McDougal, an economic development adviser to Clinton, and McDougal's wife, Susan, who also was on his gubernatorial campaign staff.

The McDougals were close friends of the Clintons and urged them in August 1978, when Clinton was confidant of his initial election as governor of Arkansas, to join in a $203,000 purchase of 230 acres in the Ozark Mountains along the White River near the Missouri border. Jim McDougal proposed to divide the property into 44 resort lots that would prospectively sell for a total of $459,000.

Kearnie Carleson, Clinton's gubernatorial campaign coordinator in the Marion County area north of Little Rock, had purchased some 3,600 acres of Ozarks land on the popular White River in a bankruptcy sale. Jim McDougal, a heavy whiskey-drinking good ol' boy with an endless gift of gab, convinced the Clintons to join him and Susan in a development partnership and buy the 230 picturesque riverfront acres at the confluence of Crooked Creek and the White River in order to "make a lot of money together."

The McDougals and Clintons bought the land with practically

no down payment on a 50-50 ownership basis. Several banks supporting Clinton's gubernatorial aspirations, including Citizens Bank and Trust of Flippen, run by part-owner of the land with Carleson, which financed some $183,000 of the McDougal-Clinton purchase.

As 50-percent partners with the McDougals, the Clintons wrote $10,000 of interest payments for Whitewater bank loans off their 1978 federal and state taxes, $12,000 in 1979, with combined taxable income of $41,000 in 1977.

Meanwhile, Hillary Clinton had arranged through her good friend, Diane Blair, wife of Arkansas poultry giant Tyson Foods general counsel Jim Blair, to invest in the lucrative cattle futures market on the Mercantile Exchange.

Bill Clinton married Jim and Diane Blair, and Hillary in her book, "Living History," recounts that she was "best person" in the marriage ceremony before Jim Blair helped show her how to become rich.

The social, political and financial triangle of the Clintons, Fosters and Blairs in Arkansas almost made polygamy in Utah look tame by comparison.

"The commodities markets were booming in the late 1970s, and Jim had developed a system of trading that was making him a fortune," Hillary Clinton recounts in her book. "By 1978, he was doing so well that he encouraged his family and best friends to jump into the market. I was willing to risk $1,000 and let Jim guide my trades through the colorfully named broker Robert 'Red' Bone. Red was a former poker player, which made perfect sense, given his calling."

To begin with, Hillary Clinton opened a small brokerage account in Little Rock, but after daughter Chelsea's birth on February 27, 1980, says she: "lost my nerve for gambling. The gains I had made [on the cattle futures market] suddenly seemed like real money we could use for our child's higher education. I walked away from the table $100,000 ahead. Jim Blair and his compatriots stayed in the market longer and lost a good deal of money they had made. The large return on my investment was examined ad infinitum after Bill became president, although it never became the focus of a serious investigation. The conclusion was that, like many investors at the time, I'd been fortunate."

Not everyone was so sanguine about Hillary's luck. Paul Greenberg—Pulitzer Prize-winning columnist for the Los Angeles Times Syndicate and editorial page editor of the

Arkansas Democrat-Gazette in Little Rock—in a May 4, 1994, column agrees with the Baltimore Sun's assessment of her "remarkable success" in the commodities market: "It certainly doesn't smell right."

Greenberg had covered Bill Clinton's rise in Arkansas politics for more than a decade as prize-winning editor of the Pine Bluff Commercial in Arkansas and was the first to label him "Slick Willy."

Greenberg also agreed with the Baltimore Sun's take on the Whitewater deal: "It doesn't smell right. That summation might apply to the whole swirly mix of fact and falsehood, impropriety and conflict of interest, suspicion and hypocrisy, excuse and indignation known as Whitewater. Nobody should be condemned on the basis of nothing more than a fishy odor, but strange smells should not go uninvestigated. They only tend to get stronger."

Yet Hillary claims in her "Living History" that she and husband Bill weren't so lucky with the Whitewater project as "passive investors." She says the idea sounded good: "The North Arkansas Ozarks were booming with second homes for people flocking down from Chicago and Detroit. The attraction was obvious: forested land with low property taxes in gently rolling countryside bordered by mountains and laced with lakes and rivers that offered some of the best fishing and rafting in the country. If all had gone according to plan, we would have turned over the investment after a few years and that would have been the end of it."

However, the Whitewater lots didn't sell, and the profit projections soon proved pie in the sky. That didn't stop the Clintons from claiming $22,000 in interest payment tax deductions on their 1978 and 1979 federal and state income tax returns, which were upheld in an Internal Revenue Service audit.

The McDougals had bought a small bank, the Bank of Kingston in northwest Arkansas, and financed Hillary Clinton's first unsecured $20,000 loan for the Clinton's initial Whitewater deposit. From there it was all downhill. The Bank of Kingston in December 1980 loaned Hillary another $30,000 to build a home for her and Bill on Whitewater's Lot 13.

The McDougals formed Madison Guaranty Savings and Loan, which became the loan engine for Jim McDougal's far-flung real estate ventures and the Whitewater resort development.

Whitewater Estates took in $300,000 between 1979 and 1983, yet assessed taxes for the property were just $2,000, which was $30,000 less than actual recorded sales values at the time. So the Clintons were posting false losses on their tax returns.

When Clinton became president, he hired Vincent Foster as his loyal deputy White House counsel to handle personal legal and tax issues involving the Whitewater real estate deal and associated tax problems, plus Cabinet nominations.

Foster was Hillary Clinton's partner at Rose Law Firm, and they had a brief but steamy affair while Bill Clinton was fooling around with other women as governor—according to many good sources, including state troopers at the governor's mansion in Little Rock when she was the state's first lady.

Vincent Foster quickly found that the claimed Whitewater tax deductions and losses were phony. He got inundated with the presidential Cabinet nominations, particularly the attorney general picks with the illegal foreigner nanny problems and Social Security issues—it was called "nannygate."

The documents in Vince Foster's White House West Wing office were taken on Hillary's orders, the night Vince Foster killed himself in Fort Marcy Park, and hidden in a closet in the president's White House upstairs residence that was off limits to law enforcement and the peering press. It was a pure and simple cover-up.

Reporter Jerry Seper did the heavy lifting on the Vince Foster story, breaking the news about Hillary's orders to move the documents from his office to the White House residence, out of reach of law enforcement investigators and court subpoenas.

Seper's stories prompted Attorney General Janet Reno's reluctant request for a court-appointed independent counsel to investigate a Whitewater cover-up, the Vince Foster suicide, and ultimately Bill Clinton's personal misbehavior and the Monica Lewinsky and Paula Jones sex scandals.

Reporter Frank J. Murray was The Times' lead reporter on the Lewinsky and Jones stories, who broke the pivotal story about Paula Jones description under oath of Bill Clinton's private parts, as proof he had dropped his pants in front of her and asked her to "kiss it" in the room at Little Rock's Excelsior Hotel.

The story led to Clinton being subpoenaed for a medical exam, where he was found to have a condition called Peyronie's Disease that causes curvature of the organ when aroused, as vividly and accurately described by Mrs. Jones. The story collapsed Clinton's defense against Mrs. Jones' sexual harassment lawsuit and forced Clinton to settle the case by paying her $800,000.

Honest first-tier reporters for major news organizations and even close White House advisers to President Clinton saw the picture: massive lying, cover-up, massive obstruction of justice throughout Bill Clinton's years as president.

Even Lanny J. Davis, Clinton's very capable scandal special spokesman in the White House from late 1996 until January 30, 1998, verified the official deceit and cover-up in his book, "Truth to Tell: Notes from My White House Education."

Regarding the crucial month of January 1998 when major news organizations started bombarding the White House with questions about Clinton's sexual affair with intern Monica Lewinsky (under investigation by a grand jury empanelled by Independent Counsel Kenneth Starr), Davis writes: "The information shutdown was complete. No one was willing to second-guess [Clinton's White House and private] attorneys. As one senior [White House] official said to me, 'Do you want to be the one responsible for saying something, or putting something out, that leads to the impeachment of a president?'" Another top Clinton adviser told Davis, "You don't want to know the facts here. It could cost you a grand jury subpoena and hundreds of thousands of dollars of legal fees."

In his book, Davis concludes that a scandal-ridden Clinton White House had taught him and others some essential truths about dealing with the press—"how we learned to get all the facts out, good and bad, early, often, and in context, thereby giving us a reasonable opportunity to comment and have our perspective reflected in the stories. I thought about the rules we had learned for coping with the scandal-beat reporters, by fighting back against their inclination to 'connect the dots' and jump to premature conclusions—not by making it difficult for them to report and get the facts, but rather by making it easy for them."

According to Davis, there is always the inherent tension in any public relations crisis "between lawyers thinking like litigators and the press and political people worrying about public opinion." Davis also states that "an essential rule for effective damage control and crisis management required some balance and consensus between the two viewpoints, and, most important, equal access for both to the facts."

Thinking about his last ten days in the Clinton White House at the height of the Monica Lewinsky revelations in January 1998, Davis says, "it appeared that the White House—now completely dominated by the president's attorneys and legal considerations—seemed to be embarked on a path regarding the Monica Lewinsky story that ignored every one of those rules. Every one. And I felt sick to my stomach."

All allegations Democrats have thrown at George W. Bush about "lying" about weapons of mass destruction in Iraq, et cetera, pale in comparison to the lying and cover-up that occurred in the Clinton White House at the time of the Vince Foster suicide, Hillary's order to political security director Craig Livingstone and others to remove and wipe evidence from Foster's White House office including her attorney billing records on Whitewater legal issues as a law partner at Rose Law Firm, and Clinton's repeated perjury and obstruction of justice during law enforcement probes of his sexual misconduct in the cases of Arkansas state employee Paula Jones and White House intern Monica Lewinsky.

CHAPTER THIRTEEN

COMMUNITY JOURNALISM

Ours was a segregated outfit. We didn't let any of you white folks belong.

—Air Force General Daniel "Chappie" James

FOUR-STAR GENERAL Daniel "Chappie" James was a six-foot-five black Tuskegee fighter pilot who flew 101 fighter missions in Korea and another 78 in Vietnam.

Known as President Richard Nixon's favorite black general, he served as assistant defense secretary as Nixon wound down the war. He told a class of graduating pilots in a memorable, funny speech at Williams Air Force Base near Phoenix that I reported for an Armed Forces Journal cover story that he didn't climb into planes, "I just strap 'em on."

James and his co-pilot, Robin Olds, later an Air Force general and commandant of the U.S. Air Force Academy at Colorado Springs, Colorado, flew F-4D bombing runs over Hanoi and the Haiphong Valley in North Vietnam and were dubbed "Black Man and Robin."

Our U.S. fighter planes flew out of Ubon Air Base in Thailand. The squadron Black Man and Robin were part of what was aptly called the Wolf Pack and had the distinction of downing seven Communist Mig-21 fighters in one day, two more the next, a record for the war. They were true top guns.

It was a heady period of my life after being the editor of my student newspaper at Old Dominion College in Norfolk, Virginia, from 1965 to 1967.

At Old Dominion College, where I was majoring in history, one of my professors, William J. Schellings, a bitter amputee from the Korean war and only professor of a required historiography course needed for graduation, said he would fail me because I editorially supported the Vietnam War and opposed the radical so-called Students for a Democratic Society who fomented anti-war demonstrations in those days.

Dean of Students G. William Whitehurst, my favorite history professor and adviser, and later a congressman from Virginia who served with distinction on the U.S. House Armed Services Committee for a decade, told me to change my major to political science, and I did.

I was drafted into the military as I graduated from college and joined the U.S. Air Force shortly after becoming an American citizen. They needed public information types to help build public support for the war and keep up morale of the troops, and I was sent to Williams Air Force Base near Phoenix, Arizona, the largest undergraduate pilot training base at the time.

I worked on the base newspaper, wrote speeches for the wing commander, and accompanied our jet-jock pilots to local civic club luncheons where they showed a film called "There Is A Way," a real-life depiction of bombing runs over Hanoi, and spoke about the war.

One pilot I accompanied for speeches to Rotary and Kiwanis Clubs in Arizona was Major Joe Victor Carpenter—the first Air Force prisoner of war released by North Vietnam's Ho Chi Minh—who was shot down and spent six years in a bamboo cage in Hanoi. Major Carpenter, a very nice man, was tortured alongside Senator John McCain, a fellow prisoner, and other hero POWs.

It was one of the true privileges of my life to be with such men in a difficult period and help tell the story. Mission journalism is very different from straight news reporting but has a distinct and important place in the panoply of American journalism going back to colonial times and the Revolutionary War.

After 10 years reporting for The Washington Times and covering Bill Clinton's run for president in 1992 and spending months in Arkansas, where all Clinton's girly stories were made known to fellow reporter Jerry Seper and me, I didn't have the stomach to keep driving 90 minutes each way from our family farm on the Shenandoah River in Front Royal, Virginia, just to do scandal journalism.

So I telephoned retired U.S. Senator Harry F. Byrd Jr., owner of a chain of newspapers in western and southern Virginia, with his brilliant publisher son Thomas T. Byrd, and became editor and general manager of The Warren Sentinel, a small weekly newspaper in Front Royal, a town near the beginning of the Skyline Drive on the Shenandoah River.

It was a tough experience for two years. Community journalism in a small town and county—where politicians and business people were at loggerheads over improving schools, bridges over the river, operation of volunteer fire departments, jobs and economic development, almost everything imaginable—turned out to be much harder than pace-setting reporting in the nation's capital.

Frankly, it was a nightmare but an experience and memory I treasure.

My first challenge came when I used my investigative reporting skills to ferret out self-dealing in the local Front Royal Fire Department after the chief, Dusty McIntosh, announced a strike and parked all the fire trucks in a show of force against the Front Royal Town Council and Warren County Board of Supervisors because they didn't fund the subsidy increase the fire department McIntosh was seeking.

I asked McIntosh and the Front Royal mayor for a look at the fire department's line-item budget request and found the requested increase was for McIntosh's $50,000-plus salary—he wasn't actually a volunteer—and for a paid medic who traveled on fire runs. The other volunteers didn't know McIntosh was raking in a big salary from the town and county subsidies, and when we broke the story that the strike was all about the fire chief getting a bigger salary, all hell broke loose in the community.

I wasn't ready for the firestorm, but Tom Byrd had an editorial advisory committee in the community, called a meeting, and supported me to the hilt. He was such a class act.

I got blackballed from the Rotary Club by local florist Carter Futtrell, a member of The Sentinel's advisory committee and one of The Sentinel's biggest advertisers, even though the county's most popular elected official, tax commissioner John Smedley, nominated me for membership.

Tom Byrd supported my view, in light of the blackball, that it was a good idea anyway for the editor of the community paper not to belong to the most elite leader's club but rather to be independent for the sake of our reporting. I attended the weekly Rotary meetings as a guest reporter, not as a member, and that relationship worked well for our reporting.

Advertising and circulation went up beyond our expectations. We topped 6,000 circulation, a one-third increase, largely because Tom Byrd bought Arthur Arundel's Front Royal News, a free tabloid newspaper, the only other weekly competition, a month after I became The Sentinel's editor and folded its masthead.

The Warren Sentinel immediately became a must-read in the community each week. Single copies were selling out. Each week, news-wise, we were beating the socks off the Northern Virginia Daily, which was our major local competition. Advertising soared.

Our photographer, Peter Wright, retired from the Associated Press and living in the area, rebuilt The Sentinel's austere photo lab and splashed the most wonderful color anchor pictures on the front page, above the fold, every week.

Those pictures were what people saw each week in the display lids of the paper boxes throughout the community. Peter and Features Editor Susan Burke, a marvelous writer and former deputy editor at The Winchester Star, won many Virginia Press Association awards. Susan ran the paper's second section and wrote riveting stories about personalities as well as the community and its history as a pivotal battleground throughout the Civil War.

We had local artist Patricia Windrow doing cartoons and special art for our section tabloids. Reporter Margo Turner churned out unbelievable amounts of copy, and Sports Writer-editor Roger Bianchini covered all the school sports games and did blockbuster local crime stories as well.

It was a formula that worked, but it was work each and every week. I had to fight Tom Byrd for pay raises for the good reporters; attend and report town council, board of supervisors, and school board meetings every week; do my writing and paper makeup on weekends; and rarely saw my family. It was a killer, but one of the most memorable experiences of my life.

We wrote stories about the town and county governments fighting and forced them to come together on some important issues. One such issue was school improvement, where we aggressively covered the campaign of local town power boss and car dealer John Marlow and others who said the community should abandon renovation of the 1939 high school and put $20-plus million into a new high school at the expense of needed investment in the community's sole middle school—where most of the youth problems existed—and the town's three elementary schools.

Economic development was vitally important because the community had lost 2,000 jobs in 1988 when the state attorney general and environmental officials moved in and closed down the Avtex rayon plant in Front Royal, the largest employer there for decades, because the plant had polluted the Shenandoah River with toxic PCBs for a generation.

After I left The Warren Sentinel and returned to The Washington Times in 1995, I got a call from Becky Norton Dunlop, secretary of natural resources for Virginia Governor George Allen at the time, who said she wanted to leak documents to me that showed the White House during the administration of President George Bush elder and his national security adviser, General Colin Powell, were responsible for keeping open the Avtex plant for several years beyond the time the Environmental Protection Agency and state wanted to close it down.

The reason the Bush elder administration kept the plant open, according to the documents, was that Avtex had an exclusive patent for the rayon used for the heat shields of U.S. space vehicles and missiles, including missiles being developed for the so-called Strategic Defense Initiative.

Governor Allen's attorney general was James Gilmore, who succeeded him as governor. Gilmore was waffling on filing a lawsuit against the federal government for $4 million in cleanup costs for the Shenandoah River related to keeping Avtex open during the elder Bush administration.

Governor Allen wanted to put some metal in Jim Gilmore's pistol, so decided to take out his cowboy six-gun and use this reporter as the recipient of a leaked documents that would translate into a big front-page story.

I drove down to Richmond and gratefully received the feed of documents and interviews with Governor Allen's key officials who explained the intended lawsuit.

On the day the story appeared, Governor Allen held a news conference on the steps of the Virginia State Capitol to announce his lawsuit, and Attorney General Gilmore's hands were tied.

Colin Powell called George Allen and chewed him out about the story, I later learned. But it worked. The federal government, then in the hands of the Clinton administration, promptly folded after the Virginia lawsuit was filed.

Journalism is war.

While I was still at the Warren Sentinel, Tom Byrd told me he wanted the paper to be a friend of the community and provide a full and feisty report to the community each and every week. We did that.

It took a marvelous team of disparate souls—Susan Burke, Peter Wright, Margo Turner, Roger Bianchini, circulation director Tammy Wright, advertising people Patty Rickard and Judy Smith, and our friends Joan Stotler, Al Armentrout, Winona Kirk, and others at The Winchester Star to make it work.

It takes a lot of disparate talent to produce any community newspaper or radio or TV news show. Teamwork and good dedicated talent are essential, especially in the news business where you're on the front lines all the time, 24 hours a day.

It takes a special breed of people and special management skills to keep things going, which is why I especially admired Publisher Tom Byrd. No one could have had a better or more supportive publisher or better businessman, and he came from the Byrd family that helped found our country, so in his heart he felt a dedication to doing it right. He wasn't one of these mega-newspaper chains like Gannett (the largest, U.S. newspaper publisher) whose people did not have a personal and historic stake in the community.

Tom Byrd's great uncle, Admiral Richard Evelyn Byrd, was the explorer who found the South Pole. His ancestors helped write the Articles of Confederation and the U.S. Constitution. So with a publisher like that, you know real history and community journalism are a sincere priority and objective.

It's very different than Gannett and the McDonalds of journalism, which are a very dumbed-down version of the kind of complete reporting communities deserve.

We're counting on the next generation of reporters, editors, photographers, producers and graphics people to save us from the myopic journalism of the media conglomerates that now control most news coverage, if one can call it that.

Sure people want all the stories about the latest car crash or murder or scam to bilk taxpayers. But we need to get back to solid community reporting that upholds the positive as well.

We need great sizzling coverage of good people and youth in our towns, cities and rural areas who work to build a better life every day, with great feature stories and pictures in community newspapers and recognition on local television and radio. That is my hope and prayer.

CHAPTER FOURTEEN

THE SPIKE FOR VINCE FOSTER

For whatever reason, Vince came to the end of his rope. In his briefcase, Bernie Nussbaum found a note that had been torn into pieces. When put back together, it said "I was not meant for the job in the spotlight of public life in Washington. Here ruining people is considered sport... The public will never believe the innocence of the Clintons and their loyal staff." Vince was overwhelmed, exhausted, and vulnerable to attacks by people who didn't play by the same rules he did. He was rooted in the values of honor and respect, and uprooted by those who valued power and personal assault more. And his untreated depression stripped him of the defenses that allowed the rest of us to survive.

—Bill Clinton, "My Life"

VINCENT W. FOSTER JR. went to elementary school in the early 1950s with Bill Clinton and his White House chief of staff, Mack McLarty, at Miss Mary Purkins' School for Little Folks in Hope, Arkansas.

He was a leading attorney at Rose Law Firm in Little Rock, the state capital, where Hillary Clinton was a partner when Bill Clinton was governor of Arkansas for 12 years. The Clintons and Vince and Lisa Foster were best friends.

As governor, Clinton said one of his few social pleasures was frequent visits to the Foster home, where he swam in the pool and partied with a close circle of friends. It was natural for President-elect Clinton to ask lifelong friend Vince Foster to be deputy counsel at the White House when he was elected as president in November 1992.

But what went wrong that led Vince Foster to blow his brains out with a .38-caliber revolver at Fort Marcy Park near McLean, Virginia, off the George Washington Parkway, on July 20, 1993?

When it happened, many conservative opponents of the Clinton administration expressed doubts that it was even a suicide. Reed Irvine of Accuracy in Media beat the drum for years saying it was not a suicide and suggested all sorts of scenarios from murder to unexplained death elsewhere and the body being dragged, by Saudi Arabians no less whose ambassador had a house near where the body was found in Fort Marcy Park.

I was assigned three years later for an anniversary story to get to the bottom of the conspiracy theories by reviewing the entire public record of Foster's death that was ruled by all authorities, including two independent counsel inquiries, as a suicide. I was given several months to work on the story.

But it was never published.

My story and graphics meticulously validated all law enforcement inquiries that ruled Foster's death a suicide and knocked down all the conspiratorial theories that had developed because the bullet wasn't found, there was a low amount of blood at the scene, and so forth. But Wesley Pruden, editor in chief of The Washington Times, didn't like the conclusions of the finally edited, lengthy special report that took two full pages of the newspaper. It was in typeset, with just the headlines and minor remaining polishing by senior editors. And at 8:30 p.m., on July 19, 1996, without even talking to me, Pruden called Joe Curl, my editor on the project, and said he was spiking the story—not just holding it for further changes after telling me and Joe what problems he had with it and giving us instructions for further reporting and work but rather pulling it altogether.

The next day was the third anniversary of the death, but since the piece was removed at the last minute, editors had to scramble to fill the pages with other stories, pictures and ads just hours before the first edition hit the presses.

Joe and I were shell-shocked. We never got a personal explanation, except Joe and Fran Coombs told me the problem was with my last sentence, which went to the heart of the conspiracy advertising campaign that Reed Irvine's so-called Accuracy in Media had waged for years in the pages of the newspaper. Fran sternly directed me not to go to Wes Pruden to question why the project was killed. So I didn't.

My unpublished story says: "Mr. Foster's death is apparently an issue that will not die so long as there are political and other incentives to keep the controversy alive. On one essential fact there is no dispute. Vincent W. Foster Jr. died tragically three years ago today."

Also, my pulled story reports that while Bill Clinton, as governor, was having sexual liaisons with Gennifer Flowers and other women in Little Rock and elsewhere, his wife, Hillary, was having her own romance with law partner Vince Foster, which ultimately became a full-blown affair. Arkansas state troopers who were members of the governor's security detail said Foster often visited Hillary at the governor's mansion when Clinton was out of town, traveling around Arkansas.

My reporting of the Hillary Clinton-Vince Foster affair was confirmed in 1996 by historian and investigative reporter Roger Morris in his book, "Partners in Power: The Clintons and Their America." According to Morris:

There would be several sources—including a former U.S. attorney, sometime aides, a number of lawyers, social friends, and many of the same [Arkansas state] troopers who

testified about the governor's illicit acts—who described the
First Lady's affair, dating to the mid-1980s, with Rose partner Vince Foster. A relationship evident in the semiprivate
kisses and furtive squeezes at parties and dinners described
by the security guards, it was also an intimate professional
bond between two attorneys who worked together on some
of their firm's most sensitive cases.

Along with Webster Hubbell, they staged a veritable
coup d'état to wrest control of the Rose firm in 1988. Many
thought that the governor was well aware of the affair and
ultimately accepted it as one more implicit bargain in their
marriage. Clinton continued to treat Vince Foster as the
close friend he had been since childhood in Hope, even
entrusting him with some of the most crucial secrets of the
1992 campaign. "Bill knew, of course he knew. But what
was he supposed to say to anybody about being faithful?"
[Morris quoted] a lawyer close to Foster who was familiar
with them all.

Morris also reports, as we found, that many Clinton friends and
associates thought Hillary Clinton's relationship with Vince Foster "was an understandable and natural response to her husband's
behavior. Foster was known to treat her with dignity, respect, and
abiding love she was missing in her marriage."

Arkansas state troopers told us that Hillary Clinton and Vince
Foster frequently spent time together at a cabin retreat of the Rose
Law Firm in Heber Springs, Arkansas, in the lake country north of
Little Rock.

Foster suddenly went into hiding just before the November
1992 election because he was afraid someone was going to blow the
fact that he was having an affair with Hillary, Rose Law Firm partner
John P. Carroll told the FBI.

In Washington, as Bill Clinton recounts in his own memoir,

"My Life," Foster tragically got in over his head quite quickly. Over the first six months of the new administration, there were several extremely stressful and contentious Cabinet nomination fights (in particular for a new Clinton attorney-general), which Vince was handling.

The issue of nominees Zoé Baird and Kimba Wood hiring foreign nannies who were illegal aliens was a big media frenzy for months.

And there was a big problem with the Clintons' unfiled personal income tax returns over several prior years because accountants had cooked numbers regarding gains and losses on the Clintons' White-water real estate investments. Foster was trying to sort that out and monitoring the various state and federal Whitewater investigations and criminal prosecutions.

Vince Foster was singled out for sharp criticism by the Wall Street Journal's feisty editorial page, which badly stung him. Also, Foster's wife and children, still back in Little Rock, were in turmoil, mainly because his high school-age son was caught up in drug abuse.

Foster fell into deep mental depression and ended up killing himself with a revolver gunshot wound through his mouth, where his body was found on a shaded pathway in the Civil War-era Fort Marcy Park overlooking the Potomac River and city of Washington on the other side.

Foster was an intensely private man, which is apparently why he chose an almost hidden path in dense underbrush at the bottom of a hillside deep within the park as the place for his suicide. He was surely unaware that the park was a hangout used by homosexual men seeking anonymous sexual liaisons.

A man who stopped at the park in late afternoon in an unmarked white construction van on his way home from work actually found Foster's body but did not get close enough to see the partially hidden gun, which police immediately found in Foster's right hand with his large thumb caught in the trigger guard.

Scared, the man ran away, drove his van to park headquarters at the next exit off the parkway, and told park employees outside taking a smoke break about the body, then hurriedly drove off toward the Washington beltway and his home in Manassas, Virginia.

When Fairfax County police got to the body minutes later and found Foster's White House pass with his neatly folded jacket on the passenger seat of his car, in the Fort Marcy parking lot, they promptly notified the U.S. Secret Service and FBI, which joined what then was labeled in police reports a "homicide" investigation.

After days of the story hitting the news, the man who first found the body called radio talk host G. Gordon Liddy to identify himself and started the conspiracy theories by saying he did not see a gun.

Liddy connected the man with FBI and congressional investigators. Political opponents of the Clintons promptly spread the story of possible foul play, saying someone might have planted the gun in Foster's hand after killing him—maybe even dumped his body in Fort Marcy after he died or was killed somewhere else.

However, my exhaustive, months-long study of the entire public record of police and FBI investigations, plus two separate inquiries by Independent Counsels Robert Fiske and Kenneth Starr, a final probe by the Senate Banking Committee, and my own interviews with key players, convinced me beyond doubt that the conspiracy theories were not true and that it really was a tragic suicide, as the medical examination at the time and all probes concluded.

Sure, there were still unanswered questions, such as what happened to the .38-caliber bullet that exited Foster's head? It never was found. But the gun in Foster's hand was identified by family members as one he inherited from his father and kept in a safe location in their rented Washington house.

Forensic examination showed it was fired at the estimated time of death and the gun had Foster's blood and DNA from his mouth on the barrel. The bullet went through the roof of Foster's mouth and exited through the back of his head into the air somewhere, maybe finally into a faraway tree but never was recovered.

The reason there was little blood at the scene was because Foster's heart immediately stopped beating and pumping blood through his body when the gun fired. Blood sank to his lower extremities as the pathway upon which he sat to shoot himself was going downhill, and his head was pointing uphill. Only a little blood trickled out of his mouth and bullet exit wound behind his head, where it pooled underneath the body.

After Foster's death, for understandable reasons, the Foster family went to great lengths to suppress detailed personal journals he kept that recounted his fondness and relationship with Hillary Clinton, then first lady.

Hillary Clinton, who had just returned to the United States from an Asian trip, orchestrated a White House cover-up of documents in Foster's office on the night he died, because they included all the Clintons' tax records for the prior four years and documents relating to their controversial Whitewater real estate investments.

On Hillary Clinton's orders, late at night on July 20, 1993, while Foster's body lay in the George Washington hospital morgue, several of their staff entered the deputy White House counsel's office suite and removed at least three boxes of Vince Foster's documents from file drawers in his personal office.

It was discovered just months later and reported by The Times' intrepid investigative reporter Jerry Seper that the removed documents included records of Hillary Clinton's involvement as a lawyer in behalf of Rose Law Firm managing partner Webster Hubbell's father-in-law, Seth Ward, who was an investor in one of the Whitewater real estate developments.

The boxes were stashed in a closet in the Clintons' White House residential quarters. This was obstruction of the ongoing Vince Foster homicide/suicide law enforcement investigation, pure and simple. The work product reflected in the documents related to Foster's death.

Hillary Clinton's staff loyalists, under directions of Craig Livingstone (known as "dirty works czar" for the Clintons), also wiped material off Foster's computer hard-drive in his office, meticulously kept by his able career civil service assistant, Linda Tripp, who immediately noticed the changes when the grieving staff arrived at the White House on the morning following the suicide.

Tripp told FBI agents about the computer tampering and missing documents when they interviewed her as part of the homicide investigation. For her honesty, Tripp was summarily transferred from the White House to another post at the Pentagon to get her out of the way.

Several years later, Clinton loyalists also transferred young White House intern Monica Lewinsky to Tripp's office at the Pentagon in an effort to save Bill Clinton from himself as he carried on his steamy sexual liaison with Lewinsky. Two women scorned got together, had sympathy for each other, and Tripp got the Lewinsky story out to the media. The rest is history.

Seper—also a former undercover cop—broke the story about the Foster documents heist in December 1993. The story forced Attorney General Janet Reno to seek an independent counsel, thus setting events in motion for both Fiske's and Starr's investigations of the president and ultimately the House Judiciary Committee probe that saw Bill Clinton impeached in February 1999.

Obviously, when Hillary Clinton ordered the boxes of documents removed from Vince Foster's office on July 20, 1993, she started a White House cover-up as first lady. She knew the documents showed that Foster had been working to extricate her and President Clinton's Whitewater land deal involving Seth Ward from the Whitewater mess—and was trying to resolve their past personal tax issues on government time, paid for by taxpayers, and the Foster files were in the White House, a government building.

So Hillary Clinton's orders for the documents to be removed from Foster's office on the day he killed himself and be hidden in a closet in the president's private residence in the White House—presumably off-limits to investigators—was the beginning of a cover-up of huge proportions that would play out for two years.

Both the Resolution Trust Corp and Starr investigated Mrs. Clinton's denials of doing substantive legal work for Whitewater investors as RTC federal bank regulators looked at suspicious loans to the deal by Madison Guaranty Savings and Loan in Arkansas, run by Jim and Susan McDougal.

Hillary Clinton's Rose Law Firm billing records were under subpoena by state and federal law courts for two years while hidden with the rest of the Foster documents in a white House residence closet.

Mrs. Clinton knew where the billing records were all along. And when the documents mysteriously appeared in January 1996 on a table in her study in the White House residence, "found" by her secretary, no one tagged her and other White House employees involved for obvious obstruction of justice.

It was ironic in February 2006 when Vice President Dick Cheney accidently shot a hunting friend with birdshot that Hillary Clinton strongly rebuked Cheney publicly two days later for being slow about getting information about the accident to the public. Yet for two entire years, as first lady, she had hidden and sat on her subpoenaed billing records wanted by the government during a corruption investigation.

As Seper reported, the records were a copy of an original version printed out from the Rose Law Firm computer in 1992. They turned out to contain important information about Mrs. Clinton's work for Madison and the Castle Grande real estate projects in which Seth Ward had invested.

Arkansas Governor Jim Guy Tucker, who was lieutenant governor when Clinton was governor, was on trial and ultimately convicted and sent to prison for fraud because he defaulted on loans over $1 million related to Castle Grande.

Jerry Seper discovered all these stories for The Times. In April 1995, the White House Correspondents Association awarded Seper the coveted Barnet Nover Award. Ironically, President Clinton himself made the award to Seper at the association's annual black-tie dinner, with Hillary Clinton staring stone-faced on the dais. The moment was caught for posterity by Times photographer Kenneth Lambert, now with the Associated Press.

It was a particularly funny moment because Wes Pruden and Fran Coombs told Seper before the dinner to make sure the picture was taken before he stopped shaking Clinton's hand, so they had a good one for the next day's paper.

Jerry watched out of the corner of his eye for a flash to go off, but Lambert was using fast film without a flash. Jerry kept pumping Clinton's hand for several seconds as Clinton only curtly said, "Congratulations," and went to pull away.

"Awkward moment, isn't it, Mr. President?" Seper said to Bill Clinton.

Ken Lambert's picture of the moment is an absolute classic.

CHAPTER FIFTEEN

NEWT GINGRICH AND HOUSE SCANDALS

*Unfortunately, perhaps, Washington is a town of fickle friend-
ships. People seem to enjoy watching others—friends or foes—
get skewered. I've never quite understood this, but certainly
learned quickly to listen to all sides on any given story. The
more I smacked them, as it were, the more they talked.*

—Paul M. Rodriguez

───────────

NEWT GINGRICH, a history professor in Georgia, was elected as a
Republican congressman in 1978. Immediately after being elected,
Gingrich joined with a band of several dozen congressional brothers
impatient with the permanent minority, go-along-get-along mindset of Republican leader Bob Michel of Illinois and other calcified
GOP seniors to found a House Republican renegade group called
the Conservative Opportunity Society.

Gingrich was an immediate national political superstar. After
Ronald Reagan's election as president in 1980, this conservative
trailblazer talked with me about corruption in Congress and his goal
to push Democrats out as rulers of the federal government.

Gingrich became House Republican whip and found a Democratic partner, Philip Gramm (former economics professor from

College Station, Texas), who organized several dozen conservative House Democrats as a group that became known as the boll
weevils.

This new partnership between minority conservative Republican general Newt Gingrich and Democratic boll weevil general Phil
Gramm changed political history.

My incestuous liberal media colleagues—Steve Roberts of the
New York Times, wife Cokie Roberts of ABC News, Helen Dewar
and Mary McGrory of The Washington Post, Elaine Povich of The
Chicago Tribune, Gloria Borger of U.S. News & World Report—
who covered the Congress and White House, smelling their own gas
every day and believing they knew all in Washington and around the
country, didn't know what hit them.

The new Gingrich-Gramm political alliance shared Reagan's values for a leaner federal government, tax cuts and economic growth
as well as an assault by the United States and global partners against
the Soviet Union and worldwide communism.

To the chagrin of the left-liberal political and media monopoly
that believed it controlled the country at the time, there was a new
conservative, bipartisan majority in the U.S. House of Representatives, and most of my Washington media colleagues did not like it
one bit.

Each and every day, I enjoyed their pain.

After covering congressional budget stories for several years, and
breaking the Geraldine Ferraro financial ethics story in 1984, the
paper put me on the political scandal beat and later twinned me
with Paul Rodriguez, an ex-policeman and political Democrat from
Texas, whose titular godfather in the U.S. House of Representatives
was Representative Henry Gonzalez, chairman of the House Banking Committee.

In 1989, when Gingrich upped the ante against congressional
political corruption that had infested the leadership and committees
of Congress under four decades of Democratic rule, Rodriguez was

there, and Henry Gonzalez and other renegade Democrats became key sources and helpers as Gingrich and his allies fed us stories.

Gingrich and fellow conservatives wanted things to change and for House Republicans to win the majority. So they sought media exposure of huge corruption in the Congress after four straight decades of Democratic majority rule.

We were happy to oblige, not because of any partisan support of Gingrich and the Republicans but rather because it was so apparent to many fair-minded people, whether loyalists of Paul Weyrich and New Right or honest liberals and Common Cause, that something was dreadfully wrong—with misuse of public office and government money and blatant, self-serving corruption on Capitol Hill.

And it all pointed back to the fact that the same party had been in power for decades, and its leaders were mostly hardened, big-government liberals and urban ward heelers with large numbers of people in their constituencies who were dependent on government largesse.

Paul Rodriguez and I knew this was a historic moment in news and helping the good of the order historically, and we fortunately had a news organization willing to run with the stories. So we went to war.

Our early Washington Times editors, Smith Hempstone and Arnaud de Borchgrave, made a commitment to cover the congressional corruption story fully. Ronald Reagan had started a sea change in Washington politics that was being blocked and stymied by the entrenched federal bureaucracy and powerful congressional barons of Capitol Hill.

We, along with other news organizations, became an integral part of the unfolding dynamic to expose the corruption and achieve change.

The media elites were with Reagan's opponents. However, some other news organizations in the decade between 1982 and 1992 such as the Wall Street Journal, National Review and talk radio hosts around the country helped even up the odds. On solid investigative stories that we broke, we could count on honest reporters with the Los Angeles Times, Miami Herald and Boston Globe to weigh in as well.

Fox News was not yet formed. CNN under leadership of Ted Turner and wife Jane Fonda tilted coverage in a left-liberal direction. CBS under doddering anchor Dan Rather, heir to Walter Cronkite, was left-liberal. NBC News followed as a lapdog of the left-liberal line under Tom Brokaw. ABC News under anchor Peter Jennings was refreshingly independent and fair.

So it fell to those of us on the national desk of The Washington Times to shake things up a little in the 1980s and 1990s. We were pleased to oblige.

Our assertive reporting of the congressional corruption story was a prickly pear for Washington's pro-Democratic Party, dominant media elites who gagged on a daily basis. They and their fellow travelers ganged up against us in the congressional press galleries and in the columns of their newspapers and on the airwaves.

That's all right. Journalism is war.

We had a few media allies, particularly Bob Merry and John Fialka of the Wall Street Journal, undercover conservative Tom Reid of The Washington Post, and Frank van der Linden of the Daily Oklahoman.

The Associated Press wire service used by almost all daily newspapers across America tilted liberal-left because of the overwhelming bias of most newspaper, radio and TV reporters for national news organizations, but the AP served everyone, and I was always impressed by the professionalism and thoroughness of AP reporters. United Press International tended to be more unbiased. Reuters, which emphasized foreign coverage, was a very good and fair news service. So was Bloomberg always fair and complete.

The major news magazines—Time, Newsweek, U.S. News and World Report—and gossip magazines such as People were predictably on the left-liberal wavelength and parroted whatever pro-Democratic party line was being pushed at any time.

Our news collaboration with Newt Gingrich became earnest in 1987 as he and about 77 House colleagues, along with the liberal good-government group Common Cause, brought ethics charges against Democratic House Speaker Jim Wright. The ethics case was launched in May 1988.

We learned with help from this band of House renegades about huge, corrupt political payoffs—involving other House and Senate leaders (including Jim Wright)—by savings and loan executives who had scammed depositors and funded illegal political fundraising boat parties for congressional politicians of both parties.

As soon as he had taken office, Gingrich had assigned a young assistant on his congressional staff to start collecting information on Wright; Rep. Tony Coelho of California, chairman of the Democratic Congressional Campaign Committee; Dan Rostenkowski, chairman of the House Ways and Means Committee; and other House leaders associated with corrupt activities of S&L executives.

At the time of this information gathering, I was running the Capitol Hill office of another Republican congressman—Eldon Rudd of Arizona, a former FBI special agent—who also used his sleuth skills to collect information about fellow members and the unbelievable corruption that was under way in those days. This experience was invaluable later as I worked as a reporter and had to get stories out on a daily basis.

Paul Rodriguez, my reporting partner, had close ties to Wright, Coelho, and other Democrats; yet, Paul and I regularly met with Gingrich and his staff during 1986 to collect their evidence and do our own reporting for stories to follow.

Paul was previously an undercover reserve policeman in Washington, D.C. and had a gift of schmoozing, which was highly effective with the invisible corps of nonpolitical permanent staffers on Capitol Hill—the furniture movers, electricians, cops, waiters and waitresses, and low-level support staff members among thousands of congressional employees in the myriad of congressional offices.

Paul picked up stuff because he befriended and got to know the real folks behind the scenes who actually make Congress run each day—the folks that most snooty and lazy members of the Capitol Hill press corps had no clue about.

The Gingrich staff research operation gave us details about the gigantic, unfolding savings and loan scandal, personalized by Charles Keating of Lincoln Savings and Loan and Donald Dixon of Vernon Savings and Loan, which cost American taxpayers more that $400 billion in bailout costs because of federal deposit insurance.

We rode the so-called "Keating Five" story about members of Congress who muscled Federal Home Loan Bank Board regulators to ease off on dicey savings and loan practices because politicians were being paid off with huge campaign contributions and expensive trips by savings and loan executives.

Senator John McCain, previously an Arizona congressman when I worked for Eldon Rudd, got mad with me because he blamed Democratic colleagues Senators Dennis DeConcini of Arizona, Donald Riegle of Michigan, and Alan Cranston of California for setting up meetings with FHLB Chairman Edwin J. Gray—formerly press secretary for Ronald Reagan as governor.

It turned out that McCain and Senator John Glenn, Ohio Democrat, had played an equivalent role in trying to get federal bank regulators to back-off in behalf of Charles Keating and Lincoln Savings and Loan. Taxpayers took it in the ear, but politicians always try to blame someone else.

Keating was ultimately exonerated by the courts because government bureaucrats horribly undersold his savings and loan real estate assets, causing the taxpayers' bailout of failed Lincoln Savings and Loan in the multibillions.

McCain, a genuine hero during the deadly 1967 explosion and fire aboard the aircraft carrier U.S.S. Forrestal off the Vietnam coast and later as a prisoner of war in Hanoi, does not suffer fools gladly. Years later, I was proudly on his bad list again when I wrote a front-page story in 2001 about his use of Democratic talking points, issued by the office of Senate Democratic leader Tom Daschle, to attack President George W. Bush in a Senate speech about "patients' bill of rights" legislation.

McCain had teamed with Edward M. Kennedy, John Edwards and other Senate Democrats in opposing the Republican Medicare bill and used the Daschle talking points verbatim to attack President Bush's proposal in his Friday speech in an empty Senate chamber, aimed mainly at the national C-SPAN audience.

McCain was very angry on the following Monday and accused me in the U.S. Capitol of "fabricating" the story, until I whipped out copies of Daschle's press release dated the day before his Senate remarks and McCain's own press release and published page from the Congressional Record. It was all identical.

McCain accused his staff of feeding him Daschle's stuff for his Senate remarks and denied knowing anything about it. Members of Congress get spoon-fed stuff by their staff and have to do things on the spur of the moment. But McCain's denial gave us a second-day story. He glared at me for weeks and wouldn't talk, but he's a media glory hound who runs after the press, and his silent treatment ultimately ended.

Paul Rodriguez was onto the savings and loan story before I was, as I was busy covering other stories in the wake of the Geraldine Ferraro scandal. My first meeting in Gingrich's office to look at his extensive files about Democratic Speaker Jim Wright occurred in May 1985. Gingrich had several file cabinet drawers full of stuff about Wright's self-puffing book, "Reflections of a Public Man," written in 1984 by Matthew Cossolotto, a government-paid congressional staffer. The files showed how Wright hit up business executives and organizations to purchase bulk copies of the book whenever he made a speech.

Wright's book was published by William C. Moore, a former campaign worker who got more than $700,000 in payments from Wright's political campaign committee and, in return, gave Wright a royalty arrangement of 55 percent—four times the industry standard. Books were sold in bulk to lobbying groups such as the Fertilizer Institute as a way around congressional limits on honoraria income.

Wright was pocketing $3.50 for every book that was, in turn, used to ply substantial political contributions to his political committee. The scam also involved employment of his wife, Betty, by Fort Worth businessman George Mallick, who Wright benefitted with lucrative government contracts and other favors.

We wrote scores of stories about Wright's misuse of his office for personal gain, culminating in a memorable front page of The Washington Times on June 1, 1989, with the banner headline: "Speaker Wright quits under fire." The full-color photo above the fold showed Wright weeping before the House of Representatives as he announced his resignation and asked the House to halt "mindless cannibalism."

Wright surely knew that our sources included his staff aide, Matthew Cossolotto, who was abused by Wright's political director, John Mack, a horrible man previously convicted of barbarous attempted murder of a woman, Pamela Small, in a Fairfax home improvement store.

Mack's brother was married to Wright's daughter, and Wright used his congressional position to get Mack out of jail after he was convicted of brutally smashing Small's head and face with a claw hammer in the store in a bizarre spontaneous attack.

Mack rose to become Wright's chief political enforcer in the U.S. House of Representatives and used his abusive qualities to put the fear in anyone who got in his way. That is until Matthew Cossolotto, in a strange turn of events after he left Wright's office and became a speechwriter for the CEO of MCI in Washington, met Pamela Small, who was MCI's communications director.

Small told Cossolotto of Mack's attack, her near death, and several reparative surgeries to rebuild her head and face. Cossolotto, who had been bullied by Mack for years as a member of Speaker Wright's staff, decided to get the justice Small deserved by toppling Mack and Wright.

Wright's reference to "mindless cannibalism" in his farewell speech was poetic because it harked back to John Mack's hammer attack on Pamela Small and to the hatred of Jim Wright and his political hammer, John Mack, among so many fellow Democrats, including none other than Wright's successor as House speaker, Democratic Majority Leader Thomas Foley of Washington state, who was a key source for our stories as Wright fell from power.

At a Democratic policy conference at the Greenbrier resort in White Sulphur Springs, West Virginia, just months before Wright was forced to resign, Foley was feeding dirt on Wright to the assembled press corps, myself included, and for months thereafter, putting his knife into his leader as Brutus killed Caesar.

Foley fed us, but his fall was yet to come—largely fashioned by wife Heather, Foley's unpaid chief of staff, who became queen of the Capitol and orchestrated a huge law enforcement cover-up that was the Democrats' ultimate undoing over the next few years.

Jim Wright, with his bushy eyebrows and smarmy, treacly, back-slapping ways, learned to be part of that chorus—having learned politics at the elbow of fellow Texan Lyndon Johnson, author of the so-called Great Society panoply of failed multibillion-dollar social-ist measures including food stamps, Medicare, and federal takeover of our nation's public schools under the so-called Equal Education Opportunity Act, which actually sent our country down the road to equal access to national public school educational mediocrity.

Wright was a Southern huckster and career politician in the

U.S. House of Representatives who flirted with the left and voted for every controlling big-government federal spending program that came along, much like U.S. Senator Robert C. Byrd of West Virginia.

Robert Byrd and Jim Wright both had Ku Klux Klan backing, yet moved with the Democratic Party's leftist movement as Robert Kennedy, Eugene McCarthy, George McGovern and Michael Dukakis took the party further and further left and ultimately into political minority status as the national mouthpiece of state socialism and big taxes, which the country resoundingly rejected under the leadership of Ronald Reagan and since.

Wright's loyalty to his friends in the Texas savings and loan industry was steadfast, to the point that Paul Rodriguez found and reported that he threatened several times in 1986 and 1987 to reveal the homosexuality of a Federal Home Loan Bank Board examiner unless board chairman Edwin Gray fired the man and agreed to listen personally to the special pleading of Wright's savings and loan backers.

The stakes were high for Wright and Democratic Party congressional campaign fund-raisers who were using a luxury yacht called "High Spirits" for parties on the Potomac River for high-roller business executives and lobbyist contributors to the Democratic Party.

They raised tens of millions of dollars in nightly sojourns that made Republican casino lobbyist Jack Abramoff look like a piker by comparison, with free airplane rides for contributors and cold hard cash from savings and loan executive Thomas Gaubert—bearded, cigar-chomping head of the deeply insolvent Independent American Savings and Loan, who also served as finance co-chairman of the Democratic Congressional Campaign Committee in the mid-1980s.

Federal Election Commission records show that between 1983 and 1986, Gaubert; his brother Jack; their wives, Barbara and Carolyn; and their children, Tom Jr., Michael, Paige, and Randy, gave $147,000 to Democratic candidates for federal office. Gaubert set up East Texas First Political Action Committee to funnel $100,920 into the 1985 special election of U.S. Rep. James Chapman. Gaubert and other thrift executives were convicted of conspiracy to funnel illegal contributions to Jim Wright and other politicians.

Don Dixon, convicted head of Vernon Savings & Loan, told us that his corporate plane was always at the disposal of Wright and other Democratic lawmakers for trips throughout the country for fund-raising and other purposes—all illegal corporate contributions that went unreported by the politicians on the take.

We found that in 1979, Wright and his wife had formed a partnership with Texas real estate developer George Mallick to sell gemstones and obtain use of a Fort Worth condominium. The House Ethics Committee found that Wright, in return, tried to steer nearly $30 million in federal grants to Mallick from a fund targeted to benefit the poor.

When Wright resigned as House speaker on May 31, 1989, following ethics charges leveled by House Independent Counsel Richard J. Phelan, he gave a belabored House speech defending his actions regarding his book profits and dealings with Mallick and savings and loan tycoons.

He ended his speech with a plea to end political cannibalism, which members of both major political parties have continued until this day.

> It is grievously hurtful to our society when vilification becomes an accepted form of political debate and negative campaigning becomes a full-time occupation—when members of each party become self-appointed vigilantes carrying out personal vendettas against members of the other party.
>
> That's not what this institution is supposed to be all about. When vengeance becomes more desirable than vindication and harsh personal attacks upon one another's motives and one another's character drown out the quiet

logic of serious debate on important issues, surely that's unworthy of our institution and unworthy of our American political process. All of us in both political parties must resolve to bring this period of mindless cannibalism to an end. We've done enough of it.

Well, the beat still goes on. Political cannibalism is still the mantra for Democrats and Republicans nationally.

CHAPTER SIXTEEN

CATHOLIC SCANDAL
SERIES SNUFFED

One cannot speak about solving a homosexual problem
among priests and bishops until you first know the extent,
the number, of homosexual priests and bishops. How
many? It is the question that no one seems to want to ask or
answer. And yet it is the first principle in solving the prob-
lem. The secrecy and silence, and absolute refusal to teach or
explain the moral truth, is the horrendous means by which
an act or agenda can be accomplished or an end achieved
that allows this homosexual problem to continue. That
silence must be broken.

—Father James R. Haley

CATHOLIC FATHER JAMES R. HALEY of the Arlington Diocese of
Virginia was on a mission against sexually deviant priests, bishops
and their supporters in the church after he attended Mount St.
Mary's Seminary at Emmitsburg, Maryland, and was ordained as a
priest in 1987.

Paul S. Loverde, Father Haley's bishop in the Arlington Diocese,
has been on the attack to defrock the whistle-blower priest since July
2002, after Haley told Loverde over several years what he knew about

sexual misbehavior and thievery by fellow priests and later explicitly revealed in a subpoenaed court deposition. This court deposition was for a civil case involving adultery by a fellow priest who got a woman parishioner pregnant and left the church to marry her.

It turns out that the biggest problem in the U.S. Catholic Church scandal is the vast extent of homosexual acceptance and practice among priests and bishops.

The Catholic Church, unlike Protestant denominations, does not allow priests and nuns to marry. They are required to make a vow of celibacy before entering the priesthood or their religious orders.

Most heterosexual priests and nuns obey their vows of celibacy and chastity—some have not. But vast numbers of homosexuals in the church go on with their sexual practices, and the church has blinked and ignored the problem.

In seminaries and church rectories throughout the country, this has caused a huge schism between holy, obedient heterosexual priests and nuns and their disobedient homosexual colleagues.

It is the homosexuals, mostly, who sexually abused teenage boys in the church and caused the scandal that cost the church billions of dollars in lawsuit settlements. And when bishops learned of a sexually abusive homosexual priest, as reporters for the Boston Globe and Dallas Morning News exposed at the beginning of the scandal, these bad priests were quickly shipped to other dioceses, their crimes swept under the carpet, and their new parishes totally kept unaware that they had sexual predators in their midst.

Catholic leaders who acknowledge the majority of homosexual priests have corrupted public awareness by confusing people about the church's requirements for chastity and celibacy.

Personally brought up in the Church of England as a youth and later in the Episcopal Church in the United States, I believe priestly celibacy is unnatural, except for very saintly men and women. But that's just my opinion. Certainly, what's been going on in the Catholic Church for years proves my instincts are correct.

The homosexuals have been jumping into bed and showering together for centuries, and heterosexual priests with hot hormones have done their share of disobedience as well, with people their own age and a lot of young people who became their predatory targets.

As a reporter on this story for many years, I say the whole thing is a dodge that the Catholic Church leadership has perpetuated—the confusion over the difference between chastity and celibacy. Church leaders have turned a blind eye to massive sexual improprieties of church priests, mostly homosexual, by saying they were faithful to their vow of celibacy—that is, they did not get married—while allowing them to do whatever they wanted (even have sexual orgies) as active homosexual partners within church rectories and other facilities. It has been a scandalous dodge. Father Haley and others tried to blow the whistle.

This was a soap-operatic story of immense proportions. Living through it was almost enough to wring all the faith out of me regarding the institutional church.

In the Protestant Episcopal Church, Bishop John Shelby Spong of Newark, New Jersey, and others in the church hierarchy have pushed a gay agenda in the church. Spong wrote a book suggesting Saint Paul was a self-hating homosexual. The Catholic Church has been ripped apart over the same issue.

At first, the story was fairly straightforward. Father Haley had caught his parish priest having sex with a married woman parishioner in the rectory in the dead of night and told the bishop, who asked Haley to provide him "concrete evidence."

Off the church computer system, Haley provided Bishop Paul S. Loverde of the Arlington Diocese in Virginia more than 300 steamy love e-mails exchanged by Father James Verrecchia and parish wife Nancy Lambert. He also provided Loverde with a stash of homosexual pornography stored by Verrecchia.

But then Loverde ignored the evidence and instead transferred Haley to another church, Saint Lawrence in Fairfax County, Virginia.

There, Father Haley found that the parish priest, Father William J. Erbacher, had stolen hundreds of thousands of dollars in church collections and, at night, in the rectory, satisfied himself with an adult toy while looking at porn pictures of aroused young boys in magazines that had been mailed to him at the church rectory.

Again, after Bishop Loverde requested concrete photographic and documentary evidence of Father Erbacher's misbehavior, Father Haley was transferred to Saint Mary's Catholic Church in Fredericksburg, Virginia, where he found that parish priest Daniel Hamilton liked homoerotic pornography featuring woman tied up in leather straps.

When Father Haley gave Bishop Loverde that evidence, the bishop told him to clear out of the church rectory in Fredericksburg within three hours, put Haley under a "penal precept of silence" under Catholic Church canon law, and stripped him of his priestly faculties. An endless saga of retaliation has continued ever since.

Father Haley's problems escalated suddenly in 2002 with a deposition he was subpoenaed to give in a civil trial, over Bishop Loverde's objections, brought against the Arlington Diocese by parishioner James Lambert of All Saints Catholic Church in Manassas, Virginia, husband of Nancy, who was made pregnant by Father Verrecchia.

Bishop Loverde tried to stop Haley's 233-page deposition and then to have it sealed, but Arlington Circuit Presiding Judge Joanne F. Alper, herself a Catholic, ruled against the bishop's lawyers each time. An orthodox lay Catholic group in Illinois, Roman Catholic Faithful, posted Haley's deposition on its Web site for all to see.

The deposition told of Father Verrecchia's sexual affair with Nancy Lambert and destruction of her marriage in excruciating detail and of the bishop's failure to investigate before Verrecchia left the church as Nancy divorced her husband and took their minor children to Atlanta, where Verrecchia joined the Episcopal Church.

The deposition also told how Father Erbacher had embezzled

more than $320,000 in cash from church collection plates and how a rectory maid had complained to Father Haley that she did not like to clean the father's room because he had lots of pornography and an adult toy in his closet, with Vaseline stains on the sides of the box.

Additionally, after the maid led Haley to Erbacher's closet, the priest also found personal bank deposit documents proving years of embezzlement by the priest, which Haley provided to Bishop Loverde. Haley also found a home video Erbacher had shot in Rome during a visit with the diocese chancellor, Father William Rippey, Father William Saunders, and other priests.

The Erbacher video showed the priests chuckling and dancing together in their vestments as two dogs copulated in the courtyard of St. Peter's in the Basilica in Rome. And much of the video focused on anatomy of church statues, especially Michelangelo's famous statue of David in Florence.

My editors at The Washington Times encouraged and supported my coverage of the Haley story until Bishop Loverde weighed in against me with Editor Wesley Pruden in December 2002.

Managing Editor Fran Coombs called me into his office to inform me that Bishop Loverde had accused me of being unprofessional and not objective because I had asked him to justify homosexual pornography found by Father Haley in rectory rooms of the three parish priests.

In e-mails with Linda Shovlain, then communications director for the Arlington Diocese, we had gone back and forth about the Haley case, and we were discussing Judge Alper's reason for unsealing the 233-page deposition that Haley had given over the Diocese's objections in the Lambert-Verrecchia case.

In one e-mail, I ask Linda: "Isn't it possible that Judge Alper saw through all the legal maneuvering and saw cover-up written all over the diocese's position? Otherwise, how does one rationalize her unsealing the Haley deposition?"

In a prior e-mail, Linda had described the pornography found in the priests' rooms in vanilla terms as "adult pornography" and "heterosexual pornography."

In my response e-mail, I called her description "pure spin":

Just the bishop's (or whoever wrote the response) unwilling-ness to call homosexual pornography "homosexual." Your response called it "adult" in the case of Father Erbacher and "heterosexual" in the case of Father Hamilton. Have you looked at that filth that is in the binder Father Haley gave Bishop Loverde? I have.

Hey, the Erbacher porn of mostly naked males was ques-tionably adult—none of the boys I saw were even shaving yet! And it was certainly homosexual. So why not call it what it is? And Father Hamilton's demeaning stuff with women in bondage, sex torture, sadomasochism! That's "heterosexual?" Give me a break! It's perverted, deviant, sick, demeaning to women. How dare anyone demean wholesome, wonderful, God-created heterosexuality by calling Hamilton's stuff by that name? Why not call it what it is?

Managing Editor Fran Coombs angrily denounced me in his office, screaming that my e-mail was "unprofessional" and would hear no argument to the contrary. "You're off the story," he shouted.

He was particularly concerned about my having challenged Bishop Loverde on the basis of our shared Christian beliefs.

In the e-mail Bishop Loverde had called to complain about, I say to Linda Shovlain: "I'm a Christian, and I have a right to filter this kind of pornography by my values and label it, appropriately, as a news reporter so I'm being accurate, fair, balanced, tasteful. But to call this Erbacher stuff 'adult' and to call Hamilton's 'heterosexual' is not truthful, accurate, fair, balanced. It's a whitewash to make it seem acceptable, if one thinks pornography of any kind is accept-able. So what was the bishop trying to accomplish? He saw what he was given by Father Haley. If those words were his, was he trying to be artful or deceitful by using these words in his responses? You look at the stuff for yourself, Linda, and make your own judgment."

Coombs stood at his desk screaming and shaking his finger at me: "You should never have said in an e-mail that you're a Christian or that being a Christian has anything to do with your reporting. That's a paper trail. That was totally unprofessional."

Well, I disagreed.

I argued to no avail that my faith is important to me and not something I leave at home when I go to work. My faith informs my journalism, bolsters my duty to report fully, fairly and truthfully, as God's tablets carried by Moses commanded, "Thou shalt not bear false witness."

I told Fran I wanted a paper trail in my series of e-mails with the Catholic bishop's press secretary, and what was wrong in saying to a Catholic bishop—shepherd of his Catholic flock—as a reporter, one Christian to another, that I wanted him to justify protecting homosexual priests with pornography or who had committed adultery? What was wrong in my asking him to justify stripping the priestly faculties of a decent orthodox whistle-blower priest and putting him under an order of silence?

Faithful Christian believers, regardless of denomination, understand the importance of living their faith and representing it to others in the way they conduct themselves at work as well as at home with family and friends.

I was, frankly, shocked and dismayed when my editor told me it was improper to tell a story subject, let alone a Catholic bishop, that I am Christian and ask him a question "as one Christian to another."

Brian DeBose, an African-American reporter, was assigned by National Editor Kenneth Hanner, tightly controlled by Fran Coombs, to particular stories affecting blacks because they wanted a black reporter covering those issues. So DeBose, to his chagrin, became the "black story" reporter under Wes Pruden and Fran Coombs. That was okay under their management.

We had openly gay reporters—Kevin Chafee and Richard Slusser—assigned to cover TV, movie, entertainment and travel beats who were allowed to tell news subjects they were gay if that helped their coverage and stories. That was okay.

We had great political reporters—Ralph Hallow and Don Lambro—who openly shared with news subjects their own conservative ideological beliefs and preferences as part of their reporting relationship, because that helped the newspaper's coverage. Don Lambro even had an opinion column all the years he was a political news reporter. That was okay.

Yet I was told I could not tell a Catholic bishop in trying to hold his feet to the fire that I was a Christian reporter and coming at the story from that perspective, as I asked him for facts regarding his sending Father Haley to purgatory while defending the likes of Fathers Verrecchia, Erbacher and Hamilton.

It was a very off scenario that challenged the very core of my beliefs as a reporter.

This was a defining moment for me as I realized anew the power of secular humanist dominance and intolerance—even within my own newspaper workplace—and how far we had come in this country away from the original commitment of our founding fathers to reporting freedom and the primacy of our Judaic-Christian heritage.

Paul Kengor, political science professor who heads Grove City College's Center for Vision and Values, reminded me that John Jay, author of the Federalist Papers and first U.S. Supreme Court chief justice, wrote to Jedidiah Morse on February 28, 1797: "Providence has given to our people the choice of their rulers. And it is the duty as well as the privilege and interest of a Christian nation to select and prefer Christians for their rulers." Jay also wrote to his wife, Sally, on April 20, 1794, "God's will be done; to him I resign—in him I confide."

John Marshall, who succeeded Jay as chief justice, wrote to Jasper Adams in May 1833, the 32nd of his 34 years on the high court: "The American population is entirely Christian, and with us Christianity and Religion are identified. It would be strange indeed, if with such a people, our institutions did not presuppose Christianity and did not often refer to it and exhibit relations with it."

I found a kindred spirit in John McCandlish Phillips, brilliant reporter for the New York Times for many years, who was an unashamed Christian in the newsroom and who kept a Bible on his desk and said he openly prayed to God to guide and help him as he reported stories over the years. I did too.

Phillips was on the front page of the New York Times for many years with riveting human interest stories. He told graduating students at a World Journalism Institute dinner in August 2001: "I prayed silently on the way to nearly all assignments. Asking the Lord to help me, to guide me, to get me below the surface, to give me all the content I needed for a first rate report."

Phillips admitted he was in over his head most of the time, as I certainly was, but God helped him through it all. And me. "Faith is a voluntary act of trust in God," Phillips said in his talk. So true.

Phillips said in a talk to World Journalism Institute students: "When you are handed something that really is beyond you, but that you have to take on, and you feel about an inch tall under a cold stone mountain that defies you, you can shrivel up inside and cringe, you can yield to panic, or you can reject either state of feeling, and just lift it to the Lord silently and tell him you voluntarily trust Him to get you through it in good shape."

Arthur Gelb, managing editor of the New York Times, and Abe Rosenthal, executive editor, certainly appreciated McCandlish Phillips' strong, outspoken Christian commitment—relishing it as a productive aspect of his journalism, not something to be diminished or tarnished with cynical secular dismissal.

They write that

> Phillips is something quite rare in newspapering, an entirely and deeply religious man, an evangelical, fundamentalist Christian, "born again" in the revelation of Jesus Christ. He keeps a Bible on his desk and turns to it from time to time during the day. Outside the Times, people sometimes ask whether his deeply religious bent does not "interfere" with his reporting—meaning, of course, whether being religious makes him distort stories in some ways or makes him incapable of handling certain assignments.
>
> The only answer to that is the editors of the paper, including the nonbelievers among them, have seen no evidence that the reading of the bible or even preaching from it, is any particular handicap to a reporter.

Gelb and Rosenthal conclude, "There are editors, indeed, who believe that if having a Bible on the desk has been of any help to Phillips, the Times might be well advised to form a Gideon Society of its own for the benefit of other reporters."

When Fran Coombs' temper was up and he was wielding his authority, he was a most impatient and angry person. The order had come down from Wes Pruden that I was "off the Catholic story," and a close aide to Pruden told me that he had been called by Cardinal Theodore McCarrick of the Washington Archdiocese about my coverage of the Haley-Loverde situation.

Pruden and McCarrick had become close. So I was off the story. And the lengthy special series on the Catholic scandal, which I had worked on for over three months with the help of Assistant Managing Editor Ken McIntyre, was spiked on orders from Pruden.

The pulling of this story occurred in the midst of the huge

Catholic Church pedophilia scandal that erupted in Louisiana in 1985 when Father Gilbert Gauthe pleaded guilty to 11 counts of molesting boys and took off like a rocket in 1992 when Father James Porter of Fall River, Massachusetts, was convicted on 41 counts of sexually molesting altar boys in five states in the 1960s and 1970s.

The scandal spread from Massachusetts to priest abuse of teenagers in Texas, Florida, Oregon, California, Arizona and other states.

As the story unfolded, it became apparent that it was not just a pedophilia problem—priests molesting prepubescent boys—but rather a problem of homosexual priests generally: "chicken hawks" going after sexually mature teenage males and having relations with fellow homosexual priests and seminarians within the walls of Catholic religious institutions everywhere.

The gay priests and bishops even had Internet chat rooms—one called St. Sebastian's Angels—where they publicly flirted with each other, from as far away as South Africa, and said crude things about sexual practices.

Former seminary director Donald Cozzens, author of "The Changing Face of the Priesthood," and A.W. Richard Sipe, psychotherapist and former Benedictine monk who wrote "Sex, Priests, and Power: Anatomy of a Crisis," said upward of two-thirds of Catholic priests are homosexual. Sipe blamed the problem on the church's requirement for priests to be sexually celibate and unmarried, which he said was unnatural.

My dispute with Washington Times editors over use of e-mail as a reporting tool to get information and comments from priests and bishops was never satisfactorily resolved.

For a reporter, documentation is lifeblood, so e-mail has become an essential tool, now more important than the telephone. News sources, even important government officials, respond to e-mail more promptly than they return telephone calls, and whatever they write or send in the e-mail is written documentation for a story—pure gold for a reporter.

But for the newspaper, a corporate news organization, e-mail also is seen by editors as a potential liability because a news source under the gun from an investigative reporter can use any e-mail selectively in a complaint or possible lawsuit, depending on how a message or series of messages is worded.

In more than two decades at The Times, covering many tough investigative stories, I was sued for libel at least three times. We were threatened with lawsuits many other times, but no one ever laid a glove on me because the documentation was always there. The first defense against any libel lawsuit is the truth, and I meticulously backed up my stories with notes of my reporting, documents and tape recordings. The paper's excellent lawyers, Allen Farber and Jay Barker, and I had a lot of time together.

However, legal cases cost a company a lot of money to defend. So with the advent of e-mail, the needs and interests of reporters and corporate management parted and became more adverse. It was something Times management needed to resolve.

Fran's position was that "common sense" told reporters what to put in written e-mails. Unlike the telephone or personal conversations, where reporters and newsmakers were totally frank and sometimes cursed each other, that wasn't appropriate in e-mails because it left a paper trail. I couldn't say to a Catholic bishop, to press a point and elicit a response regarding pornography in priests' rooms, how do you justify this, as one Christian to another?

The story became even more bizarre after I left the Times and started writing this book. Father Haley had been in purgatory for three years; his canonical trial overseen by Bishop Thomas G. Doran of Rockford, Illinois, had dragged on endlessly. Bishop Loverde had tried to drag up an old case against Haley before he came to Arlington in March 1999 involving a lady who came on to Father Haley romantically. When that didn't work, Loverde accused Haley of going to the media and causing scandal for the church, which wasn't true. Haley was not responsible for release of his deposition in the

Lambert case. That was done by Lambert's attorney and Stephen Brady of Roman Catholic Faithful.

In the meantime, Loverde protected the priests who stole money from the church and had pornography stashes at church expense as well as the chancery officials who protected these perverts with church collars.

I was writing freelance for Insight magazine online, a publication resurrected by The Washington Times Corp., and offered them a piece about Cardinal Theodore Edgar McCarrick sleeping with seminarians at a beach cottage in Sea Girt, New Jersey.

McCarrick is a close friend of Bishop Loverde and Washington Times Editor Wesley Pruden.

Insight's editor, Jeffrey Kuhner, was nervous about the piece because Robert Ciolek, a Mount St. Mary's seminarian and best friend of Father Haley's seduced by McCarrick in 1985 had left the priesthood and become a lawyer.

Cioleck called Kuhner and threatened litigation if his name was used in the story. But when Kuhner talked to Ciolek on the phone, Ciolek admitted the accuracy of the report that McCarrick had seduced him into bed, and said he'd confirm it on the record if Insight promised not to reveal his name.

He was a successful attorney working for a big pharmaceutical company in Manhattan, married with three children.

However, Fran Coombs was upset with Insight's online success and, according to Kuhner, was "on a jihad" internally against the magazine.

Pruden had sent out a memo prohibiting Washington Times reporters from writing for any other publication without permission from their desk editor on a case-by-case basis, because some Times reporters were writing some of Insight's best stories on the side. The McCarrick story was an additional complication that Kuhner said apologetically he did not want to tackle.

But the facts were clear: McCarrick, as bishop of Metuchen and

Newark, N.J., dioceses from 1981 to 2000, kept a beach house at Sea Girt, N.J., where he took young seminarians studying for the priesthood for weekend sleepover soirées. Participants and priests told this reporter that McCarrick had years of bedtime enjoyment with young men and promoted many to high offices in the church.

The story was partially broken in December 2005 on an Internet Web site by Matthew C. Abbott, reporter for Catholic World News and the Wanderer, who quoted Father Haley's revelations that Cardinal McCarrick had seduced his best friend at Mount Saint Mary's, Emmitsburg, Md., in summer 1985. The posting gave the seminarian—Rob Ciolek—a pseudonym, but Haley had revealed the man's name to me.

Haley said Ciolek was exceptionally handsome and that McCarrick pursued him insistently. He told me McCarrick lured his friend to the Sea Girt beach cottage alone and took him to bed. The seminarian did not complain to church officials about McCarrick's advances and the two became close friends.

Haley and Ciolek were ordained as priests in May 1987. But within several years, Haley said Ciolek got a divorced Catholic school teacher pregnant and obtained McCarrick's help to abandon his priest's vows.

He married the pregnant woman in a Protestant ceremony after McCarrick had traveled to Rome to convince Pope John Paul II to sign an order absolving Ciolek of his lifetime priestly vow of celibacy, Haley said. "It was highly unusual; the pope was reluctant to do it, but McCarrick made a special effort" for the friend, Haley recounted.

With McCarrick's assistance, the ex-priest graduated from Seton Hall University School of Law in 1996, was a senior environmental official in New Jersey, and practiced environmental law for a prominent national law firm in the Garden State before joining the pharmaceutical company in Manhattan.

Haley said Ciolek "consented to sleeping in the same bed with the archbishop but said, 'nothing occurred.' He never listened, however, to my argument that very much had actually occurred by his easy compliance, by his lack of shock, and by his later refusal to report the incident. To whom [would he report]? Who would believe him? McCarrick, on the other hand, had almost all the information he needed about [him]."

Subsequently, Ciolek, as a seminarian, was "the recipient of almost weekly handwritten letters sent to him by McCarrick, many of them speaking of the bishop's delight in one day raising young seminarian [name deleted] to the heights of splendor as a bishop himself," Haley writes.

"I always thought the letters were amazing, since I had never even met my bishop in the whole four years of my seminary studies, let alone was I being encouraged with intimate letters to Episcopal splendor. I always wondered how our bishops are selected so quickly in their young days as priests

Father Carlos Miguel Viego of Irvington, N.Y., confirmed McCarrick's habit of luring young male seminarians to bed with him at the beach cottage. Viego said he was chosen by McCarrick as a bedmate in the summer of 1988. "My reaction was, do what the boss says," the father told me. He said he regretted his acquiescence. "It is an abuse of authority. He abuses his power in order to fit into the moral atmosphere. That's perverse and unacceptable," Viego said. "Do I think McCarrick is a homosexual? No. But he has made it appear he is a homosexual."

Viego said he was "not good at reading things. I was part of a choice group of seminarians, always invited [to McCarrick's cottage]; it was a privilege to go. That's where the coercion came in. It's just a strange position to put a seminarian in. I thought priests believed in holiness. It never appeared to me that priests would live unholy lives. When I came down the next morning, [the other seminarians] were all looking at me. They were wondering, what happened, what were you thinking when you went up to sleep with McCarrick?"

Haley said McCarrick's beach house slumber parties came to the attention of Archbishop Agostino Cacciavillan—the Vatican's diplomatic papal nuncio in Washington in the late 1990s—who saw a growing potential scandal and directed the cardinal to sell the cottage.

Susan Gibbs, McCarrick's spokeswoman for the Catholic Archdiocese of Washington before he retired in 2006, refused comment.

CHAPTER SEVENTEEN

FEMINIST PARTY AT
U.N. CHINA PARLEY

Men weren't really the enemy—they were fellow victims suf-
fering from an outmoded masculine mystique that made
them feel unnecessarily inadequate when there were no
bears to kill.

—Betty Friedan, author of "The Feminine Mystique"

O NE OF MY STRONGEST MEMORIES during two decades at The
Washington Times is the day in September 1995 when I arrived in
Beijing, China, after 30 hours of air travel, on assignment to cover
the United Nations Fourth World Conference on Women—and
found myself homeless.

Josette Shiner, then assistant managing editor, met me and columnist Suzanne Fields at the Beijing airport—after we both cleared
through customs—and explained our predicament.

Josette often traveled to countries throughout Asia and had independently booked our reservations at the huge downtown China
World Hotel, owned by the prominent Shangri-La chain. But at
the last minute, as we were on our way to China, First Lady Hillary
Clinton decided to go as head of the U.S. delegation.

As I left the United States, Secretary of State Madeleine Albright
and Geraldine Ferraro were designated as co-chairs of the U.S.

delegation. But Mrs. Clinton's last-minute decision to go and bring an entourage of about 200 government and interest-group people with her changed everything while I was in the air between Washington and Beijing.

After I arrived, Josette explained that Chinese government officials had gone to the China World Hotel to find the 200 rooms needed for Mrs. Clinton's entourage. They had checked registrations and ordered all media kicked out—us, ABC, CBS, NBC, Associated Press, United Press International, Reuters, and enough others to make room for Mrs. Clinton's planeload of people.

So we were homeless when Suzanne Fields and I arrived and scrambling with Josette, our editor, to find a place to stay.

Because of Josette's good relations with the China World management, they were most helpful and told us they had another hotel on the west side of Beijing near the zoo.

We had to go to the U.N. check-in center to organize the new accommodations. The Chinese agent at the desk said we could not stay at the Shangri-La Hotel because the government had reserved it only for TV people.

I promptly said, pointing at Josette, "She's TV." Josette stared at me with a puzzled look. I repeated, "She's TV. She's a weekly regular on 'Capital Gang' on television in America."

The Chinese guy responded, "Oh, you TV," and rushed off to see if we could be booked into the Shangri-La. Within ten minutes, he came back and said we would be booked into the hotel.

The China World's manager provided us a car and driver to take the three of us and our luggage across Beijing on three-lane, almost vacant super-highways to the other hotel, which was a breathtaking view of the city more than a decade ago.

The next morning, as I came out of my room at the same time as a lady across the hall, I looked at her as I followed her to the elevator, and it was feminist leader Betty Friedan, an icon of the American left-oriented women's movement.

We became quick friends as we waited for the elevator to arrive on the fifth floor to take us to the lobby and a waiting bus for us to go to the nongovernment organizations meetings at a village 40 miles outside Beijing.

Friedan confided that she was being hosed down by former Congresswoman Bella Abzug of New York, Gloria Steinem, and other feminist leaders who wanted to continue the political sex wars against men.

Oh boy, here I was in China and had a huge story in the making. The wars of the women. I'd get in trouble if I described it as shock jock radio host Don Imus would have. On our first 45-minute bus ride to a week-long meeting of nongovernment women's organizations before the formal U.N. conference, Friedan told me she had teamed up with Maureen Reagan, President Reagan's daughter, to advocate "communitarian feminism" as an alternative to the hate-men agenda of Abzug, supported by President Clinton's Undersecretary of State Timothy Wirth. She also told me that the two opposing camps would lock horns with pro-women's rights men to push for more sensible policies.

This turned out to be a great story. Both Betty Friedan and Maureen Reagan held alternative seminars at the China conference and gave me exclusive interviews for The Washington Times as the U.N. conference unfolded.

The feminist forces demanded United Nations guarantees of employment quotas for women and "reproductive rights," meaning permissive safe-sex education for kids going down to elementary school, abortion-on-demand, and government assurances of homosexual rights in every country.

An alliance forged by the Vatican, Muslim countries in the U.N., and Christian groups in Europe and the United States—fundamentalist Baptists, nondenominational Christians, Mormons, conservative Anglicans, Methodists, and Presbyterians stopped the feminist agenda at this conference and another United Nations Children's Summit some years later.

The China experience introduced me frontally to the global culture war, as I saw lesbian women at the U.N. conference rally one Sunday morning in the Australian tent to invade nongovernment organization exhibits of women from Muslim countries—Afghanistan, Iraq, Iran, Saudi Arabia.

I went over to the lesbian tent and talked to leaders from many countries. They expressed outrage that so many Arab women wore scarves and garments to hide their faces, saying this was all a product of male suppression. They disparaged the religious beliefs of the Muslim women and said they were enemies of women's rights.

I asked Betty Friedan, who was Jewish, about this. "These radical lesbians are intolerant," she told me. "All they want is to force their views onto everyone.

"They're not for women's rights. They're only for their own secular rights, as they see them. They are intolerant of Muslim women and Christian women who live according to their religious and family traditions. We need to move toward a more tolerant communitarian vision."

The lesbians from all countries who gathered in the Australian tent in the center of Huarou one Sunday, the Chinese village where the week-long NGO meetings took place, proved Betty Friedan's point.

As church services of all faiths were taking place throughout the village, the lesbians ran as an army into exhibits of women from Muslim countries (Iran, Iraq, Saudi Arabia, and others), ripped off the veils of Muslim women, squirted red blood-type juice on them, and tore down their exhibits in a Ride of the Valkyries rage.

I was at a tent attending an Anglican church service with U.S. Rep. Christopher H. Smith of New Jersey (a leading Republican human rights advocate), Diane Knippers (leader of the Institute for Religion and Democracy), Mariam Bell, and others when the rampage began.

We watched in horror at this intolerant hate crime. U.N. officials did nothing to stop the attack or afterward to provide justice to the women who suffered from the lesbian assault. Congressman Smith and others joined in solidarity with the attacked Muslim women.

I wrote that story and The Times put it on the front page. The experience made an indelible impression on me, particularly as we have since seen so many scenes of intolerance and unnecessary violence against innocents by Muslim, Christian, and secular extremists, particularly since 9/11 and America's declared war against terror.

The backdrop for this story occurred a year before. Fran Coombs, my national editor, called me into his office and said he was unhappy with the foreign desk's coverage of the United Nations by our correspondent in New York, Betsy Pisik, saying the coverage was too lapdog, pro-U.N. He said he wanted me to cover the U.N. story aggressively from the national desk as a domestic political story.

Coombs instructed me to call congressional sources and people who had oversight of U.S. spending for U.N. programs—particularly critics such as U.S. Senator Jesse Helms of North Carolina, chairman of the Senate Foreign Relations Committee, and Congressman Christopher Smith of New Jersey, the House GOP's leading champion on global human rights matters.

So I began working on a series of stories after interviewing congressional people who were questioning our monetary outlay to the United Nations, heard loads of horror stories about monetary waste and corruption, and then the paper sent me to New York to see things for myself and start writing stories.

At first, Betsy Pisik was not pleased but was very cooperative nonetheless in introducing me to Secretary General Kofi Annan's American press spokesman, Frederic Eckhard, and his staff.

At the United States Mission to the United Nations, across the street from the tall U.N. secretariat building in East Manhattan— then headed by President Clinton's Ambassador Bill Richardson—I got the cold shoulder.

But Linda Shenwick, a budget officer and whistle-blower within the U.S. Mission from Madeleine Albright days, helped and led me by the hand in understanding the bureaucratic quagmire of the United Nations.

Shenwick gave me a roadmap of how the United Nations works in both the General Assembly and Security Council. She also told me where the translation operation was located and how to forge a bond with friendly translators at all the U.N. committee meetings.

Shenwick also told me how the Russians had control of the U.N. library operations and the United Nation's budget committee was run by a Tanzanian national who had been in New York for decades at a six-figure, tax-exempt salary and lived on New York's Long Island in luxury with his common-law wife.

The corruption was unbelievable when I started covering this story in 1995, and the United States was footing 30 percent of the costs—30 percent of the corruption upfront, plus everything New York State was kicking in to support this nest of thieves from countries throughout the world.

I used to roam the upper floors of the U.N. Secretariat building on New York's East side and find people playing chess and cards all hours of the day, drinking alcohol, sleeping on couches, and several times even caught people having sex. There are so many places in that skyscraper building where mischief was occurring, not to speak of the corruption involved with unreported scandals preceding the Iraq food-for-peace scandal.

Every time I entered the U.N. headquarters building, I was reminded of a right-wing bumper sticker when I was in college that said, "Get the U.S. out of the U.N. and get the U.N. out of the U.S."

The whole place was rife with waste and corruption. The diplomats there from all foreign countries, making tax-free, six-figure salaries and enjoying diplomatic status, knew they had it good. They had no plans to return to their home countries if they could avoid it. All their rhetoric about justice and world peace was a farce. Their goal was simply to line their own pockets.

Genocide in Bosnia and Darfur were just incidents they hoped people would never pin on them so long as they lived in New York luxury with huge, tax-exempt salaries, lucrative expense accounts, long lunch breaks, and diplomatic tags on their cars.

Father Frank Julian Gelli—an Anglican priest in England who befriended and advised Diana, Princess of Wales, after her separation from Prince Charles and until her tragic death in the August 31, 1997, car crash in Paris with Muslim fiancé Dodi Fayed—certainly shared my view that something was very wrong with the United Nations and expressed strong opinions to me and others about leftist, feminist intolerance against people of faith across the spectrum.

"I know many Muslims women, who are religious and wear the badges of their religion proudly. Let Muslim women decide what is right for them," Father Gelli told me in a personal communication long after I met him in New York about a decade ago at a U.N.-related conference hosted by United Families International. He writes a very erudite weekly commentary that he calls "Father Frank's Rants," which goes out to his own large e-mail list.

Father Gelli is a Church of England iconoclast with tremendous historical knowledge going back to Herodotus and the Greek-Persian wars 500 years before Christ. He is not opposed to theocratic regimes in Iran and elsewhere, opining that the Islamic Republic is principally an affront and provocation to Western secularism.

Gelli writes in one of his weekly rants: "A state run by clergy? Boy, you nuts? Never mind that Iran has a parliament and parties and elections. Religion, ecrasez l'infame! We can't tolerate a working religious polity in the brave new world of globalization. But why not? Isn't diversity a good thing? Haven't nations a natural right to self-determination? Why has the whole universe got to be fashioned after the capitalist-consumerist Western political model? So, is it Islam, in its Shia version, that the West longs to be at war with? It certainly looks that way."

Princess Diana's priest says: "Feminism, of course, is a ragbag.

Some views are acceptable, others absurd. In principle, militant feminists have no more right to speak out for women as a whole than the Communist Party had when it spoke for 'the workers.' Most workers wanted to have nothing to do with them. Communism was in fact their bitterest enemy, in practice."

When Barry Goldwater accepted the Republican presidential nomination in 1964, he uttered a memorable line, "Extremism in defense of liberty is no vice; moderation in pursuit of justice is no virtue."

The problem we see today, it seems to me as a reporter, is that the extremism around the world is not in defense of liberty. It is in defense of violence and terror to spread intolerance, suppression of people, and ultimately fear, defeat of democratic values, and totalitarianism.

CHAPTER EIGHTEEN

THE CULTURE WAR

Freedom is the recognition that no single person, no single authority or government has a monopoly on the truth, but that every individual life is infinitely precious, that every one of us put on this world has been put there for a reason and has something to offer.

—Ronald Reagan, speaking at
Moscow State University, May 1988

———————

THE BIG CULTURAL ISSUES OF OUR DAY—abortion, drug trafficking and abuse, the push for feminist and homosexual rights, global trafficking of humans as economic and sexual slaves, immigration—were always stories in the forefront as a national news reporter.

There wasn't a day I woke up and one of those issues wasn't grabbing our attention, a daily story that had to be covered.

My first libel lawsuit as a 28-year-old staff writer for The Arizona Republic in Phoenix came after an investigative editorial I wrote about an abortion mill in Los Angeles, the 22-bed Avalon Memorial Hospital, where hundreds of Arizona women went on weekends as outpatients to terminate their pregnancies before the Supreme Court's 1973 decision in Roe v. Wade forced all states to permit abortion.

Abortion was illegal in Arizona, and those promoting its legalization spoke of the dangers of "back-alley" abortions. Little did they know about the medical atrocities at this little hospital in Los Angeles, where more than 1,000 women a month went to get abortions, left bleeding and moaning on gurneys in the hospital hallways and later sent home—many with internal hemorrhaging and other medical complications their own local doctors had to take care of. Planned Parenthood and other referral agencies got kickbacks of $30 to $50 per patient for their referrals, so it was big business for them.

Doctor Carolyn Gerster, an internal medicine physician in Scottsdale, called me about the problem in the summer of 1972. Gerster was a co-founder with Doctor Jack Willke of the National Right to Life Committee.

My editor at The Arizona Republic, Edwin McDowell, told me to get in my Volkswagen bug and drive out to L.A. to take a look. It was about a nine-hour drive.

I walked around Avalon Hospital on Saturday and Sunday as Doctor Edward Allred, chief abortionist, and other doctors and nurses performed hundreds of outpatient abortions. I took a lot of notes and pictures, then drove back to Phoenix.

I wrote the most devastating Sunday lead editorial I could write. McDowell liked it but toned it down a little.

The editorial, "Out-of-state abortions," was published as the paper's lead editorial on August 6, 1972. It concludes, "If Arizona agencies have directly or indirectly referred women to Avalon and other hospitals guilty of overcrowding and unsanitary conditions, they are guilty of the worst form of negligence."

The editorial called on the state to investigate "the true relationship between these local agencies and doctors involved in the mercenary out-of-state abortion business."

Doctor Allred and Avalon sued The Republic and me personally for defamation and sought a lot of money. But the paper had superb attorneys, and Doctor Allred dropped the suit after just a few depositions where we laid out our evidence. We had them dead to rights in our call for action to protect women caught up in the mercenary abortion mill enterprise that he was running.

There was a feminist writer at the Republic in those days, April Daien, who was after me and invited me to a party where I met her visiting Japanese roommate from when they attended Hollins College together in Roanoke, Virginia, Noriko Wakabayashi.

Noriko was visiting April and got pregnant by one of April's male friends. Noriko loved the guy and didn't want to succumb to their pressure to get an abortion. She called me, because I had spoken out against abortion at a party in defense of the editorial I had written.

Noriko and I had lunch. She told me the situation and said she didn't want to have an abortion. I told her I would call Doctor Carolyn Gerster so she could get a medical exam to make sure she was pregnant, and she could go from there.

Doctor Gerster agreed. This was in the fall of 1972. I drove Noriko to Scottsdale for the exam, which confirmed she was pregnant. Doctor Gerster told Noriko she would continue to give her free prenatal care throughout her pregnancy (if she wanted), deliver the baby, and if Noriko could not keep the baby would help her find a family for adoption.

Noriko wanted this, but her father, a top executive with Nissan Motors in Tokyo, ultimately forced her to go back to Japan, where he made her have an abortion. Some years later in Japan, after time in a mental hospital, Noriko took her own life.

This experience had a tremendous impact on me and opened my eyes about many issues involving male-female relationships, pregnancy, and those who are for and against the biblical injunctions regarding the sanctity of all human life—from conception to old age—whether handicapped or not.

The abortion issue dogged me again more than a decade later.

My second libel lawsuit came at The Washington Times after I broke a series of stories during the Reagan administration about the U.S. Peace Corps under Director Loret Miller Ruppe, who was sending single American women volunteers who were promiscuous and got pregnant in Africa and elsewhere, for taxpayer-funded abortions at a military hospital in Frankfurt, Germany.

Ronald Reagan read our front-page story and, I was told, angrily hit the Oval Office ceiling and personally demanded that the taxpayer-funded abortion operation be closed down.

I afterward rode the Peace Corps scandal in Africa and was tipped off by Scot Faulkner, a newly-appointed Peace Corps country director in Malawi, that the son of his predecessor, Anna Marie Hayes, had a cocaine, drug-running operation going with the Peace Corps deputy country director, Charles Blake, and Malawi nationals.

Ruppe shipped Anna Marie Hayes to Botswana as Peace Corps country director to get her out of the way. She was a former Michigan school teacher and close personal friend of Loret Ruppe, who had run George H.W. Bush's successful presidential primary campaign against Ronald Reagan in Michigan and owed her appointment as Peace Corps head to Vice President Bush.

I exposed the Malawi drug-running operation in a series of stories, based on Scot Faulkner's information.

To box in Loret Ruppe, who did not want to get rid of her political hack, his son, and dirty deputy country director, Faulkner cleverly got together with Reagan's ambassador to Malawi, Weston Adams, and documented all of his evidence about the drug operation in a confidential cable that Adams sent to the State Department. Adams, Faulkner, and Deputy Peace Corps Director Edward Curran then made sure that the cables were leaked to me.

I picked them up from Curran's secretary, Connie Boggs, at a Friendly's restaurant in Oakton, Virginia, where we often met surreptitiously mid-evening so I could pick up internal Peace Corps documents that Curran regularly leaked to me.

I even had Loret Ruppe's detailed travel schedule and met her one evening at Dulles International Airport to question her about some controversial appointments as she returned alone from a trip somewhere.

She had obviously enjoyed a few drinks on the plane, as I was advised she would, and she was surprised to see me there to greet her off the airport shuttle before she collected her baggage.

At the baggage carousel, I questioned her from documents I had for the story I was pursuing. Suddenly, she lunged at me and tried to grab my file. "Let me see those documents," she yelled.

I jumped away and others waiting for their luggage looked in surprise. "This is Loret Ruppe, director of the Peace Corps," I said to the waiting travelers. Ruppe backed off promptly as passengers gazed and, for obvious reasons, answered none of my questions.

She just knew I was on the job. Journalism is war. Sometimes this is all you want an important government official, a news target, to know (even if you cannot get answers to legitimate questions)— that as a reporter you are on the job, that they cannot avoid you, and that they have a responsibility 24/7 to be accountable, as they are working on the public dime.

The day after our Dulles encounter, I was told that Ruppe went on a rampage, yelled and screamed all over her office about my knowing her arrival details, and instructed her staff to keep her schedule secret, even from Curran (her deputy Peace Corps director) and other officials of the agency. Her outburst just bolstered good public servants within the agency and doubled my sources overnight.

Charles Blake, the assistant Peace Corps country director in Malawi involved in a drug scam there, ultimately sued The Washington Times and me—and the Peace Corps, strangely enough—for defamation when I broke that story. So we were oddly co-defendants.

The Peace Corps, in legal maneuvers, moved to obtain my vital source documents and tape-recorded interviews. Allan Farber and Jay Barker, The Times' longtime attorneys, said we had to turn over my reporter's notes and tapes to the Peace Corps lawyers.

Those notes and tapes inadvertently burned Scot Faulkner and deputy Peace Corps Director Curran as my heroic whistle-blower sources. It was an unfortunate price in the ongoing journalistic wars. But Blake withdrew the lawsuit after several dozen depositions.

The ultimate defense in any claimed defamation or slander lawsuit is the truth, and we had our published stories fully validated in all respects with government documents, tape-recorded interviews, and my reporter's voluminous notes.

In another series of stories, there was no chance that Kevin Jennings of the Gay Lesbian Straight Educators Network was going to sue; although, he blustered about stories I wrote about his relationships with male students who he encouraged to be gay when he was a private school teacher in Massachusetts.

One of Jennings' students, Brewster, was a 15-year-old sophomore at Concord Academy in 1987, a private boarding school in Concord, Mass. Jennings writes in his book, "One Teacher in Ten" (a reference to biology researcher Alfred C. Kinsey's disputed conclusion that one-tenth of our population is homosexual), that Brewster was using "substance" and having a homosexual relationship with "an older man" in Boston whom the student met in a bus station restroom.

What in this scenario is right? Jennings told Brewster's story and gave public speeches that he knew the kid was using substance and in a sexual relationship with "an older man," which he encouraged.

Hello? Why weren't the school's administrators and the student's parents told? What was going on here?

Jennings was fired from a prior teaching job at historic Moses Brown School in Provincetown, Rhode Island, because he openly told faculty and students that he was homosexual.

During his first year at Concord Academy in 1987, Jennings writes that teenage Brewster came to him about the encounter with the older man in a Boston bus station restroom and his travels against school rules to and from the state capital for their ensuing homosexual relationship.

Neither Jennings nor school officials told Brewster's parents or state child protection authorities about the boy's problems and delinquency.

When conservative members of the 2.4-million-member National Education Association school union complained about Jennings' ethical failure in violation of state law, as the union bestowed upon him their annual human rights award in 2004, I covered the story alone among the national media. This story was ignored by all other news organizations as it unfolded.

Brewster was a charming but troubled kid. His grades did not match up with his potential, his attendance could be irregular, and he often seemed a little out of it. He was clearly using some substance regularly, and was not very happy with himself. Jennings states in his book that he did not know what was wrong with Brewster at first but found out and gave him sympathetic support.

Jennings says he went to the Concord Academy headmaster to talk about his own homosexual lover and students' questions about his ring. "Tell them it's a gift from someone you love," the headmaster said.

Jennings told his students about his male partner. "They didn't seem to care much at all about my being gay," Jennings writes.

> Toward the end of my first year, during the spring of 1988, Brewster appeared in my office in the tow of one of my advisees, a wonderful young woman to whom I had been "out" for a long time [as an active homosexual]. "Brewster has something he needs to talk with you about," she intoned ominously. Brewster's eyes widened briefly, and then out spilled a story about his involvement with an older man he had met in Boston. I listened, sympathized, and offered advice. He left my office with a smile on his face that I would see every time I saw him on the campus for the next two years, until he graduated.

The story shocked me. I was a boarding school student in my youth. The rules prohibited us leaving the campus unsupervised. Yet here was a young teenage student, leaving his boarding school campus and traveling to Boston during the week for his relationship with the older man, coming back in wee hours of the morning, and missing classes.

Jennings not only knew about the situation but encouraged it in violation of Massachusetts state law that required school teachers to report their awareness of such situations threatening the well-being of minor children to school administrators for required reports about potential child abuse to state child protective agencies. Jennings did not do this and, thus, broke the law.

Jennings and GLSEN since 1990 have formed more than 2,500 Gay-Straight Alliances in public schools nationally with the aim of promoting acceptance of the homosexual lifestyle among school children, under the guise of anti-harassment and anti-bullying.

Jennings and GLSEN are relentless proponents of the notion that homosexuality is a genetic, inborn trait, which justifies their civil rights claims for homosexuals—another important legal device to promote the lifestyle. But important members of the American Psychological Association, Robert Spitzer of Columbia University and Warren Throckmorton of Grove City College, have successfully refuted these claims with scientific research.

In a speech Jennings made to a GLSEN conference in Iowa in 2000, where he promoted a gay rights agenda in the schools, Jennings talked about Brewster's situation at Concord Academy. He said he was in his first month on the job, and his advisee, Brewster "was missing a lot of classes. He was in the boarding school, so I said to his first-period teacher, 'Next time Brewster misses a class, I want you to tell me, and I will go find him.' So I went and found Brewster one morning when she had called, and he was asleep in his dorm room."

Jennings woke him up and asked Brewster why he was skipping class again. "Well, I'm tired," Brewster said. "I was out late last night." Jennings said he asked, "What were you doing out late on a school night?" Brewster responded, "Well. I was in Boston"—45 minutes away by train. "I met someone in the bus station bathroom, and I went home with him."

And in that speech to GLSEN activists, Jennings continued: "High school sophomore, 15 years old, that was the only way he knew how to meet gay people. I was a closeted gay teacher, 24 years old, didn't know what to say. Knew I should say something quickly, so I finally said my best friend had just died of AIDS the week before. I looked at Brewster and said, 'You know, I hope you knew to use a condom.' He said to me something I will never forget. He said, 'Why should I? My life isn't worth saving anyway.'"

The issue blew up at the National Education Association convention in Washington, D.C., in July 2004, when several conservative state NEA delegates with strong opinions against advocacy of the homosexual lifestyle in schools objected to Kevin Jennings getting a "human rights" award from the union at a black-tie dinner during the 2004 convention.

Diane Lenning of California, chairwoman of the NEA Republican Educators Caucus, led the charge along with Jeralee Smith, chair of the NEA's Ex-Gay Educators Caucus.

Lenning and Smith both wrote to NEA President Reg Weaver as individual delegates to complain about the award on grounds that Jennings knew as a teacher of possible sexual and emotional abuse of Brewster by an adult, homosexual male but did not report the situation to officials of Concord Academy, and to the state child protection agency in Massachusetts, as required by state law.

The proverbial stuff hit the fan when the letters from Lenning and Smith went to the NEA president, and I covered the story as it unfolded at the NEA's convention in Washington, D.C. in July 2004.

Led by the NEA's chief lobbyist, Randall Moody, who calls himself a Republican, NEA delegates Shawna Adam and Ron Ward from

California, joined by Sarah Simoneaux from Texas, recruited about 100 NEA delegates from the union's Democratic and gay-lesbian caucuses to pay $10 dues and flood the NEA Republican caucus at its annual business meeting, with the purpose of overwhelming the real Republican caucus members and changing the caucus bylaws to oust Lenning as chair and install Adam and other pro-Democratic and pro-gay officers on the caucus's executive committee. It was a raw power play to help the Democratic and homosexual agenda within the NEA union.

The coup against Lenning was also designed to help the John Kerry-John Edwards Democratic presidential ticket as it formed before the 2004 Democratic National Convention, because Lenning had organized Bush-Cheney placards and a pro-Bush show of force by Republican and conservative delegates during the NEA convention when Kerry and Edwards spoke to the 10,000 delegates after Kerry chose Edwards as his vice presidential running mate.

But coup leader Adam and her conspirators in the NEA hierarchy shut down the planned Republican show of support when television cameras splashed the Kerry-Edwards appearance by video at the NEA convention over national cable television. There were no Bush-Cheney posters, just a sea of 10,000 NEA delegates waving thousands of hurriedly produced Kerry-Edwards posters rushed over to the D.C. Convention Center by the Democratic National Committee.

The NEA hierarchy also moved quickly in Kevin Jennings behalf to flood the NEA convention delegates with 10,000 copies of a union-sponsored publication from many years earlier that opposed the notion of ex-gays and so-called "reparative therapy" to help people recover from same-sex attractions.

In an interview with NEA President Reg Weaver, I asked him why the union had gone to such lengths to resurrect 10,000 copies of this old publication and distribute it to NEA convention delegates, while blocking the NEA Ex-Gay Educators Caucus from distributing to delegates its own response to the pro-gay publication.

Weaver, a very fair man, told me he'd give me an answer the next day, and he did. He said he had ordered NEA officials to allow NEA delegates to distribute the ex-gay publication.

Delegates distributing the ex-gay piece stood at the top of escalators and in front on the convention doorways and handed out their publication. They were insulted by many delegates.

One member of the NEA's Gay Lesbian Bisexual Transgendered and Questioning Caucus yelled at Sissy Jochmann, chair of the NEA's Conservative Educators Caucus, "There's a special place in hell for people like you!" Others called them Nazis and other endearing terms. Tolerance and a commitment to diversity were not in abundance that day of the NEA's 2004 convention.

The controversy over pro-homosexual advocacy in the schools, led by Kevin Jennings' GLSEN group and others, has become a huge issue in many communities across the country.

The fight is pretty simple to explain: The gay lobby, led by Jennings and others, takes the position that homosexuality is an in-born genetic trait and that gays are wired as homosexuals at conception. With this argument, they claim a legal civil rights privilege for gays, just like blacks and other minorities—which has offended many blacks.

Many Christians, ex-gays, and members of the mental health profession—notably Warren Throckmorton of Grove City College, Robert Spitzer of Columbia University, and Dean Byrd of Brigham Young University—who have fought out this debate in their professional associations and done peer-reviewed published research say homosexuality is not genetic but rather a learned behavior and can be acquired or rejected by men and women at will.

This is very threatening to the gay lobby, because if this is true, sayonara to the gay lobby's civil rights claims and their efforts to promote the homosexual lifestyle as equal to heterosexuality in the schools. This of course would be detrimental to Kevin Jennings and

GLSEN since they have a big presence through their large network of Gay Straight Alliance clubs in thousands of schools.

So the battle has been waging. At some point with stories like this, a reporter has to reach a conclusion. After covering more stories than I wanted about sexual permissiveness of public officials and libertine activities in society generally, here is mine: Warren Throckmorton was three-time president of the Association of American Mental Health Counselors. He and Robert Spitzer of the American Psychological Association from Columbia University, Charol Shakeshaft of Hofstra University, and others have done peer-reviewed published research in this area and believe that homosexuality is a response to upbringing and other experiences in a person's life, governed by temperament and interaction with others as one grows up.

A person is born with heterosexual biology, but same-sex attractions during youth are not unusual and should not be seen as a definitive sign of homosexuality. These research scientists believe that people are not born homosexual. They say the notion that homosexuals are wired gay is false.

Homosexuality is an acquired behavior, just like any other. People who have same-sex attractions as youths or who go on to live in a homosexual lifestyle as adults can modify their sexual behavior and be heterosexuals, according to their social, moral, and religious beliefs at any time in their lives. It's just like anything else in life. It's a matter of personal choice, based on whatever other social and family pressures exist in one's life and what makes one happy.

The gay lobby doesn't like the idea that sexual preference and activity is a matter of choice. The gay lobby wants to knock that on the head in today's cultural environment because the notion of choice and homosexuality not being in the genes strips the gay lobby of purported civil rights claims and the right to use government powers, schools, and all public forums to promote the same-sex homosexual lifestyle as normal and equivalent to man-woman heterosexuality, particularly among children as early as elementary school age.

That's the ongoing struggle and the ongoing story.

It's a cultural clash that needs to be reported fully and honestly without people in the news media taking sides. Unfortunately, pro-gay reporters and editors and radio-TV producers have skewed the story to promote the GLSEN objectives.

On the other side, groups like Focus on the Family, Concerned Women for America, the American Family Association, and ex-gay groups with a Judaic-Christian orientation such as Exodus, have argued against GLSEN and the pro-gay lobby. As a result, the story is easy to cover completely and honestly if news organizations want to do so.

If those in the news media would not take sides in the culture war and would treat people equally, they would point out, as in the debate over display of the Ten Commandments, that public display of "gay pride" materials and books with gay themes are offensive to parents with religious views opposed to the homosexual lifestyle and should not be supported with taxpayer dollars.

Similarly, school curriculums introducing children as young as age five to the deadly HIV-AIDS sexually transmitted disease while not promoting sexual abstinence are definitely offensive to many parents.

Such school programs promote the idea that any kind of sexual activity is okay, and here's how you do it—supposedly safely—but research shows these so-called comprehensive sex education programs have been a horrible failure for generations.

Interestingly, three groups representing gay and feminist lobbies did a recent survey of all 50 states to pick the best and worst on the issues of "gay and reproductive rights."

According to news reports, the National Gay and Lesbian Task Force, the Sister Song Women of Color Reproductive Health

Collective, and Ipas (an international nongovernmental organization based in Chapel Hill, North Carolina) chose 25 specific laws for the rankings.

Tied for first place with the best record, according to the survey, were New Mexico and New York. Tied for last with the worst records were South Dakota and Ohio.

The 25 laws used for the survey included nine governing availability of abortion, five on use of contraceptives and family planning, five on "lesbian, gay, bisexual and transgender" (LGBT) issues—including "hate crimes," same-sex marriage and adoption by same-sex partners—and six laws opposed by the groups concerning abstinence-only sex education and fetal endangerment laws.

Thomas Ashcraft, formerly U.S. attorney in North Carolina appointed by President Reagan and a good source of mine for many years, reacted to the survey succinctly in a column in The Charlotte Observer by pointing out how far we have come from the Judaic-Christian values upon which the United States was founded, "Earlier generations have labored to expand the realm of legitimate human freedom," Ashcraft writes. "These new activists focus on expanding the range of human genital activity. Two visions of America: One old, broad and bright; the other new, narrow and dark. The second, should it succeed, will not only remake our 230-year-old country but also sack the 'shining city on a hill' others have sacrificed to build. We cannot let that happen."

CHAPTER NINETEEN

COVERING THE SCHOOLS

Education will not take the place of persistence. The world is full of educated derelicts. Persistence and determination alone are omnipotent. The slogan "press on" has solved and always will solve the problems of the human race.

—Calvin Coolidge

COVERING THE NATIONAL EDUCATION BEAT for The Washington Times for five years from 2001 through 2005 forced me to go back to basic principles as a reporter and taxpayer.

How was I to cover the Congress's and the Bush administration's federal imposition of the "No Child Left Behind Act" on America's state and local public school systems?

The legislation had noble objectives:

—To force some accountability for the hundreds of billions of local, state and federal taxpayer dollars spent each year on the schools and to require some needed additional competence and rigor in America's classrooms.

—To close the horrible learning achievement gap nationally between white and minority students.

—To give parents a report card on their local schools with a choice to send their children elsewhere or get after-school tuition for children if the nearest public school was substandard.

As I became the paper's national education reporter, the first question that came to mind was, "What are we as consumers getting for our money—more than $440 billion in taxpayer spending a year?"

A second question was, "Why is there such a huge literacy and other learning achievement gap between white and minority students in public schools, particularly in the big cities?"

A third question: "Why is there such antipathy within the public education establishment for parents to have alternate choices—charter schools, private schools—if the local public schools where they live are substandard and not to their liking, for whatever reason?"

I soon found out that public school administrators and teachers don't like these questions. When the George W. Bush administration's congressionally enacted, federal "No Child Left Behind Act" went into effect in 2002, we were spending nationally an average of $11,915 for each of the country's 45 million public school students, kindergarten through 12th grade.

The per-public expenditure obviously varied from state to state, but why were nearly half of all children in fourth grade and beyond unable to read or compute arithmetic at their grade level and testing "below basic" according to testing by the National Assessment of Educational Progress?

The idea of social promotion—pushing children from one grade to the next so they kept up with their peers, even if they hadn't mastered the expected grade-level skills, obviously had been a massive mistake and disaster over many decades.

But I found as both a parent of four daughters who went through public schools and as a reporter covering the school beat that you get all kinds of answers and excuses.

Educators argue correctly that public schools are required to accept everyone, including children with disabilities and misbehaving children who cause problems in classrooms. They argue that parents aren't sufficiently involved in their children's schooling and that school teachers aren't paid enough.

Except isn't this a myth about teacher pay? In Fairfax County, Virginia, the 12th largest school district in the country, a new teacher fresh out of college makes $40,000 for a 194-day contract, while the average salary in the D.C. metropolitan area for new workers is $29,604 for 235 days of work.

The average teacher salary nationwide was $60,201 in 2005. For teachers making that amount, Fairfax County added $23,348— 39 percent—for Social Security, health insurance, retirement, and other benefits, so each teacher slot ended up costing taxpayers at least $83,348 per year.

And at 30 years, teachers could retire with something like 90 percent of their annual salary, a much better deal than people in the military who—after 30 years of getting shot at, family separations, et cetera—got 75 percent of their base pay, which did not include housing, food, and other allowances.

But a reporter must use the facts and keep going back to the basic questions: With all this money we spend each year for public schools, why can't we expect children to learn reading, math, science and so forth at grade level before they are moved from grade to grade?

They do so in China, Singapore, England and European countries. Why should we put up with less? Why should we congratulate a school industry that has been producing a nation of dummies? We have a lot of exceptional students from good families. But there's a big divide in our country between achievers and nonachievers, and the public schools have not found a way to breach the achievement gap, despite an announced philosophy of equality.

Let's congratulate success where it is happening and denounce failure where it is happening. I know school people don't like that. They don't want the kind of grading system I grew up with and

come up with a slew of excuses that go to social reasons why they
can't help children achieve.

These excuses don't explain how some schools can't help children
achieve, but a school leader such as Marva Collins can, in inner-city
Chicago, teaching children from the poorest of poor families, many
one-parent families without the resources of rich upper-crusties.

It's a matter of standing for proper values, helping children
pull themselves up by their bootstraps, teaching literacy to children
the proper way at a young age, putting the bar high so children
have to keep flexing their intellectual as well as their physical and
humanitarian muscles.

As a reporter, I just looked at the situation by the numbers and
asked my questions accordingly—not much liked by public school
administrators and school union leaders of the National Education
Association.

In the 2004–05 school year, according to data issued by the
U.S. Department of Education and the Council of the Great City
Schools, which has 7.5 million kids in 49 urban public school
districts—including more than a third of our country's minority
kids with parents mostly below the poverty income line:

   —42 percent of fourth graders and 60 percent of eighth graders in
      public, inner-city school districts were below grade-level profi-
      ciency in reading and math.

The disparity between white and black students on national
tests was huge, with black and Latino students scoring as much as
16 to 35 points below white students on reading and math tests in
fourth and eighth grade in most of the largest urban public school
districts.

Abigail Thernstrom of the Manhattan Institute—a presidentially
appointed member of the U.S. Civil Rights Commission—and her

husband, Stephan Thernstrom of the Harvard University history faculty, have done some of the most profound published research on our country's racial gap in learning. They conclude in their seminal book "No Excuses," published in 2003, that the gap in academic achievement between white and black children that we see today in public schools "is actually worse than it was 15 years ago."

While the white-black learning achievement gap in the United States was closing in the 1970s and through most of the 1980s, their research finds that it began to widen around 1988 "with no turnaround in sight."

The Thernstroms resolve that the problem is easy to see. With middle-class families of all races fleeing to the suburbs, large public, urban school systems with mostly minority children from poverty-stricken families, more social problems, and a smaller property tax base lack professional and financial resources to beat their dysfunctional situation.

Minority poverty-stricken school systems, with more disorder in classrooms, cannot provide incentives to attract highly motivated, well-qualified teachers to come in to repair the damage inflicted by dysfunctional education programs that lack discipline, rigor and motivation for students who need it most.

"Students in schools with high minority enrollment were considerably less likely to turn up in class at all," the Thernstroms find. In San Francisco, their research shows that as many as 39 percent of black middle school students were absent from school for 3-1/2 weeks, or 10 percent of the academic year, compared with 15 percent of whites. In San Francisco high schools, two-thirds of black students and one-third of whites were absent for 3-1/2 or more weeks of classes.

No wonder the high school graduation rates have continued to plummet in the country.

"The process of connecting black students to the world of

academic achievement isn't easy in the best of educational settings—
and such settings are today few and far between," the Thernstroms
conclude.

Why can't highly paid school administrators figure a way to solve
problems the same way the military and successful corporations do?
Where's the bang for the buck?

Why are almost a majority of children in our public schools
not meeting even basic literacy and computing skills from fourth
grade, age 10, onward? And what are the alternatives for parents and
families in so many large urban communities where public schools
are failing?

I found that public school people don't like the label "failing." I
never understood that. The teachers I had in school were quite honest in giving me an "F" grade if I didn't pass their requirements. So I
asked the question, why can't we grade teachers and schools that fail
to progress students in literacy and other academic competency?

It's a reporter's job to ask these questions and to get answers.
This leads to news stories that force those in authority to explain
failure and ultimately help the good of the order. It's not our job as
reporters to defend mediocrity and failure. It's the job of highly paid
administrators who run our public schools to explain failure and how
they intend to get us back on a track of success and superiority.

If the method of reading instruction being used is not properly
teaching children how to master the language and read books, it
needs to be changed to a proven method that works.

Reid Lyon, President Bush's chief reading advisor in his first
term, a child development and brain specialist at the National Insti-
tutes of Health, was a champion of scientific-based reading methods
that teach phonemic awareness and other proper language skills.

But I found it was difficult to get the colleges of education and
school establishment generally to abandon the failed reading method
called "look-guess," which was the fad starting in the 1950s.

Harvard educator-researcher Jeanne Chall proves in her seminal

book, "Learning to Read," in 1967 that teaching children to read is
a developmental process that requires use of a phonics approach and
exposing children to challenging literature. But this is tough work
for any teacher and requires committed teachers willing to use this
approach and stay the course with children, year in and year out.

The National Council on Teacher Quality studied 222 required
courses for prospective elementary school teachers at 72 teacher colleges throughout the country and reported in May 2006 that only
11 of the 72 colleges taught all five components of the science of
reading—phonemic awareness, phonics, fluency, vocabulary, and
comprehension.

The NCTQ report said a third of the college syllabi "make no
reference to reading science in any of their reading courses." The five
best teacher colleges for reading instruction, the report said, were
Texas A&M, Rhode Island College, Clarion University of Pennsylvania, the University of North Carolina at Greensboro, and the University of Oklahoma.

The education establishment and school unions affiliated with
the National Education Association have for decades resisted a sci-
ence-based approach to reading instruction, so a big shake-up was
needed. That shake-up started with the No Child Left Behind Act,
but as with all federal laws, it was far from perfect.

As a reporter, my interviews with hundreds of school teachers
and administrators identified at least six fundamental flaws in our
public school system nationally because of so-called "progressive"
ideas that took root in the days of Columbia University philosophy
professor John Dewey, a pragmatic psychologist who had tremendous influence on American education colleges in the early 1900s:

—The first flaw is the mistaken social-promotion idea that was
   rooted in the John Dewey notion that school teachers should
   make children "feel good" and have a good self-concept. That
   meant failure was bad. No one was to be allowed to fail, even

if he or she hadn't learned enough to be promoted to the next grade.

So teachers up the line were sent children who hadn't mastered the basic skills needed to do their work at a higher level. That meant classrooms were filled with frustrated students who couldn't read their books and keep up with the work assigned to them. When frustrated children reached adolescence in middle school or junior high school, many acted out badly, caused discipline problems for teachers, or dropped out of school and became problems in society generally.

As Cheri Yecke—former chief state school officer in Virginia and Minnesota and now K–12 chancellor in Florida—writes in her marvelous book, the whole middle school paradigm must be changed so children from sixth to eighth grades get more rigorous instruction and rich course content.

All the touchy feely pablum since the 1960s should be ripped out of the middle schools, where adolescents need more discipline, rigor, and to be taught to accept the responsibilities of burgeoning adults.

As Yecke wrote in her 2003 book "The War Against Excellence: The Rising Tide of Mediocrity in America's Middle Schools," most schools for sixth to eighth graders are boring adolescent students to death and pouring their minds and character development down the toilet.

Mediocre middle and high schools sow the seeds of adolescent student frustration, dropouts, and failure for too many students, particularly from poor and single-parent families.

Our school dropout rate each year over the past decade has been about 5 to 10 percent starting in ninth grade, with children from low-income families comprising the largest number of school dropouts before high school graduation.

The dropout rate is mainly rooted in the frustration of students because the school system failed to teach them basic literacy and arithmetic skills in early grades and keep them interested so they could master their work in later grades. This is not rocket science.

The public school system has let us down throughout the country because it is riveted in failed ideology and lack of commitment to discipline and academic rigor to keep both teachers and students motivated.

—The second flaw is the pernicious school union idea of teacher tenure and opposition to merit pay for teachers, which has swelled teacher ranks with a lot of mediocre people who just enjoy their jobs while shuffling children up through the system.

There are tens of thousands of wonderful, excellent teachers in our public school system, but there are also a lot of mediocre and bad teachers who should have been weeded out.

The pay system that gives bad teachers the same pay and advancements as excellent teachers is absurd. We should move to a system that rewards excellent teachers and figures out a way to get rid of mediocre teachers.

—Thirdly, we need to get back to the proven system of old that rewarded excellent students and used them as role models to help pull up children who need help and maybe need to try harder.

The idea in many schools of holding ice-cream parties for children from low-income families, just to make them feel better, is a nice gesture, but shouldn't children who perform best, regardless of their family situation, get the ice-cream parties?

There is nothing wrong with merit, and it should be rewarded and used as a model for students who need to do better.

—Fourthly, school choice is a good idea, and the hostile opposition of the unions and the monopoly public school establishment to parental choice regarding the schools their children attend must be overcome.

The charter school movement within the public school systems of the country has proven to be a huge success, despite some isolated problems and attacks by the New York Times based on disingenuous data produced by public school unions.

School vouchers—I call them school stamps—for parents whose children are trapped in bad public schools are also a good idea. Milwaukee, Cleveland, and the state of Florida have had very successful school voucher programs where families can get a check for the pupil expenditure from the public schools and move their children to a public or private school of choice. Thousands of private and parochial schools in communities throughout the country do a far better job at much less cost than public schools.

Voucher programs have been vigorously opposed by the public school unions and liberal interest groups but upheld by the Supreme Court and other courts as a basic right of taxpayers and parents in behalf of their children; although, state courts in Florida and elsewhere have balked.

Congress approved a plan in 2003 for about 2,000 District of Columbia families to get scholarships up to $7,500 so their children could leave bad public schools infested with crime and mediocre teaching and go to private or parochial schools.

A study of this federally approved voucher program by a group of independent researchers affiliated with Georgetown University gave it high marks.

Other independent studies by the Manhattan Institute, researchers Carolyn Hoxby and Paul Peterson of Harvard University, Frederick M. Hess of the American Enterprise Institute, and Chester

Finn's Fordham Institute have similarly shown that charter school and voucher choice programs are good for public school improvement because, in their view, they inject needed competition into the school marketplace and force improvement in local public schools.

Defenders of a monopoly public school system continue to throw legal, political and other monkey wrenches in the way of parental school choice however they can, but groups like the Alliance for School Choice in Phoenix; Center for Education Reform in Washington, DC.; Landmark Legal Foundation in Herndon, Virginia; Liberty Counsel in Orlando, Florida; the Milton and Rose Friedman Foundation; and others have kept pushing for choice and provided news for reporters who are open to stories about better school opportunities.

—Fifthly, discipline in the public schools is a huge problem because liberal school administrators do not support teachers, school bus drivers, and others who have problem students, some of them maniacal.

After the Columbine massacre in Colorado, we are now used to seeing police in the schools and shakedowns of students for weapons and drugs. This is not a problem that is hard to figure out.

Great state school administrators such as William Moloney in Colorado, Cheri Yecke in Florida, Patti Harrington in Utah, and others have no problem figuring out a solution: Schools need greater structure, much better supervision of children and teachers, and according to Patti Harrington, "proper discipline by adults who are unafraid to be authority figures, which kids are seeking, in truth, and schools with high expectations for performance, dress and deportment."

A good example is Shaw Junior High School in Washington, D.C., which has administrators who require a strict dress code, good manners by students, and use an almost military manner to control their student body. The same at George Junior Academy, a privately run reform school in Grove City, Pennsylvania.

Students at George Junior acknowledged to me in interviews that they were one step from jail when they were sent from Philadelphia and other places to this strictly run school that has marvelous athletic and vocational education facilities.

One memorable story from Dean John Stephens of the education school at Grove City College involved a naïve student teacher who gave a geography lesson at George Junior about major oceans and waterways of the world, and two students came up to her after class to inquire where Pennsylvania was on the map.

She showed them the world map, where the United States was, where Pennsylvania was, and where Grove City was. The two wide-eyed young punks from Philadelphia asked the teacher if they could study the area map, so she made them a copy.

The next thing reform school authorities knew, the two punks "were outta there," Stephens told me. "They wanted to find a road and hit the road." They took the map, left the unwalled George Junior campus, hot-wired a car at an adjacent used car dealership in Grove City, and off they went.

The story doesn't detract from a central truth: We need to get back to academic rigor and strong moral values in our schools that support community values.

One has to admire the ingenuity of the escaping George Junior kids in figuring out their way to freedom, but then civil society also has to stay ahead of criminals. Liberals, unfortunately, usually side with amorality and criminals.

The unhappy truth is that the public school system for too long has promoted a secular relativist agenda, anything goes. So the public schools are to blame as much as anyone for the cultural and social breakdown all around us.

They've perpetuated permissiveness and libertine behavior, patted punks on the back while handcuffing teachers, and concerned school administrators so proper discipline in the schools has been forbidden and prevented by political correctness.

—And finally, the sixth flaw is the way sex education is conducted in the schools. When I was in eighth-grade health class in 1958, they showed us the body parts of boys and girls, told us how babies are created, and so forth.

Now in sex ed. classes, according to videos I've seen that are used in even elementary school classrooms, they have lovely young girls using a cucumber to show boys how to put on a condom.

This is pornography the Federal Communications Commission would rule off television, yet this kind of stuff is being shown to young children every day in our public school classrooms throughout the country. They say it is needed to prevent unwanted pregnancies, sexually transmitted diseases, and HIV-AIDS.

Well, sex education programs in the schools have become a how-to method for adolescent kids with raging hormones. This has been going on for many years. We wonder why we have so many criminal sex incidents involving adolescent children, predatory teachers, and other adult perverts.

The sex education fiasco is now even raging in Catholic parochial schools, where liberal bishops, such as Paul Loverde in Arlington, Virginia, have ditched abstinence programs that worked very well for many years in order to implement touchy feely "how-to" sex education classroom stuff that should properly be left to parents to discuss with their children in the privacy of their own homes.

I admired greatly the message of Erika Harold, Miss America 2003, who went to high schools and told teenagers to respect each other and abstain from sex, drugs and alcohol. I followed her around one day as she traveled to Washington, D.C. schools and told this message to the young ladies, and they stomped and shouted "yeah."

And when the young ladies shouted yeah, there were a lot of young gentlemen who shouted yeah as well.

In each school, Erika crowned one young lady, chosen by students, as queen and one young gentleman, also chosen by students, as king. Liberals would complain that this is a process to separate the cream from the milk. Yes, it is.

But it was apparent in all these school sessions as I followed Miss America 2003 Erika Harold through inner-city Washington, D.C. schools that there were a lot of lovely black young ladies from poor families, living in homes with single working moms, who wanted better lives and young gentlemen who treated them with respect and not just as sex objects. So this is a message that works.

Why are liberals and the public school establishment so opposed to this message?

Lately, the public school establishment has adopted the agenda of the Gay Lesbian Straight Educators Network (GLSEN) to put Gay Straight Alliances in the schools so children as early as age seven can be encouraged to accept homosexuality as a norm.

Excuse me, schools that are not properly teaching children to read and do arithmetic and have wholesome, honest values should not be promoting homosexuality or other secular relativist values to precious children in their early years of development.

They should get back to the task of preparing our next generation for jobs in a very competitive world and to be moral, upstanding people.

Let's cut all the baloney and spend the public's money properly. It's every reporter's job to hold their feet to the fire and expose schools and school administrators who are not doing that.

My biggest frustration on the national education beat was that so many of my reporter colleagues from other news organizations were in the pocket of the education establishment and were spoon-fed; they did not do their own independent, aggressive reporting.

There were some exceptions, but the education press was mainly a lapdog for the monopoly public school establishment and its liberal political supporters at the local, state and national levels.

This is a major obstacle to school improvement. The media has an accountability role and responsibility. There is no more important arena than the continuing public education story.

There are many who believe it is impossible for public schools to improve so long as the government runs them, and a current movement within the Southern Baptist Convention similar to Catholic Jesuit independence would set up a parallel private parochial school system affiliated with local churches in order to collapse a failed public school system.

This movement challenges the John Dewey and B.F. Skinner ideological assumptions that government schools are an essential means for social cohesion against chaos, children must be socialized by government agents in order to tolerate each other, children must be protected from parents and conditioned by government-certified experts, and it is necessary to remove children from their parents' influence and family/religious moral value system so they can develop their intellect.

It seems long overdue to this reporter that the public should question assertively the liberal notions that general education of all is more important than independent schooling and liberty—and that state control is vital to protect us all from people who think independently for themselves and from families with different beliefs and backgrounds who question or contradict a community-driven group ideology.

A mass exodus from public schools would be extraordinary, but students leaving public schools for other alternatives is most certain to continue to happen as public schools keep wasting so much taxpayer money while failing to deliver real improvement and renew the spirit of liberty among succeeding generations of children.

The public school establishment appears sorrowfully mired down in bureaucracy, complacency and arrogance that stems from an elitist, socialist attitude that militates against the essential free-inquiring spirit of every person.

News reporters in every community should seriously challenge all excuses from apologists of the status quo and assertively ask why public schools cannot dramatically improve. Why should all families in communities throughout America be bound to a communal, government-run public school system if it is failing, yet not have unlimited school choices for the education of their children?

Just as reporters every day challenge the Defense Department and our country's war on terror throughout the world, they should ask the tough questions that challenge the precepts and ideology of a certainly substandard and mediocre public school establishment.

This should not be an inside, second-section story each day, where most newspapers put it. This story about school reform, improvement and wider choice for families regarding the education of their children should be kept on the front pages, each and every week. It's certainly a story as important as the daily weather, sports results, and latest car pileup on the local interstate.

Just one reporter's opinion.

CHAPTER TWENTY

MISS AMERICA MUZZLED

Quite frankly, and I'm not going to be specific, there are pressures from some sides to not promote abstinence. I will not be bullied.

—Erika Harold, Miss America 2003,
National Press Club October 9, 2002

ERIKA HAROLD, 22, was crowned Miss America 2003 on September 23, 2002, and like Queen Elizabeth I of England, the proverbial Virgin Queen of today had an immediate fight on her hands with beauty pageant bureaucrats who wanted to run the show and control her message.

But like her feisty role model six centuries before, Erika took decisive charge and told the bureaucrats who was boss. The proverbial Tower of London loomed for these challengers of the queen.

The gorgeous and eloquent woman of American Indian, African-American, and Caucasian ancestry had stumped her home state as Miss Illinois 2002 to urge adolescent school children to abstain from drugs, sex and alcohol.

More than 14,000 students at schools across the state of Illinois, and thousands more in her two prior tries for the state beauty title, had heard her message of abstinence from sex, drugs and alcohol.

Erika Harold was a lovely role star who brought to thousands of teenagers —particularly lovely, young ladies—a message of chastity and self-respect.

She had stood firm in every session I attended. She told her own story to students about how she was bullied in school as a child of mixed parents in Urbana, Illinois—her father white from Europe and mother half African-American, half Cherokee Indian. And she was ruthlessly bullied in high school in Urbana, Illinois, because she was a half-caste.

But she was beautiful. She and her parents had great hearts. They read together, her parents taught her history honestly, she listened to good music (staying away from vulgar music), decided what she wanted in life, and realized life is not a white-black situation.

Why can't we all realize that?

Erika Harold, Miss America 2003, is a true hero because she not only broke through the color barrier but also stood up to people who told her she could not stand for the values she believed would help people break away from a racial and economic divide that still existed in our country—plus she added a moral-cultural asterisk.

Erika Harold's message to America's youth as Miss America was that what happened to her as a youth should not happen to any child. Her message was that no child should be bullied because of his or her parents' situation, income, whether it's an intact family, inter-racial, whatever. Children are innocent. Period.

We should nurture children. And as they grow up, we need to teach boys to respect girls and vice versa. But most girls won't respect boys who just want to get into their pants. And most girls won't respect boys who don't have anything upstairs intellectually.

So the message I heard Erika Harold tell young people was simple: Respect each other. Work hard to make yourselves the best you can be. Look to having a loving mate and family. Work as hard as you can to get all the skills you can to make this happen. Have fun, because that's important. But young ladies and young gentlemen, please keep your eye on the ball.

We need a future that will be good for our children, and it is our responsibility as parents to provide that, as did all before us. We need solid families. That means good men as fathers and good women as mothers, who will raise strong children.

The Bill Cosby model.

Yet immediately upon beating all other state contestants to be crowned Miss America 2003, Erika Harold was told by pageant officials and handlers she could no longer talk to youth about premarital sexual abstinence in her coming year's travels throughout the country. She was told the theme of her reign was a national campaign against youth violence, bullying and harassment, but premarital sexual abstinence was not to be mentioned as part of the message.

The abstinence message, pageant officials told her, was "too controversial." And so the new Miss America was muzzled even before her reign began.

Erika was furious and called several good friends for advice and help. They included Kathleen Sullivan—founder of Project Reality, a group with a pro-abstinence school curriculum—for whom she worked as spokeswoman while Miss Illinois and Connaught Coyne Marshner of the Leadership Institute, who helped train her in public persuasion as a college student and abstinence advocate.

Sullivan and Marshner for many years long before my tenure at The Washington Times, when I was a congressional aide for many years in Washington, were both sources of mine on education, family life and feminism issues. They promptly called me to say there was a big story brewing over Erika Harold's dispute with the Miss America Pageant bureaucrats.

After the Miss America pageant in Atlantic City, New Jersey, Erika was first taken on a whirlwind tour of advocacy groups in New York City, including the Anti-Defamation League, which featured her on their Web site in opposition to "hate crimes" and the ADL's promotion of a pro-gay rights agenda in the schools.

Kathleen Sullivan called to say Erika was then coming to Washington October 8, 2002, for a press conference at the National Press Club as guest of a sponsoring group called Fight Crime: Invest in Kids.

"Why don't you go to the press conference, and ask why she's been muzzled on abstinence?" Kathleen asked. After the Washington press conference, Erika was to return to Illinois for her first appearances as Miss America in her home state.

I told my Washington Times National Editor Kenneth Hanner about the potential story and asked if this should go to our very capable family issues reporter Cheryl Wetzstein. He said Cheryl was busy with something else and that I should go to the 9 a.m. press conference.

I went to the photo desk assignment editor to request a photographer. He wanted to know what the story was. I told him.

Award-winning photographer Michael Connor arrived for the press conference about a half-hour early, as I did. We discussed the story I was after. Michael, genius at work, camped out with his gear in the hallway for Erika to arrive, and I settled into a front row seat for the press conference.

Connie Marshner arrived, and surprised to see her, we discussed her role advising Erika who then arrived in the hallway outside the room. Connie dashed to meet her, and they huddled. I saw Michael snapping shots.

When Connie came back into the room just before the press conference started, I went over and asked her what was going on. "Erika's furious," Connie said. "They told her again as they walked from the J.W. Marriott Hotel to the Press Club to be sure she said nothing about abstinence."

I told Connie, "Fasten your seat belt. We'll see about that."

In the meantime, Erika was standing, arms folded and scowling outside the National Press Club room where the press conference was to occur with Sanford A. Newman, an executive of Fight Crime: Invest in Kids, and their publicist Philip Evans, who ironically was an original assistant managing editor of The Washington Times.

Michael Connor was snapping priceless pictures of a very unhappy queen that absolutely made our story in the next day's newspaper.

The press conference opened with an introduction of the new Miss America. Erika Harold looked pained in Connor's pictures, made a few remarks about her own childhood being bullied as a mixed-race high school student in Urbana, Illinois, her planned campaign over the next year to reduce youth violence, and then asked for questions from the press.

I sat for a few seconds, not wanting to be the first, looked back at the TV cameras in the rear, and when no other reporter spoke up, raised my hand.

"Yes," Miss America said.

I rose and introduced myself, offered congratulations on her selection as Miss America, then asked my question: "When you were Miss Illinois campaigning for the Miss America crown, you visited a lot of teenage school children while talking about the value of abstinence from sex, drugs and alcohol. But since you've received the Miss America crown, you've said nothing in your public appearances about abstinence. Why is that?"

I saw the shocked look of her handlers on the dais and thought they would fall off the stage.

Erika Harold's eyes widened, she looked right at me, gripped the podium, and gave a general response about a larger national message against youth violence and having to tailor her message for a larger audience.

I pursued with a follow-up question: "But I'm told you've been told not to talk about abstinence, that you've been muzzled. Is that true?"

Again, Erika Harold responded directly, "Quite frankly, and I'm not going to be specific, there are pressures from some sides to not promote it [abstinence]."

I followed up: "Well, you just went to New York for some visits to the Anti-Defamation League and others, and the ADL Web site has you pictured and projecting you as supporting their campaign against hate crimes and for a gay rights agenda. I've downloaded their Web page. Are you in agreement with the way they're positioning you, as you're not allowed to talk about sexual abstinence?"

Suddenly, a Miss America Pageant handler got up and tried to cut me off, saying they wanted to allow others to ask questions.

Erika said, "Wait, would you come up afterward and show me what you're talking about?" I said I would and sat down.

When I went up to Erika at the end of the press conference, Miss America pageant handlers and people for the local host group tried to stop our conversation. Phil Evans, an original assistant managing editor for The Washington Times and press consultant for the host group chided me, "George when are you going to mellow?"

I responded, "Hey, Phil, mellow doesn't fit with going after the story."

Erika Harold was eager to see how she was being positioned on the Anti-Defmation League Web site in favor of its pro-gay, anti-hate crimes agenda, and I showed her what the ADL had posted.

"I do not support a gay agenda," she said. "This is not what I support. Thank you for showing this to me."

The handlers again tried to cut me off, but Erika waved them off and said she wanted to keep the discussion going.

I asked her, "So you were muzzled on the abstinence message, right?"

She repeated that there were "pressures" from Miss America pageant officials and various sponsoring groups, such as Planned Parenthood and the so-called comprehensive safe-sex condom crowd.

I said, "But you're the queen now. Can't you tell them what you want? Are you going to be bullied?"

She looked at me and responded, "I will not be bullied."

The Miss America pageant handlers grabbed her at this point and said they had to go. But I saw her eyes as she looked at me quite directly in a very, shall I say, thankful way that the question was asked and she could respond, and I could report the story with her on the record. It was like she was a prisoner being taken to jail as they walked out of the National Press Building room, she turned and gave a look I shall never forget. It was like a thank-you. It was one of my most happy memories as a reporter. We had defeated the enemy, and we told the story.

My editors did a phenomenal job packaging the story, which was on Page One below the fold on October 9, 2002. The headline was masterful: "Miss America told to zip it on chastity talk: Says abstinence for teens frowned on as 'platform.'"

Michael Connor's three column picture of Erika Harold showed her looking miffed as she was introduced at the National Press Club press conference. A picture on jump page A-11 showed her with arms folded in front of her and frowning in the hallway before the press conference began. And a front-page story by Cheryl Wetzstein was twinned under her story with the headline: "Abortion rates decline in late 1990s: Teens show biggest drop, but numbers rise for poor." The story reported that abstinence education was a major cause of the reduced abortion numbers.

The next morning, my phone rang, and the voice on the other end said, "Hello, Mr. Archibald, this is Erika Harold." I quickly told her how sorry I was about the pictures showing her not so gorgeous.

"Oh, no, they were great," she said. "The story was great. You liberated me. I just want to say thank you. I'm on my way to the airport to return home. You liberated me. Thank you." And she hung up.

I learned from Connie Marshner and Erika's close associate, Libby Gray, that Erika had furious arguments with Miss America officials after the press conference and into the evening and next morning after the story appeared, insisting that she be allowed to speak about premarital sexual abstinence as she wanted. She even threatened to give back the Miss America crown if they did not give her full voice on the issue that meant so much to her.

Pageant officials ultimately folded before her return to Illinois. So she was liberated, as she said, and went on for the rest of her reign in 2003 to speak eloquently throughout the country to tens of thousands of school children about teenage sexual abstinence.

I covered her tour of Washington, D.C. public schools in the fall of her reign, just before the next Miss America pageant, and the "young ladies" stomped and clapped as she gave them her message of self-respect and telling the boys "no" when they pressured them for sex.

She crowned a young Miss America, selected by fellow students, and a young Mr. America, with her own crown, and it brought tears to my eyes as I saw the impact of this recognition on these young people.

When she had called on October 9, 2002, to say, "You liberated me," she also liberated me, because she showed me so personally the importance of the ongoing culture war and necessary efforts to confront powers arrayed to stop good people like herself from helping the good of the order.

I knew that journalism was war. But once in a while, even a battling reporter needs a courageous newsmaker with a firm moral foundation and platform to remind him that it's important to keep going to the next sniper hedgerow.

As Winston Churchill said, "Never give in."

CHAPTER TWENTY-ONE

REGIME CHANGE AT THE WASHINGTON TIMES

All I have ever really cared about is who is the best and hungriest reporter. Resumés are often a joke. I could care less about people's backgrounds or private lives. All I want is their best effort for the paper when they're on the job.
—Francis B. Coombs Jr., managing editor
(2002–January 2008), The Washington Times,
in an email to the author, March 3, 2006.

═══════════

THE WASHINGTON TIMES was in crisis many years before the 2006 congressional elections because its senior editors did not respect good seasoned reporters.

They pitted young, immature and inexperienced reporters hungry for advancement against the higher tier of experienced reporters who could get stories the younger reporters could not imagine, let alone report. That's just the way the world works in dog-eat-dog journalism.

As a result, there was a serious debilitating morale problem in the newsroom and a constant exodus of veteran reporting talent from The Washington Times in the late 1990s through 2007, when the owners suddenly retired Editor In Chief Wesley Pruden Jr. and Managing Editor Francis B. Coombs Jr.

A fresh team took over the newsroom headed by newly-recruited Editor in Chief John F. Solomon, who previously ran The Washington Post's investigative reporting unit and before that was assistant bureau chief for the Associated Press in Washington for several years. David Jones, The Times' foreign editor, where he had served admirably for many years, was elevated to managing editor to succeed Coombs.

Coombs, who grew up in a military family, was national editor during the time of our best exclusive big-hit stories—the 1989 Washington summer sex and Barney Frank scandals, the House post office and bank scandals of the early 1990s that toppled Democrats from decades of iron-fisted control of Congress, and all the seemingly unending Clinton-era scoops that made The Washington Times a must-read in Washington for so many years.

When we'd meet in Coombs' office to revel over our latest skewering stories, Coombs would joyously slam his fist on the desk and yell out, "Journalism is war!" Unlike Pruden, who was a reclusive Southern gentleman with a similar go-for-the-jugular, right-oriented ideological bent, the ebullient Coombs unfolded their take-no-prisoners approach each day in the newsroom. It was the modern form of print muckraking in an era dominated by tabloid and radio-TV journalism.

Pruden, a highly gifted wordsmith with an innate sense for the fundamentals of journalism, came to The Times' national desk as a political reporter in mid-1982 wearing a rumpled suit. He'd had a checkered career as a reporter for Dow Jones' weekly National Observer, which didn't trouble Times' founding Editor in Chief James Whelan and Executive Editor Smith Hempstone, who quickly moved him up the ladder. Pruden was soon wearing nice seersucker suits, spats, brown-and-white patent leather wingtips, and fedora hats in the mold of legendary newspaperman H.L. Mencken.

Pruden's comfort was his regular column, "Pruden on Politics," where he skewered liberals, socialists, political correctness, feminists, gays and the "lavender bund," bad manners, and constantly stood up for courtly Southern gentility and civility.

Pruden didn't want to roll up his sleeves by mixing with the hoi polloi in the newsroom as top editors Hempstone and Arnaud de Borchgrave had done before him, so he tapped Coombs who shared his neo-Confederate affections to run the newsroom for him as managing editor, keep reporters hyped-up to bring in zinger-stories, put together a nice newspaper package each day, and make the production trains run on time.

Both Pruden and Coombs, in the privacy of their offices, displayed horrible tempers and scared the daylights out of fellow editors and the most productive reporters. Too many of them couldn't put up with the disparaging treatment and trod a steady path to the door as, one by one, they left The Times for nicer pastures.

The newspaper's parent company, News World Communications, ultimately conducted an internal management probe in 2006 to figure out ways to save the newspaper from plummeting employee morale and its decades-long advertising and circulation morass.

The abysmal advertising and circulation numbers of The Times were an unfortunate joke. No one on the editorial side of the newspaper could understand why The Times' total classified advertising was no more than one or two pages a day, while competing The Post's Saturday edition alone had five or six separate sections of classified ads totaling more than 100 pages.

Also The Times' consistent, large ideological ads, many of them full-page, taken by various cause-oriented groups, were a major source of regular embarrassment to professionals in the newsroom. They included a steady stream of religious and political ads placed over the years by groups financed by The Times' founder, the Reverend Sun Myung Moon—head of the Unification Church and worldwide fishery, mining and manufacturing businesses—through a variety of political front groups such as CAUSA, Collegiate Association for the Research of Principles (CARP), Family Federation for World Peace and Unification, Holy Spirit Association for the Unification of World Christianity, and Women's Federation for World Peace.

The paper from 2004 onward inexplicably published 30 ads placed by neo-Nazi Stan Rittenhouse, head of a group called Exhorters with a white-supremacist Web site called Stormfront. Many of us asked, why would any respectable pacesetting newspaper accept such ads, let alone be dependent on them for needed revenue?

How the owners of The Times tolerated the lack of sufficient sales by its advertising and circulation staffs for so many years was a complete mystery to us in the newsroom. The Times' advertising hole was less than almost any small, successful suburban paper in Virginia and Maryland. Even the competing give-away Washington Examiner tabloid, which started in 2005, had more advertising and circulation on its first day than The Times had built up over almost a quarter century.

On top of the advertising and circulation problems, the far-right orientation of the Times under Pruden and Coombs, who as managing editor was a supporter of white supremacists, caused major angst for reporters and editors who just bit their tongues as unfortunate serfs dependent on their jobs and paychecks, constantly reminded by Coombs as part of his regular intimidation spiel that there were hardly any jobs to be had out there in the newspaper world.

The eventual downfall of the Pruden-Coombs regime came in the wake of a devastating investigative cover story in the October 9, 2006 issue of The Nation, a leftist magazine, titled "Hell of a Times: Succession Battle Rages in Right-Wing Message Factory." Reported and written by Max Blumenthal, son of famed veteran-retired Washington Post reporter and Clinton adviser Sidney Blumenthal, the story accurately catalogued a devastating series of horrible truths known only by insiders:

—That Coombs had repeatedly told those of us in the newsroom that he believed blacks were "born genetically 15 to 20 IQ points lower than a white person" and that abortion was necessary "to keep the black and minority population down in this country."

—That Coombs' wife, Marian Kester Coombs, had voiced the same views to many of us during a social occasion at their home and confirmed this on the record in a taped interview with Blumenthal.

Blumenthal asked Marian Coombs directly in the interview whether she and her husband shared the same political and racial views. "Pretty much," she said, while insisting that Fran Coombs' personal views were not reflected in the pages of The Times.

That was not true. Fran Coombs directed and micromanaged news stories as much as possible. He and Pruden would go into stories late at night and rewrite leads, restructure stories and add whatever they wanted, which was the reason a lot of people left the paper over the years.

Many of us in the Times newsroom knew Fran and Marian Coombs to be unreconstructed racial nationalists who reviled blacks and other minorities, but we were grateful to be working for a respected daily newspaper in Washington and suffered in silence, trying to ignore, as Coombs voiced his extreme views on racial and cultural issues. It would have done no good to register disapproval to Pruden, who backed Coombs unconditionally.

Marian Coombs had written for white supremacist magazines as a self-proclaimed "white nationalist" and lunched with neo-Nazi leaders such as William A. White of Roanoke, Va., commander of the American National Socialist Workers' Party. White had lauded Fran and Marian Coombs and Robert Stacy McCain, a Times assistant national editor and another vocal white supremacist and staunch anti-black segregationist advocate, who Coombs hired and appointed to run The Times' page A2 daily culture page.

Under McCain's control, the culture page often prominently ran columns by racist White, who on his neo-Nazi Web site, Over-throw.com, had described McCain as "a pretty good friend of mine." I sat right across from McCain on the national desk, and when I was infrequently in the newsroom had overheard him on the telephone with Mrs. Coombs discussing pieces he was running.

Mrs. Coombs also was a close friend of Jared Taylor, notori-ous white supremacist and founder of the neo-eugenicist group, American Renaissance. She acknowledged in her interview with The Nation's Blumenthal that she had attended American Renaissance conferences to meet with her old friend, Nick Griffin, leader of the neo-fascist, whites-only British National Party (BNP).

On American Renaissance's Web site, she posted this comment in 2001: "Whites do not like crowded societies, and Americans would not have to live in crowds if our government kept out Third-World invaders." She had frequently written for Occidental Quar-terly, an openly white supremacist and anti-Semitic publication. In one article, she wrote the United States had become a "den of iniquity" because it allowed too many minority immigrants into the country. In another piece, she criticized interracial marriage, stating: "White men should 'run, not walk' to wed 'racially conscious' white women and avoid being outbred by non-whites."

Fran Coombs voiced these same views and exerted pressure on Times reporters Jerry Seper, who covered the Justice Department, and Audrey Hudson, who covered the Department of Homeland Security, to reflect his views in their immigration stories.

Seper, one of the best investigative reporters at the paper, and Hudson, a steady professional, resisted these efforts as much as pos-sible and were always straight, honest reporters who let the chips fall where they may. But Coombs and Pruden were always in their sto-ries when Seper and Hudson left the national desk—after editing, rewriting and recasting—to make the stories more to their liking.

That's what senior editors are supposed to do, but in this case there was a racist agenda afoot. Coombs also had a habit of front-ending stories to skew them by going over the top of his national editor, Kenneth Hanner, to tell reporters what he wanted the story to be and what to get for it ahead of their reporting.

They didn't tamper with my copy very often as I fortunately had other good editors—notably Jeffrey Kuhner, Victor Morton, Chris Dolan, Jason Hargraves, Joe Curl , Ken McIntyre and Kathleen O'Malley—whose good work usually kept me clear of major late-night changes.

But on two troubling and hurtful occasions involving the tragic suicide of Vincent Foster Jr., President Bill Clinton's close friend from Arkansas and his deputy White House counsel, and the Catholic priest homosexual scandal, Pruden and Coombs spiked my stories involving more than a year's work on both projects because Pruden disagreed with the results of my reporting.

In the case of the Foster story, Pruden wanted me to prove advertiser and right-wing advocate Reed Irvine of Accuracy in Media's conspiracy theory that Foster was actually murdered or died in another place and his body clandestinely carried to the spot where it was found in Fort Marcy Park overlooking Washington on the Virginia side of the Potomac River.

My reporting thoroughly went back over all the evidence and investigations, and I interviewed most principals in the case. There is no doubt it was a suicide. The full-page special report meticulously edited by Joe Curl, with a genius graphic put together by Greg Groesch, told that immutable conclusion, but Pruden didn't like it and killed the story as dead as Foster—had the typeset ripped off the camera-ready page at 8:30 p.m. on the eve of the third anniversary of Foster's self-inflicted shooting in July 1996.

The written and edited three-part Catholic series also was killed and never ran because the church's Arlington bishop Paul S. Loverde, with help from Washington's prelate at the time, Cardinal Theodore McCarrick—a friend of Pruden—successfully muscled him to take me off the story.

Bishop Loverde claimed in a fax to Pruden that I was "not an objective reporter," as supposedly shown by intrepid questions I had sent for the bishop via email to Arlington Diocese Press Spokeswoman Linda Shovlain. I had asked about horrible homosexual magazines with pictures of sexually-aroused naked boys and leather-strapped naked women in bondage that were found by Catholic Father James R. Haley in other priests' rectory bedrooms, along with proof of embezzlement by one priest totaling almost $100,000 stolen from church collection plates.

Haley had provided photos and documents of the evidence to me, which I asked the editors to review after Loverde complained about my objectivity, but my request was denied. "You're off the story," Coombs shouted, slamming the desk with his fists as he told me, "Now, get out of my office, and get back to work."

Pruden had revealed in a televised CNN interview in 2006 that he would retire in 2008, and he named Coombs as his probable successor—a public announcement that greatly upset the paper's corporate chiefs. Why would they want an admitted white supremacist and neo-eugenicist, with a wife who had publicly written yards of copy admitting such racism, as The Times' top editor? I was told by a key highly placed source in the third-floor corporate offices of The Times and News World Corporation that revelations of Pruden's long countenancing of Coombs' bigoted worldview was too much of a threat to the integrity of the newspaper on its own.

Enough was enough and a huge editorial housecleaning was going to happen.

My sources told me that, with the impending Nation story, The Times' corporate owners commissioned a report about Coombs' management and ideology from the Nixon Peabody law firm in Washington. The owners were worried enough about what they had gleaned of Blumenthal's intrepid reporting that they were embarking on a damage control strategy, of which the Nixon-Peabody internal investigation was the principal shield.

The report was to be submitted to Dong Moon Joo, South Korean president of The Washington Times Corporation (who had anglicized his name to Douglas M. Joo) before The Nation story hit the newsstands several months hence. The report eventually documented testimony of numerous employees who related in detail Coombs' extensive racist comments and abusive, unpopular management style.

As Blumenthal conducted interviews of current and former Times employees for The Nation article from May through September 2006, a lot of Times reporters and editors felt they could finally express themselves without fear of retaliation, although upper editorial managers certainly tried their best to intimidate and threaten those who they learned were talking. The result was a practical revolt in the newsroom.

I was surprised at the time to find out how many of my former colleagues at the newspaper were willing to talk to Blumenthal about Coombs' rampant racism and abusive management behavior, supported by Pruden. It took a lot of courage for Times people to speak out.

In fact, nothing illustrated this better than the joint reaction of Pruden and Coombs to The Nation piece. They refused to answer the serious points raised by Blumenthal's many sources in The Times newsroom but instead went on a hunting jihad to intimidate everyone in sight and try to discredit and smear anyone who had been willing to put his or her name on a quote.

But the Nixon-Peabody report had validated the thrust of The Nation story. In one telling fact, the report revealed that several Times employees who attended a party at an editor's home in Spring 2003 said they were told there by Coombs after he'd loosened up with a few drinks, "I would never want to be born black. This would mean that I would be born genetically 15 to 20 IQ points lower than a white person."

At the party, the report disclosed, Coombs repeatedly said he was "unequivocally for abortion…Since abortion disproportionately impacts blacks and minorities, it helps to keep the black and minority population down in this country."

I personally heard Coombs express the same comments over the years. Coombs claimed in an interview with Blumenthal that he never said such things. Yet Blumenthal reported that at least three Times sources, plus me on the record for attribution, said Coombs directly made such statements to them. They all said they personally heard, as I had, Coombs laud abortion as a means to stem the tide of black, brown and Asian babies—a form of ethnic genocide.

The high-powered Nixon Peabody law firm, was retained to go around Allen Farber, The Times' longtime attorney on workplace and libel issues, in order to uncover the unvarnished truth regarding explosive allegations being investigated by Blumenthal for The Nation.

This was appropriate and a good move for conflict of interest purposes. Farber, himself a brilliant attorney, over the years had well-represented the paper, Pruden, Coombs and others —even me—in at least three dismissed libel actions over a 20-year period. But for this sort of sensitive, needed, thorough, independent internal investigation of the newspaper's top management, the owning company needed to go outside to retain best firm it could find.

The Nixon-Peabody probe was fiercely resisted by Pruden and Coombs, who in turn went to Joo and convinced him to try to block it and hire instead the public relations firm Hill & Knowlton to do a damage control inquiry in-house, with interviews of employees, before and after The Nation piece hit the newsstands.

When Joo, a South Korean who for many years has served as founder the Reverend Sun Myung Moon's translator, attempted to do Pruden's bidding to end-run Nixon-Peabody's inquiry, the entire matter was taken out of his hands as president of The Washington Times Corporation by the Reverend Moon's son, Preston Moon, president of the parent company, News World Communications.

Getting wind of the corporate turmoil in August 2006, Pruden flew back to Washington from vacation in Memphis to plea with Preston Moon, whose offices are in New York and Washington. I was told by senior corporate officials familiar with what happened that Preston Moon told Pruden the Nixon-Peabody inquiry was proceeding and ordered Pruden to cooperate fully.

Then Pruden, who was used to telling the Koreans he was able to get an interview with President Bush and top administration officials anytime he wanted, and even get the president on the phone, overplayed his hand.

He threatened Preston Moon that he would hold a news conference where he would publicly accuse the owners of "editorial interference" if they continued with the probe of editorial management and alleged racial prejudice, anti-Semitism, and sexual harassment on the part of Coombs.

Pruden no doubt believed he had the upper hand and would hit a nerve with the reference to "editorial interference" by the owners, because it was something written in stone as a no-no by The Times' first founding editors in 1982 regarding possible Unification Church control of the paper's editorial product. The owners' pledge of editorial independence for the newspaper was a part of the contracts of the first editors and their successors over the years.

But this was a failed strategy because Pruden and Coombs had made The Washington Times a marginalized and irrelevant ultraright newspaper, and Preston Moon knew they were driving the newspaper into the ground with far-right ideology.

Moon was not intimidated by Pruden's threats to try to embarrass further the owners. He dismissed them and stuck to his position that this was to be a probe of management and workplace propriety. Racial bigotry and harassment or intimidation of employees by managers on grounds of race, color, ethnicity, religious beliefs, or birthplace origin are against the law and valid areas for corporate review of any owned company, including a newspaper.

A review by corporate owners of allegations that editors of a company-owned newspaper published in the United States might be skewing stories for racial, religious, gender, or place of origin reasons was an area of particularly legitimate concern for the owners.

Nixon Peabody's attorneys had already scheduled interviews that would result in sworn depositions by National Editor Kenneth Hanner and Deputy National Editor Victor Morton, which had panicked Pruden and caused him play the "editorial interference" card.

This was a blatant stonewalling and cover-up attempt by Pruden and Coombs in the face of impending devastating charges in The Nation, but it didn't work. It took the owners another year to get their ducks in a row for a complete regime change at one of the foremost and only reliably conservative pacesetting daily newspapers in the country.

Pruden and Coombs apparently knew the jig was up by the time The Nation issue hit the newsstands. Pruden stayed on at the paper to organize a nice golden parachute for his ultimate retirement exeunt and to keep his column in the paper.

Coombs promptly went to Deputy Managing Editor Ted Agres to tell him he was ready to start discussions to get a buyout of his contract if the owners wanted him to go. Pruden and Coombs hunkered down and hoped the company's senior corporate leaders and owners would back down and allow them to retain their perquisites until they ultimately were asked to go, which happened toward the end of 2007.

The bottom line for the owners was impatience with the huge money drain and ideological sclerosis at The Times and its management's failure to get on the leading edge of a much more vibrant information age with its news product and Web site.

Thomas P. McDevitt, who was there when owners founded The Times, was named Joo's successor as president of The Washington Times Corporation. McDevitt's announcement of Solomon's appointment as Pruden's replacement on January 14, 2008, was telling: "He is a working journalist, innovative manager, and skilled leader who can navigate the complicated media landscape while maintaining traditional news values and credibility."

For those at the newspaper and past employees who rejoiced the regime change, it boiled down to the fact that no honest reporters, editors or producers worth their salt want top-down skewing of news in an ideological or political direction.

The same challenge had faced talented reporters and editors at The New York Times, USA Today, other newspapers, and television giant CBS News, whose longtime nighttime news anchor Dan Rather was caught up in a fake story pushed by partisan sources about President Bush's National Guard service.

Rather told viewers of CBS Evening News on September 8, 2004, and separately 60 Minutes, that "exclusive information, including documents" purportedly showed that President Bush shirked his duties when he was in the Texas Air National Guard in the 1960s and 1970s. But within hours of the documents being posted on CBS News' Web site, typography experts questioned that they had really come from the late Lieutenant Colonel Jerry Killian, Bush's former commanding officer. The documents were actually faked.

However, according to Bernard Goldberg, best-selling author of "Bias" and veteran CBS producer, the story fit Rather's preconceived anti-Bush views. He wanted it to be true and ran with it despite all the red-flag warnings of fraud that a responsible news professional with integrity would have vetted before rushing the story onto the air.

Certainly journalism is war. But the badge of honor for most of us in the trade—regardless of our own personal, political and religious beliefs—is an honest, complete report for readers and listeners and a commitment to counter those media operations that do not provide reliably consistent, factual and thorough reporting.

It is dishonest in the news business to go over the edge in any particular ideological direction and spin news to further or promote just that perspective. In addition to being honest and complete, reporting must be balanced and fair.

To get that in our trade is another form of journalism warfare that was certainly fought, with some casualties to be sure, during the first quarter century within the walls of The Washington Times.

ACKNOWLEDGEMENTS

This book is based on a lifetime of relationships and professional partnerships with literally thousands of news sources, fellow journalists, committed ideologues, and plain wonderful people I have been blessed to know over the years—plus many jerks one encounters in the toss-and-throw of daily news and political discussion. I acknowledge and thank them all.

I am particularly indebted to my late mother, Rusty, her son's best comforter and friend for 62 years, who until her last gasp was always there with a helping hand and sound advice; ex-wife, Blair Smithson Belkin, who supported and put up with me for 18 years and gave us four lovely daughters—first Washington Times baby, Leslie, mother of first beautiful granddaughter, Carmen, and also her good mate, Noah; Ali, gorgeous mischief; Leigh Anne, lanky beauty; Lizza, the horsey girl who carries on five generations of equestrian champions since Great-Great-Grandfather George Blackwell trained Rock Sand, grandsire of America's winningest stallion, Man O'War.

Also Blair's lovely parents, D.R. and Betty Lou Smithson; late grandparents, Tommy and Mildred Mayo and Margaret Smithson; Kitty Landauer; Berch and Cathy Smithson; Brian and Sugi Dewan; and my dear sister, Valerie Embrey, who I wholeheartedly love but have always embarrassed, her ex-husband, Ronnie, and their good sons, David and Kevin.

From formative days as a young British émigré to America, thanks to the late Mutual Radio news commentator Fulton Lewis Jr.; Thomas S. Winter, Allan Ryskind and Cleo Grant of Human Events; Kenneth Y. Tomlinson, college friend and former Readers' Digest chief editor, and mate, Rebecca; M. Stanton Evans, once youngest editorial page editor in America who founded the National Journalism Center; titan publisher Eugene C. Pulliam who gave me my first break at The Arizona Republic and first editor Edwin S. McDowell; former Congressman John B. Conlan and former mate Irene, current mate, Julia; the late Congressman Eldon Rudd and widow Ann—they entrusted me as wordsmith and strategic aide in helping move the peg forward; spiritual mentors the Reverend Charles Fuller (Baptist), the Right Reverend Marc Handley Andrus (Episcopal) and mate, Sheila, and the Reverend James Gould (Catholic); caring neighbors Janice Albany in Virginia and Roy Miller in Arizona, longtime friend from Air Force days at Williams Air Force Base.

Also the late Major Dick Cox, base information officer at Willie, then the country's largest undergraduate pilot-training base in the Vietnam era; enlisted colleagues Don Andrews, Jimmy Walker, George Economides; Tech Sergeant Johnnie Fletcher; late retired Army Light Colonel Jack Moser; Captains Paul Cormier and George Upchurch; First Lieutenant Marilyn Shoemaker Jones who was my immediate boss; Lieutenant Colonel Jack Becko who flew me over the high skies and Grand Canyon in a Northrop T-38 jet as I chased his daughter, Lenore; Colonels Roger Ludeman and A.K. "Duffy" Koeck, our Air Force uppers at Willie who always pushed the limits for freedom's cause.

In Washington, friends and mentors for more than 30 years, Charlene Luskey; Edwin Feulner; Phil Truluck; Becky Norton Dunlop and mate, George; Ed Crane; Checker Finn; the late Diane Knippers; Wendy Wright.

And in the heartland, Phyllis Schlafly of Eagle Forum in Clayton, Missouri; Professors Douglas Tarpley of Biola University in La Mirada, California, Warren Throckmorton of Grove City College in Pennsylvania, and Michael Smith of Campbell University in North Carolina; Tom Boney, C.K. Ramsey and Tom Ashcraft in North Carolina; Dena Suarez in New York; Margaret and Lynn Dayton in Utah; Syl and Donna McNinch in Wyoming; Bob and Kath Case in Seattle.

Also in and around horsey Middleburg, Virginia, dear friends and kind neighbors: Always cheery, optimistic, Eileen Hackman, who understood and supported our family through thick and thin; Jim Atkins and mate, Sandi; Emmanuel Church organist Wendy Oesterling and mate, Jim Greene; the late Bob Humphrey who installed the red-phone for JFK at Glen Ora; the Reverend "Froggy" de Bordenave, long departed; son the Reverend Tad de Bordenave and sister Rachel Saffer; the Reverends Kira Myers and Lupton Abshire; Dody Vehr; Nancy Manierre; Norris Beavers; Tyler Gore; Reggie Dawson; Natasha Curry Kurfees and mate, John; Jerry and Charlene Curry; Lillian Griber; Roxy Hill and Nancy of Haute Fabrics; champion saddler Punkin Lee; Howard and Nancy Allen of Photo and Fun Shop Frame; Betsy Allen Davis; Paige Allen; Mark and John Tate of Middleburg's Coach Stop Restaurant; Sheila Johnson who bought the house next door; Matt and colleagues at the Middleburg Exxon; Jay Trier and crew at the Hidden Horse Tavern; John and Marny Birkitt and crew at the French Hound; Nancy and Turner Reuter and crew at the Red Fox Inn; Carol Hartley; Hazel Piscopo; Terry at the post office; all the Safeway and Salamander folks, particularly Barbara, Jennifer, Sam, Debbie, Nicole and Adam.

In Arizona, where I wrote the book, very special thanks to Royann Jordan Parker and lovely mother, Lillian, husband, Dave, children, Katie and Leann; longtime friend and mentor Marcia Sielaff and mate, Ernie; Edith Richardson and mate, Wade; Jon and Caryll Kyl and son John; veteran congressional aide Tim Glazewski; Joan and Jim Skelly and sons Jim and Chris; Ann Rudd and daughter Carolyn; Irene Conlan and sons Chris and Kevin; Roy Miller and family; Alexis Wilson and mate, Toby; Drs. Carolyn and Joe Gerster; Jake Logan; Sarah Morgan; Hank and Margaret Kenski; Barry Goldwater's telephone man Nick Volcheff; Flossie Melby and Anna Cocklin, the congressional mobile office pioneers.

At The Washington Times over the years, particular gratitude goes to longtime colleagues and friends: Ralph Hallow, original founding reporter, and mate, Millie; founding pre-publication organizers Jonathan Slevin; Paula Gray; Jim Gavin; Tom McDevitt; Denny Duggan; Matthew Lohmann; deskmates John McCaslin and Jennifer Harper; reporting partner Paul M. Rodriguez and mate, Katharine; champion reporters Jerry Seper and mate, Carol; Rowan Scarborough; Bill Gertz and mate, Debbie; Willis Witter and mate, Naomi; Tom Carter; Julia Duin; Amy Fagan; Sonsyrea Tate; Cheryl Wetzstein; Stacey Urban and mate, David; marvelous publicist Melissa Smigley Hopkins and mate, Gary, who headed both sports and photo departments at TWT; indefatigable librarians Clark Eberly, John Haydon, John Sopko and Amy Baskerville; incorrigible foreign desk Marxist curmudgeon Gus Constantine.

Also desk editors over the years: Bill Kling, Donald Lambro, Robert Morton, Frank Murray, Fran Coombs, Ken Hanner and lovely ex-mate Donna, David Jones, Mary Lou Forbes, the late Anne Crutcher, Bill Cheshire, the late Tony Snow, Tony Blankley, Debbie Simmons, Cathy Gainor, Carleton Bryant, Ken McIntyre, Joe Curl, Chris Dolan, Jeff Kuhner, and Victor Morton; chief editors over the years Jim Whelan, Smith Hempstone, Arnaud de Borchgrave, and Wesley Pruden; their man-Friday Jeffrey Lea; magnificent attorneys for all causes Allen Farber and Jay Barker; and tireless Ted Agres, the newspaper's original founding administrative editor, and mate, Marie; and loyal assistants Lois Carlson and Christine Reed, who always kept the ship afloat.

At Anomalos Publishing, great thanks to Tom Horn and mate,

Nita, for getting this baby out of intensive care, with heavy lifting by superb editor Michelle Warner and mate, Steve Warner, graphics and photo genius. And to George Doumar, very able and patient attorney, who pushed the book along.

All gave me footing—a platform to serve my country as a thinker and writer, do news and advocacy, help get out the message, and train the next generation, while providing constant encouragement focused always on the first principles of truth, honesty, personal integrity, beauty, love of freedom, and dignity for all humanity.

INDEX

JOURNALISM IS WAR 295

ABOUT THE AUTHOR

GEORGE ARCHIBALD, three-time Pulitzer Prize nominee as investigative reporter for The Washington Times during four presidential administrations, covered waste and corruption in Congress, federal agencies, the United Nations, and in public education. A native of England, he has four daughters and lives in Middleburg, Virginia.